ANCIENT SYNAGOGUES REVEALED

Editor: Lee I. Levine
Administrative Editor: J. Aviram
Layout: E. Jacob

PHOTO CREDITS
W. Braun; H. Burger; H. Cohen; S. Eldar; A. Glick; D. Harris; Israel Department of
Antiquities and Museums; Israel Museum; National Parks Authority;
Z. Radovan; J. S. Schweig

Maps drawn by Carta, Jerusalem

ISBN 965–221–000–5

Printed in Israel by Academic Press, Jerusalem

ANCIENT SYNAGOGUES REVEALED

EDITED BY LEE I. LEVINE

THE ISRAEL EXPLORATION SOCIETY · 1981

האוניברסיטה העברית בירושלים
THE HEBREW UNIVERSITY OF JERUSALEM

THIS VOLUME IS DEDICATED TO THE FRIENDS OF
THE HEBREW UNIVERSITY
TO MARK THE UNIVERSITY'S RETURN TO MOUNT SCOPUS

Contents

MAPS

COLOUR PLATES

following page 128

COVER PHOTOS:

Front: Section of mosaic panel from Ḥammath-Tiberias synagogue. Torah shrine flanked by Jewish symbols
Back: Autumn season as represented on mosaic floor of Ḥammath-Tiberias synagogue

Foreword

To anyone even remotely aware of the extent and nature of archeological discoveries in Israel during this century, a presentation of the remains of ancient synagogues requires little explanation. Such remnants are ubiquitous, scattered over the length and breadth of the country. To date, over 100 synagogal remains have been recorded in Israel alone, and even more in the Diaspora.

As its predecessor, *Jerusalem Revealed*, the present volume was initially intended to provide the English reader with a selection of articles taken from the popular Hebrew archeological journal, *Qadmoniot*. However, it soon became apparent that while the *Qadmoniot* articles offer an up-to-date review of excavations during the last decade or so, particularly those in Israel, they do not provide a comprehensive picture of ancient synagogues from either an archeological or an historical perspective. Moreover, the rapid rate of discoveries in this area renders a publication based on articles even five or ten years old somewhat obsolete. Finally, it was deemed desirable to present contrasting views with regard to the central issues in the study of ancient synagogues. As a result of these various considerations, almost half the articles in the present volume come from sources other than *Qadmoniot*, and of these, most are being published for the first time.

The two introductory essays, offering an overview of synagogue research and its implications in a variety of areas, are followed by a survey of Second Temple synagogues. The remains of three buildings — Masada, Herodium and Gamla — are discussed and analyzed, with various suggestions being made regarding the origins and typology of these buildings. The synagogues of the Galilee, constituting the richest single corpus of synagogal remains, then receive extended treatment. Two major issues are addressed by a number of authors: the origin of the "Galilean-type" synagogue, and the dating of these structures.

A special addition to this section is the presentation of two preliminary reports of excavations recently conducted in the Galilee, at Gush Ḥalav and Ḥorvat ha-'Amudim.

The ever-increasing number of synagogal remains in the Beth Shean region are presented next, followed by an extensive treatment of recently discovered Golan synagogues. Since this latter material has never been published in English (and only very recently in Hebrew), a relatively long chapter is devoted to an examination of these structures. The historical and artistic dimensions of these finds are also discussed at length, as well as their relationship to the nearby Galilean remains. A section on synagogues in the southern part of the country, from 'En-Gedi in the east to Gaza in the west, concludes this survey by geographic area.

A summary of epigraphic data, especially the Hebrew and Aramaic material, is offered in the first essay of the section on inscriptions and small finds. Separate chapters are devoted to the two major inscriptions found during the last decade, the enigmatic communal inscription of 'En-Gedi and the Reḥob halakhic inscription. A translation of the latter has been prepared by R. Grafman. A number of smaller finds are also presented, each interesting in its own right, and together reflective of the many less dramatic discoveries, which constitute the bulk of archeological contributions to the study of ancient synagogues.

Finally, in the last major section, we turn to a brief survey of Diaspora synagogues. An introductory chapter offers an overview of the important remains throughout the Roman Empire, and is followed by two others relating to the major Diaspora synagogues found to date, Dura Europos and Sardis. After a brief article on Corinth, a concluding chapter treats the fascinating remains of Mopsuestia (Asia Minor).

It is a pleasure to be able to acknowledge the help extended by a number of people, thus enabling publication of this volume. First and foremost, thanks are due to Mr. J. Aviram, Director of the Institute of Archeology, Hebrew University, and Honorary Secretary of the Israel Exploration Society, for initiating this project, and lending full support and cooperation throughout the entire process of completing this book.

We also wish to acknowledge the work of R. Grafman, who translated most of the articles, and that of Sue Gorodetsky, with regard to editing. Thanks are also due to M. Levine and D. Saltz for their translations, to H. Davis, I. Karp and D. Tritt for their conscientious work on the proofs of this volume and to N. Naveh for preparing the index.

Lee Israel Levine
Elul, 5740   The Hebrew University
September, 1980   Jerusalem

Ancient Synagogues — A Historical Introduction

Lee I. Levine

The emergence of the synagogue constitutes one of the most revolutionary developments in the history of ancient Judaism. This institution represented a wholly new concept of religious observance. Cultic practice was no longer confined to a small coterie of priests and professionals, and the masses of people ceased to be relegated to the outer courtyards of the Temple precincts. Leadership in the synagogue was open to all, and the ceremonies there were conducted in full view of the participants. The form of worship likewise shifted dramatically, with prayer and study replacing sacrifice as the means of serving God. The synagogue differed from the Temple in one other respect. According to Jewish tradition, as crystallized in the biblical account, there could be only one Temple, and that on the sacred site in Jerusalem. A synagogue, however, could be built anywhere, in large and small cities, within and outside city walls, in the Diaspora as well as throughout the Land of Israel. Thus, the synagogue brought officially recognized sacred worship to every corner of the Jewish world. The fact that, in ensuing centuries, church and mosque derived their inspiration from the synagogue further attests to the significance of this institution in the history of religion generally.

Despite the importance of the synagogue, its origins and early history are shrouded in mystery.[1] We simply do not know where and when this institution crystallized. The earliest literary sources which mention it stem from the first century C.E., and describe the synagogues of that period in Palestine and throughout the Roman Diaspora (Egypt, Asia Minor, Greece, Rome, etc.). Archeologically speaking, the earliest synagogues in Roman Palestine also date from this century. The buildings at Masada and Herodium were constructed during the war against Rome in 66–74 C.E. (see pp. 19–29), and the Gamla building, if indeed a synagogue, was built somewhat earlier (see pp. 30–41). A monumental Greek inscription found in Jerusalem in 1913–14 provides the earliest archeological attestation we have (from the late first century B.C.E.) for the existence of a Palestinian synagogue. Evidence from the Diaspora is somewhat earlier. In Egypt, synagogue inscriptions from the third and second centuries B.C.E. have been preserved, and a building often identified as a synagogue dating from the first century B.C.E. has been found at Delos.

Given this paucity of material, it is but natural that opinions vary considerably as to when the synagogue first evolved. Some have suggested a date as early as the First Temple period (seventh century B.C.E.). It has been assumed that this was the most propitious time for the emergence of an institution like the synagogue, this on the basis of scattered biblical allusions to prayers, hints regarding regular meetings with a prophet on a holy day, and the fact that local shrines were abolished during this century in deference to the central Jerusalem sanctuary.[2] At the other extreme, some have advanced the emergence of the synagogue to the Hellenistic period, this

---

[1] See J. Gutmann, "The Origin of the Synagogue," *Archäologischer Anzeiger* (1972), 36–40.

[2] L. Finkelstein, "The Origin of the Synagogue," *PAAJR*, 1 (1930); I. Levy, *The Synagogue: Its History and Function* (London, 1963); J. Weingren, "The Origin of the Synagogue," *Hermathena*, 98 (1964).

SYNAGOGUES OF ERETZ-ISRAEL

Mediterranean Sea

Bar'am
Sasa Gush Halav Dabbura
Meiron 'En Neshut Dabiya
Nabratein Kazrin
H. Shema' H. Dikke 'Assalieh
Zumimra
Chorazim Gamla
Capernaum H. Kanef
Veradim Lake Kinneret Umm el-Kanatir
H. Ha-'Amudim
Arbel
Husifah Kefar Kana Hammath Tiberias
Sepphoris
H. Summak Beth Shearim Japhia Beth Yerah Yarmuk
Hammath Gader

Kokhav Ha-Yarden

Caesarea Beth Alpha
Beth-Shean Ma'oz Hayim

Rehob
Tirat Zvi

Gerasa

Jordan

Na'aran

Sha'albim Jericho

Huldah

Jerusalem

Ascalon Herodium

Beth Govrin Dead Sea

Gaza
H. Kishor
'En-Gedi
Eshtemoa
H. Rimmon Susiya
Ma'on

Masada

0   20   40 km

© carta, JERUSALEM

Map of ancient synagogue sites in Israel

on the basis of the earliest evidence from Egyptian inscriptions,[3] and its omission from earlier Jewish literature.[4] However, the bulk of scholarly opinion has taken a middle course, and there is general consensus today that the development of the synagogue followed the destruction of the First Temple in 586 B.C.E., either during the Babylonian exile or soon after, when Jews returned to Judaea during the Restoration period. The need of the exiles for a substitute for the Temple, the newly instituted fast days for mourning its destruction (*Zech.* 7:5), and perhaps the inauguration of public scriptural readings, dated by tradition to this period, were all factors leading to regular meetings which eventually became the basis of what we know as the synagogue. Evolving over the course of centuries, the synagogue finally appears in literary sources as a fully developed communal institution playing a central role in Jewish life.

Thus, for some 500 years the synagogue appears to have developed parallel to the Temple. It served the religious and social needs of Jews, yet never during this period did it replace the Temple as the cultic focus of Judaism. The functions of synagogue and Temple were complementary, not antithetical. The former borrowed much from the latter in the realm of prayer and other ritual observances. The prayer service itself was conceived as a parallel to sacrifices offered at the Temple. When priests of a particular locality traveled to Jerusalem to participate in the Temple ritual, special services were held by their fellow townspeople in the local synagogue (M *Ta'anit* 4, 2–3).

By the middle of the first century of this era, the synagogue represented the central Jewish institution in any given community. The variety of activities which took place there

is even more extensive than the many roles played by Diaspora synagogues today. The most frequently mentioned activities include the following:

1) Prayer — Whether regular communal prayer services were held in the synagogue before the destruction of the Second Temple is a matter of conjecture. On the basis of scattered information culled from the New Testament, the Theodotus inscription and several early rabbinic traditions, it would seem that communal daily prayers were institutionalized only after the destruction. In any case, already at an early period regular Sabbath and holiday services were held and attracted large numbers of worshippers.

2) Study — This activity might take one of a number of forms: schools for children, reading and expounding Scriptures at prayer services, regular study sessions for adults generally, or for local sages (in the absence of an academy).

3) Sacred meals — Josephus, rabbinic literature and archeological evidence all attest to the practice of holding sacred meals at the synagogue. Such festivities were probably associated with the Sabbath or holidays, but may have taken place at other times as well. A triclinium or dining hall is mentioned in synagogue inscriptions from Caesarea and Stobi (in Yugoslavia).

4) Repository for communal funds — The synagogue served as a center for communal charities, with monies being collected, deposited and dispersed there. In the Diaspora, contributions to the Temple were collected annually, kept at the local synagogue until their transfer to a central regional bank, and were then forwarded to Jerusalem.

5) Courts — Communal law courts sat in the synagogue, and numerous sources tell of punishments meted out to offenders within the synagogue precincts.

6) General assembly hall — As the largest communal institution, the synagogue also functioned as a place of meeting. In a vivid description of the tensions within Tiberias in 66–67 C.E. over the question of whether to join the war effort against Rome, Josephus

[3] M. Hengel, "Proseuche und Synagoge," *Tradition und Glaube: Festschrift für K.G. Kuhn* (Göttingen, 1971).

[4] E. Rivkin, "Ben Sira and the Nonexistence of the Synagogue," *In the Time of Harvest: Essays in Honor of Abba Hillel Silver*, ed. D.J. Silver (New York, 1963); *idem*, "Pharisaism and the Crisis of the Individual in the Greco–Roman World," *JQR*, 60 (1970).

describes the various political meetings held in the local synagogue, some scheduled immediately following religious services.

7) Hostel — Synagogues also served as hostels for Jewish travelers. If they were located in Jerusalem, then the need to service the tens of thousands of pilgrims who flocked to the city several times a year was paramount. But even synagogues outside Jerusalem and throughout the Diaspora appear to have had rooms set aside for the poor, for itinerants, and for Jewish merchants.

8) Residence for synagogue officials — Both rabbinic and archeological materials attest to the fact that a communal official not infrequently resided within the synagogue complex. The official named in rabbinic sources is the "ḥazan."

While a plethora of activity revolved around the synagogue in the first century, it would nevertheless seem that first and foremost the synagogue, in its formative stages at least, served as a place for the reading of the Torah and its study. All of our earliest sources point in this direction. The first century Theodotus inscription from Jerusalem mentions study of the Torah and fulfillment of the commandments as the principal activities of the synagogue (see p. 11). Josephus likewise emphasizes the centrality of scriptural reading and study, a practice he ascribes to the days of Moses:

> He appointed the Law to be the most excellent and necessary form of instruction, ordaining, not that it should be heard once for all or twice or on several occasions, but that every week men should desert their other occupations and assemble to listen to the Law and obtain a thorough and accurate knowledge of it, a practice which other legislators seem to have neglected.[5]

Although not mentioned specifically, it is quite certain that Josephus had in mind (at least for his own day) the synagogue as the setting for such activity. The author of *Acts*, in fact, makes this connection quite explicit:

> For from early generations Moses has had in every city those who preach him, for he is read every Sabbath in the synagogues.[6]

Such an activity would appear to have stemmed originally from the days of Ezra, who came to Jerusalem around the year 450 B.C.E. with a royal mandate to judge and teach the Torah to the Jewish inhabitants of the area:

> And you, Ezra, according to the wisdom of your God which is in your hand, appoint magistrates and judges who may judge all the people in the province Beyond the River (i.e., the Euphrates), all such as know the laws of your God; and those who do not know them, you shall teach.[7]

In the late Roman period, large Jewish communities were not limited to just one synagogue. It is reported that Tiberias, in its heyday of the third and fourth centuries C.E., boasted 13 different synagogues, Rome had at least 11, and Sepphoris 18. Jerusalem itself is reputed to have contained hundreds of synagogues in the last decades of the Second Temple period, but this estimate is probably greatly exaggerated. Worship was directed toward Jerusalem, and whenever possible the building was erected near a source of water to facilitate ablutions, or on a high spot for greater prominence. Benches were always a fixture in these buildings, highlighting the communal aspect of the worship, and laver basins for hand washing have been found in excavations (see pp. 116–119, 157). Other elements — the number and location of entrances, the plan and dimensions of the building, the number of columns, their placement, and artistic decorations — varied

---

[5] Josephus, *Against Apion* 2, 175 (LCL, p. 363). See also Josephus' comment in his *Antiquities* 16, 43 (LCL, p. 225): "Nor do we make a secret of the precepts that we use as guides in religion and in human relations; we give every seventh day over to the study of our customs and law ..."

[6] *Acts* 15 : 21.
[7] *Ezra* 7 : 25.

greatly, depending on the cultural proclivities, size, and wealth of the community, as well as the architectural forms then in vogue. In later synagogues of the Byzantine period, the Torah shrine was accorded a permanent installation; earlier it appears to have been portable, introduced into the main sanctuary when needed. In some synagogues a special place known as "the seat of Moses" was set aside for the leader of the community (see pp. 135, 165, 173).

Synagogue remains are not only significant in their own right, attesting as they do to the existence and function of a central institution in the Jewish community. They also provide precious information regarding a wide range of issues affecting Jewish life in ancient times. The importance of these archeological remains cannot be exaggerated. The late Roman–Byzantine period, known in Jewish historiography as the talmudic era, was perhaps the most formative period in the evolution and development of Judaism as it is known today. Judaism in the last 2000 years differs markedly from the beliefs and practices of the biblical period. At most, one can say that Judaism of today is largely the religion of the Bible as reinterpreted, reworked and carefully elaborated by the sages of the first five centuries of the present era. This pivotal era is both richly and sparsely documented. It is rich in the sense that rabbinic literature does tell us a great deal about the life of the Jews of the period, and particularly about the legal and homiletical material of the rabbis themselves. Nevertheless, the sources can also be considered sparse in that there remain innumerable areas of Jewish life almost totally ignored by rabbinic material. In the absence of comprehensive literary data, the numerous synagogue remains are indispensable for a fuller understanding of Jewish life at the time.

The very location of ancient synagogues tells us a great deal about patterns of Jewish settlement in antiquity, both complementing and supplementing rabbinic sources. That Jewish settlement was focused in eastern Galilee during late antiquity is borne out by both literary and archeological evidence. The greatest concentration of ancient synagogues was there and, not surprisingly, this was also the center of rabbinic life. Few rabbis lived at that time in the Golan region or in Judaea in the south; thus very little is known of these areas from rabbinic literature. However, the numerous synagogue remains found in the Golan and Judaea attest to a flourishing Jewish life there as well. Some of these structures are strikingly similar to those found in Galilee; others are rather unique in their plan and decorations, raising interesting questions as to the nature of Jewish communal and religious life in these locales (see pp. 98–132). Regarding the Diaspora, in addition to remains in places mentioned in literary sources (e.g., Sardis, Corinth), synagogues have been found in cities with hitherto unknown Jewish communities, e.g., Dura, Ostia, Stobi (see pp. 163–183).

The hundreds of inscriptions found in the various synagogues have opened new vistas in our understanding of Jewish life in antiquity (see pp. 133–158). The scores of names of officials and donors have added immensely to our knowledge of Jewish prosopography (the study of personal names). The study of such names can be an immensely fruitful area of research in the determination of social and cultural influences affecting any given community or region. Moreover, the offices listed have enhanced our familiarity with the many functionaries within the Jewish community. At times inscriptions offer dates for the erection (or restoration) of a synagogue building, valuable information in and of itself (see pp. 127, 130, 164, 171–172). Some inscriptions give the exact year of dedication, as at Dura, Apamaea, Gaza and Nabratein (see pp. 14, 130, 164, 172). In other cases only the reign of an emperor is indicated (Beth Alpha), although at times an inscription is so badly damaged that even this information is incomplete (see p. 127). Other bases for dating that appear are the era of a given city, the prevalent Seleucid era, dating from the destruction of the Temple, from Creation, or according to the sabbatical year cycle.

Reconstruction of Capernaum synagogue

Besides the usual dedicatory inscriptions, several have been found whose size and importance warrant mention. The 'En Gedi inscription cites the names of the ancestral generations of mankind as listed in the book of 1 Chronicles. Then follow the twelve names of the zodiac signs, the twelve months of the year, the three Patriarchs, and three companions of Daniel. The main paragraph includes a list of donors and an enigmatic statement referring to community secrets and other information forbidden to be revealed to outsiders. While the nature of these secrets is unclear (political, communal or economic), the communal discipline and the suspicion of Gentiles reflected therein offer a rare view of the workings and attitudes of one 'particular Jewish community (see pp. 140–145).

Of no less significance is the lengthy Reḥob inscription which reproduces several paragraphs from rabbinic literature dealing with the areas of Jewish Palestine to which the biblical agricultural injunctions pertain (see pp. 146–152). Moreover, new information is provided regarding the area of Beth-Shean (Scythopolis), as well as a list of hitherto unknown towns in Samaria. By and large the places enumerated reaffirm Jewish settlement patterns known from other sources, and also provide an early independent version of rabbinic traditions heretofore preserved only in manuscripts dating from later centuries. Finally, the Reḥob inscription reflects the concern, at least of this community, for agricultural laws mandatory for Jews living in the Holy Land.

Synagogue inscriptions also provide an invaluable gauge of the cultural climate among Jews. The large percentage of inscriptions in Greek and numerous names of Greek origin indicate the extent to which Greek influence had penetrated many parts of the country. As might be expected, not all sections of the country were similarly affected. Greek was particularly pervasive in the coastal area where large Greco–Roman cities (Gaza, Ascalon, Joppa, Caesarea, and Acre) were concentrated. Even in the cities of the lower Galilee and Jezreel Valley, Greek was a very significant factor (Beth Shearim, Tiberias, Sepphoris, Beth Shean, Beth Alpha). However, in the Golan, Judaea, and smaller Galilean villages — places somewhat less exposed to the prevalent cultural currents — Hebrew and Aramaic inscriptions predominate.

The acculturation process had other manifestations as well. The art and architectural forms of ancient synagogues also exhibited considerable outside influence. The art of the large Galilean synagogues shows remarkable affinities with the pervasive art forms of southern Syria in the second and third centuries C.E., while that of the Byzantine synagogues is strikingly similar to Christian art of the time (see pp. 15ff.). Architecturally, the basilica form of later synagogues appears to be an imitation of contemporaneous church buildings, while the "Galilean-type" synagogue may, in fact, derive from the Nabatean temple courtyards of southern Syria (see p. 48).

At the same time, some synagogue buildings are *sui generis* and display little affinity with other structures in the same region. Ḥorvat Shema' (see pp. 70–74) is a classic example of a synagogue, located in eastern Galilee, which finds no parallel in the area. In fact, only two other synagogues in the entire country approximate its plan and orientation toward the long, rather than short, wall. Both examples are located in southern Judaea, at Ḥorvat Susiya and Eshtemoa (see pp. 120–128). This type of synagogue, commonly referred to as the broadhouse type, appears in the Diaspora at Dura and Naro (see pp. 170, 172). The source of this plan remains enigmatic, as does the reason for a particular community preferring this type of arrangement to others more commonly used. Perhaps it reflects a different religious orientation, a different conception of the place of the congregation in synagogue worship, or might there be economic factors involved here? It certainly is not a regional feature, as this type appears in the northern and southern parts of the country, on the Euphrates (Dura) and in North Africa (Naro).

We have referred to the art preserved among the various synagogue remains. In fact, were it not for these archeological discoveries we would know next to nothing about Jewish artistic expression in late antiquity. Rabbinic literature either opposes such activity, particularly as regards figural representation, or only grudgingly accords approval, *ex post facto*. Indeed, until the deluge of archeological discoveries during this last half century, it was widely held that Jews simply did not indulge in art, on the assumption that the Second Commandment forbade depiction of human or animal features (*Exod.* 20 : 4–5). Synagogue remains, however, have alerted us to the fact that Jewish artistic expression was very much alive and widespread in late antiquity. In fact, there is little doubt today that Jewish art was so developed as to have been of considerable influence in the shaping of early Christian art. In this regard the Dura synagogue is of cardinal importance (see pp. 171–176), attesting as it does to fully developed pictorial cycles of biblical narratives used to decorate the building from floor to ceiling. If this was the case in a remote settlement like Dura on the eastern frontier of the Roman Empire, how much more so in the large centers of Jewish population with their stronger demographic and economic base, and their well documented proclivities towards acculturation!

The fact that Jews so willingly embellished the synagogues of late antiquity with all sorts of decorations reflects a major change in attitude. The last centuries of the Second Temple period witnessed a strong aversion among Jews — particularly, although not

Lintel from Capernaum: eagles (l.) and capricorn (r.)

exclusively, in Judaea and Jerusalem — to any kind of figural representation. That had not been the case during the biblical period, and may well reflect the traumatic effects of the persecution under Antiochus IV (167–164 B.C.E.) when pagan deities were introduced into the Temple precincts. Nevertheless, within two centuries following the destruction of the Temple in 70 C.E., Jews were using symbols and designs previously regarded as anathema. To cite but one example. Herod erected an eagle over the entrance to the Temple around 6–5 B.C.E., touching off a major riot led by several sages, who paid for the insurrection with their lives. Yet, by the fourth century C.E. the eagle had become one of the most ubiquitous symbols gracing the synagogues of Galilee! Undoubtedly the decline of paganism as well as the ever-increasing acculturation among the Jewish populace go far in explaining this surprising development. It is apparent that the tastes and attitudes reflected in ancient synagogues are strikingly different from those which had previously been considered normative.

Furthermore, even within late antiquity itself, Jewish artistic expression underwent significant alterations. Until the early fourth century C.E., for example, very few Jewish symbols appear in a synagogue context. For all the rich remains of Capernaum, primarily in the form of intricate and sophisticated stone reliefs, only one clearly recognizable Jewish symbol (a *menorah*) appears. In Byzantine period synagogues, however, Jewish symbols appear with regularity. Representations of a Torah shrine, *menorah, shofar, lulab, ethrog* and incense shovel became regular features in

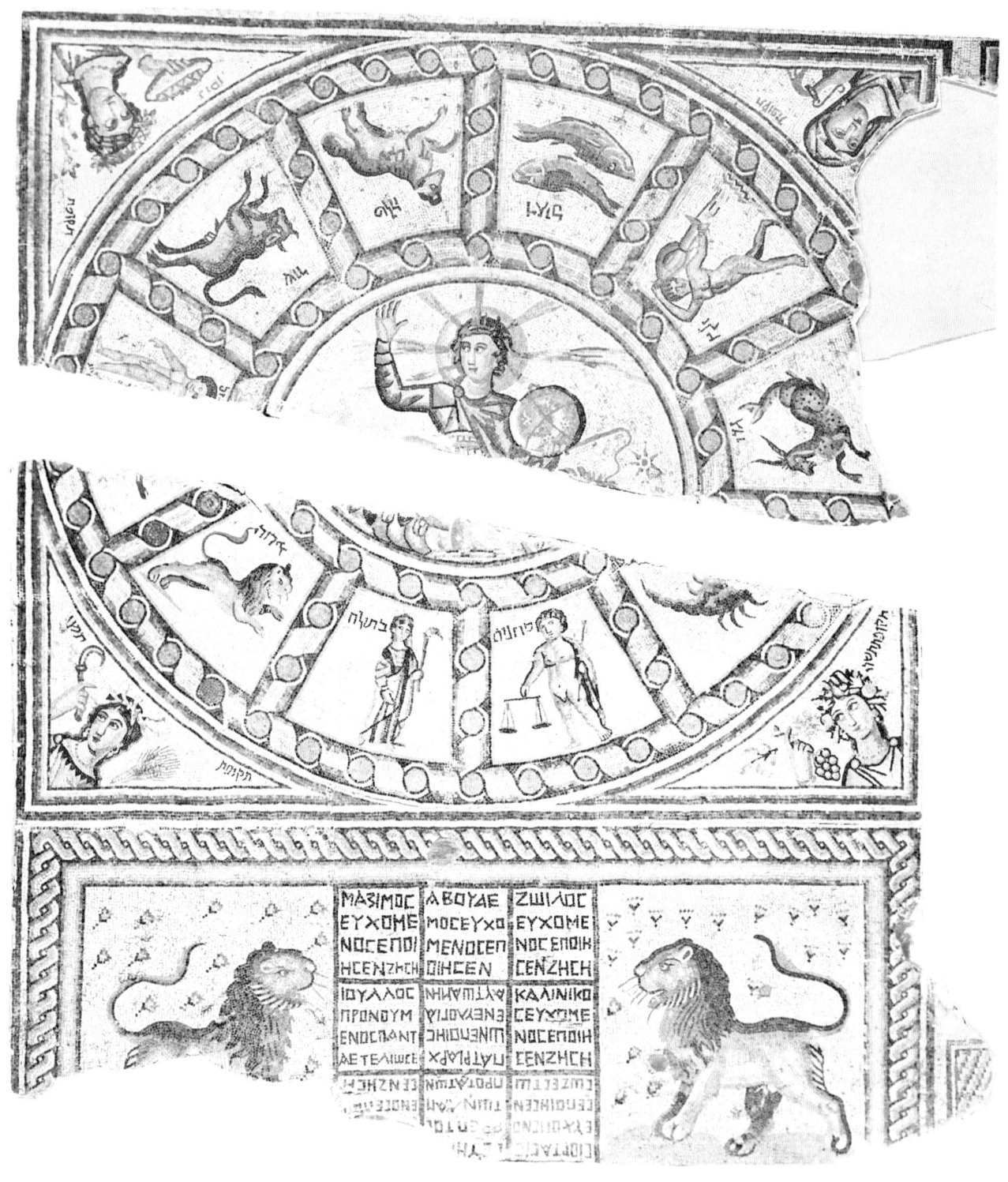

Part of the mosaic floor — Ḥammath-Tiberias

these synagogues. The reason for this development can only be conjectured. It would appear that it was, at least in part, a response to the rise of Christianity in the fourth century C.E. The introduction of Christian buildings and symbols into Byzantine Palestine on a large scale, beginning with Constantine, may well have given rise to the need of Jews for more tangible representations of their own unique symbols.

Another innovation within the Byzantine synagogue may also be related to the ascent of Christianity. The Torah shrine now became a permanent feature of the synagogue, so much so that the Jews were accused by certain antagonists, John Chrysostom for example, of exaggerated veneration for their Holy Ark. Such a permanent location for the Torah ark was facilitated by the adoption of a basilica-like hall; with its orientation (i.e., apse) facing Jerusalem, the ark could conveniently fit there. The need for such a permanent installation and the accompanying veneration may also have been part of the Jewish response to the disquieting political supremacy of the Church.

One of the most striking types of mosaic floors in Byzantine synagogues represents Helios, zodiac signs, and the four seasons. The appearance of such representations in ancient synagogues initially startled most modern observers. The immediate reaction was to interpret them as the gift of an emperor, or as the expression of some fringe group in Judaism. However, with the discovery of at least four such pavements — dating from different centuries and located in different areas, including one at Tiberias, the very center of Jewish life at that time — it became clear that we are dealing here with a popular and accepted form of artistic expression. What, then, did such a depiction mean to the contemporaneous Jewish community? Was it merely a decorative motif, or did it bear some religious significance? Was this kind of panel intended to reflect the importance of the Jewish calendar in the community's life? Did Helios represent the power of God in creating the world anew each day, each month, and each season? Or perhaps Helios stood for the Divine Himself? All the above have been offered as explanations of this enigma; none has won general acceptance.

One other possibility deserves mention. During this same Byzantine period, a work called *Sefer Harazim* ("The Book of Secrets") was composed by a Palestinian Jew. A work of practical magic, it lists the angels in the various heavenly spheres, to whom one could turn with specific requests: healing the sick, winning one's love, punishing an enemy, gaining wealth or power. Even determining the outcome of a horse-race at the hippodrome was in the hands of one particular angel. To effect the desired result, one but needed to know the name of the proper angel, the requisite formula and other necessary preparations, all provided for by *Sefer Harazim*. Another possible request was to see the sun at night, at which time one could ask for whatever one wished, and learn the secrets of the universe as well. The following prayer, in Greek, was then to be recited:

> I adore you, Helios, who rises in the east, the good sailor, faithful guardian, trustworthy leader, who from of old set the great sphere on its course, the holy orderer of the stars, he who rules the heavenly byways. Lord! Illustrious leader! King! Orderer of the stars.

The above leaves no room for doubt that certain Jewish circles of Byzantine Palestine did not regard Helios as merely a decorative element, or even as representing the power of God as creator of the universe. Rather, he functioned as a kind of super-angel capable of affecting one's life. The question then arises: Is there any relationship between the Helios of the synagogue mosaics and the Helios of *Sefer Harazim*? Do the mosaic panels reflect a conception of Judaism differing somewhat from that which finds expression in rabbinic literature? On the basis of the material available to date it is impossible to answer these questions definitively. However, it should be clear at the very least, that the implications of synagogue art are far-reaching, and may, in fact, touch upon our very understanding of Judaism as perceived and practiced by different groups at that time.

Finally, the developments in the study of ancient synagogues these past few years have suggested a totally new perspective on the history of the Jewish community in late Roman Palestine. Heretofore it has been commonly assumed that the late Roman–Byzantine period witnessed a steady decline of

Jewish life and the recession into a kind of Dark Age which was to last for centuries. Large-scale emigration, loss of political status, lapse of key communal institutions, economic hardships and religious discrimination bordering at times on persecution, were assumed to have had their cumulative effect, leaving the Jewish community in an impoverished state. This perception has been challenged on a number of fronts. The Cairo Geniza has revealed a series of literary works dating from this period, indicating the existence of a creative cultural life among Jews. This impression is the result of the now-accepted dating to late antiquity of a series of liturgical, apocalyptic, halakhic, and mystical works, previously thought to be medieval in origin. To these examples can now be added the ever-increasing number of Byzantine synagogues being found throughout Israel. Moreover, other synagogues, products of a somewhat earlier age, continued to undergo extensive renovations, and were in use down to the Arab conquest of Palestine and beyond.

Truly revolutionary in this regard are the latest finds from Capernaum (see pp. 52–62). The Franciscan archeologists who excavated the site claim that the monumental synagogue there was not built in the second–third centuries C.E., as hitherto assumed, but rather in the fifth century! They further suggest the application of this new dating to other "Galilean-type" synagogues. If this might be granted, and many scholars have indeed been convinced by their findings, then our perception of the nature and position of the Jewish community requires serious readjustment. The monies required to erect such edifices, and the secure political position to which they attest, assume an established and flourishing Jewish populace far different than heretofore imagined.

Such a conclusion, however, raises numerous questions. Why were so radically different types and styles of synagogues (as Capernaum and Hammath–Tiberias, for example) being built at one and the same time? If all existing remains date from the Byzantine period, what archeological evidence do we have for synagogues from the second and third centuries C.E.? How then would one explain the all but total absence of structures from the earlier period, and the plethora of later types and styles? Since Capernaum reflects a Roman style of the second and third centuries, could Jews in the Byzantine period have built some of their synagogues in this fashion? These are only some of the important issues raised by the excavations. Nevertheless, even if the Franciscans have erred in the interpretation of their findings, and the Capernaum synagogue was not actually built in the fifth century C.E. but only extensively renovated (see pp. 57–62), such repairs in themselves would presuppose a vibrant and economically thriving community supporting such an enterprise. The fact that at this same time a rather modest church stood in the shadow of this monumental synagogue is a further indication of the secure political and religious position of the local Jewish community. Thus, in any case, our perception of Jewish life in the Byzantine period requires serious re-evaluation.

We have tried to indicate, albeit in rather summary fashion, some of the ways in which ancient synagogues reveal a great deal about Jewish life. Because of the comparative paucity of literary sources from this period on the one hand, and the relative abundance of archeological finds on the other, one cannot even attempt to draw a complete picture of the synagogue, or of Jewish life generally, without incorporating the data offered by material remains. The volume at hand is intended to supply the information which has come to light in the course of recent excavations.

Ancient Synagogues in Israel:
An Archeological Survey

A. Kloner

The synagogue, as noted, was the religious, cultural, and social center of the Jewish community in every settlement of the Roman and Byzantine periods. Archeological investigations have considerably extended our knowledge of this institution as compared with even two generations ago, and a rich and varied picture has emerged; remains of more than a hundred buildings or architectural elements identifiable as synagogues are known throughout the country, over half of which have a discernible plan. The buildings are found in various parts of the country from Upper Galilee to the Beersheba basin. We also know of numerous Samaritan inscriptions, attesting the existence of Samaritan synagogues in the places where they settled.

Ancient synagogues were identified as such by Jewish travelers from the thirteenth century onward and have been a subject of study since the nineteenth century. Various scholars, including Robinson, Renan, Guérin, Kitchener, Conder, Schumacher, and Oliphant, have each made a significant contribution. The comprehensive research of Kohl and Watzinger in 1905 and 1907 is a fundamental work of unparalleled importance to this day regarding the buildings in the Galilee. Following World War I, synagogues were also found in other regions of the country, and significant research was carried out by Sukenik, aided by Avigad. The latter also deciphered a number of synagogue inscriptions. Sukenik and Avigad, together with Avi-Yonah, who studied buildings with mosaic pavements in various locations throughout Israel, raised the generation of archeologists who have contributed most of the studies appearing in this book.

Synagogues from the Second Temple Period
As mentioned above, the institution of the synagogue was already in existence during the Second Temple period. It is unclear archeologically when buildings began to accommodate the functions associated with synagogues. The existence of this institution in the Second Temple period is evident from its frequent appearance in written sources. A monumental Greek inscription found in Jerusalem during excavations in 1913–1914 reads as follows:

> Theodotus, son of Vettenos the priest and *archisynagogos,* son of a *archisynagogos* and grandson of a *archisynagogos*, who built the synagogue for purposes of reciting the Law and studying the commandments, and the hostel, chambers and water installations to provide for the needs of itinerants from abroad, and whose father, with the elders and Simonidus, founded the synagogue.

Theodotus inscription — Jerusalem, 1st century C.E.

The text of the inscription, which originally seems to have been set in the wall of a building of which nothing remains, is presently on display at the Rockefeller Museum in Jerusalem. It is reminiscent of the passage in the Talmud:

> R. Pinḥas quoted R. Hoshaya as saying: 'There were four hundred eighty synagogues in Jerusalem, each of which had a school and a *bet talmud;* the school was for (the study of) Bible and the *bet talmud* for (the study of) Mishnah; and Vespasian destroyed them all' (J *Megilla,* III, 1, 73 d).

More recent excavations at Gamla, Masada, and Herodium have uncovered buildings thought to have been synagogues in the final years before the destruction of the Second Temple. The archeological data are important both for the idea they convey of the public buildings themselves and for the influence they may have exerted on the plans of later buildings. These three buildings from the Second Temple period have stone seats extending along each of the walls; their entrances are located on the short side.

Opinions differ as to the origin of this building plan. One approach regards it as stemming from the assembly halls found in the East — at Dura Europos and Nabatean sites — where the arrangement of benches resembled a small theatre. Another view sees it as originating rather in public buildings found in the West. However, its source may perhaps best be sought in a local type of assembly or reception hall from the Second Temple period, such as those recently uncovered at Jericho. Whatever the case, the discoveries of the last fifteen years have made an important contribution to the study of synagogues. Previously, "Galilean-type" synagogues, dating from the second and third centuries C.E., were thought to constitute the earliest stage of synagogue buildings.

"Galilean" Synagogues

There are remains of over fifty synagogues in Galilee and on the Golan Heights. The term "Galilean" synagogue refers to a characteristic

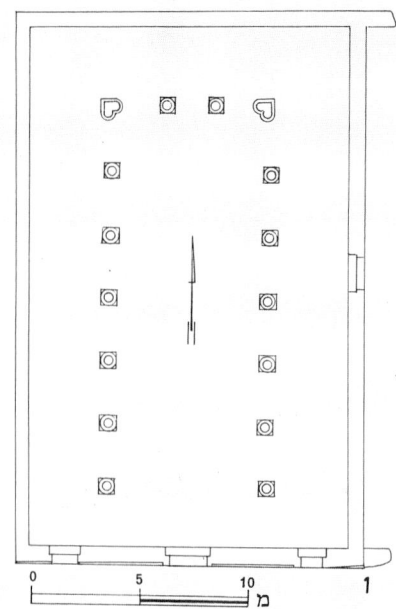

Ḥorvat Ha-'Amudim: a "Galilean-type" synagogue plan

group of structures whose lines of construction and ornamentation are similar in conception and design. These buildings, constructed in ashlar, were rectangular in shape, with their entrances usually on the short side. As a rule, the façade was on the southern side with three entrances facing towards Jerusalem. Most of these synagogues were paved in stone slabs, with columns running along three walls of the hall, two lengthwise and one crosswise. Some of the buildings contained heart-shaped columns where the rows met (columns with heart-shaped cross-sections have also been found in various buildings from the Second Temple period). Reconstruction of some buildings includes a second story of columns, which increased the capacity of the prayer hall, but scholarly opinion is divided as to whether this balcony served as a women's gallery or rather housed other activities associated with the synagogue. One or more stone benches ran along the walls of the hall to provide seating for the congregation. There was no fixed place for the Torah ark in most of the buildings, nor were there any signs of a *bema.* Decorations were carved in stone on friezes, walls, lintels, and capitals. They included a combination of floral motifs, classical images, and even human and animal figures, some resembling definite mythological characters.

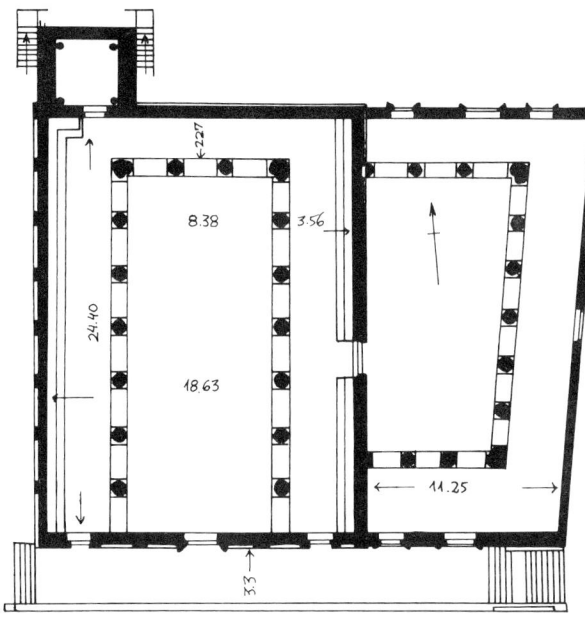

Plan of Capernaum synagogue

The most complete example of this type of building is the synagogue at Capernaum. Its main building is a rectangle 20.5 × 18.5 m. wide, bordered on the east by a courtyard whose width at the façade is 11.25 m. The façade contained three entrances, the middle one larger than those on either side; all were decorated with images of palm trees, vine-scrolls, eagles, and lions. The upper half of the façade wall contained windows surmounted by a gable of the "Syrian" type, consisting of a pediment with an arch cut into its base. The interior decorations included Corinthian capitals, some of which incorporated seven-branched *menorot*. Along the walls were vaulted friezes decorated with rosettes, grape clusters, pomegranates, geometric designs, a Torah ark in the shape of a cart, mythological sea creatures, etc.

Although "Galilean" synagogues share certain characteristics, there are no two buildings which are identical in size or interior plan. Nor is this fact surprising, for there are few examples in ancient architecture of identical buildings even among those of the same period. One also finds buildings with a single entrance and various orientations: at Kazrin the single entrance faces northward; at Kanatir, Ḥorvat Somek, and Arbel the entrances faced eastward; and at Ḥorvat Dikke, westward. Buildings like those at Ḥorvat

Dikke and Nabratein had only two rows of columns running lengthwise. Thus, even given an overall likeness of the "Galilean" synagogues, at each site the common model was altered and adapted in accordance with its geographical setting, the abilities of local craftsmen, the budget available to the community, and the wishes of those who commissioned the work.

The most logical theory assumes that the remains of synagogues in the Galilee represent an advanced level of building whose plan and architectural components evidence a well-established tradition. Yet, though this tradition probably stemmed from Second Temple times, the structural design also reflects the influence of the Syro–Roman building tradition, as is most evident in the Syrian gabled façade with its three entrances. In the absence of identical structures in either Syria or Galilee, we may assume that the local craftsmen copied models popular in the larger society and adapted them to their needs (see pp. 42–51).

Scholars had generally agreed that these buildings were erected at the end of the second and during the third centuries C.E. This supposition was also in keeping with the political situation of Roman Palestine at the time: the concentration of Jewish population primarily in the northern part of the country,

Capital from Capernaum synagogue with *menorah, shofar* and incense shovel

13

Portion of frieze from Capernaum synagogue

View of interior of Capernaum synagogue with benches along the walls

the good relations between the local leadership and the Roman government, and the power and prestige of the Patriarchate in internal affairs. The assertion that "Galilean" synagogues were built as early as the second century C.E. has generated much debate, and there are those who contest even a third century date for most of the Galilean buildings. Recent excavations at Capernaum have considerably intensified this dispute. The excavators assert that the synagogue was built in neither the second nor the third century, but rather at the end of the fourth or beginning of the fifth century C.E. Acceptance of this late dating implies the use at the turn of the fifth century of a style of building and decoration previously considered typically Roman (see pp. 52–62).

The only building among "Galilean" synagogues bearing an inscription with a date is at Nabratein. The inscription, which dates the building to 564 C.E., has been attributed to a later period of repairs. However, if taken as the date of original construction, this inscription clearly corroborates the latest Capernaum finds.

The synagogue at Ḥorvat Shema', although not of the "Galilean" type in all its details, was constructed in the third century C.E. According to the excavators, the synagogues at both Meron and Gush Ḥalav were established in the middle or towards the end of this same century.

All the above data would seem to indicate that "Galilean-type" synagogues were built as early as the third century C.E., and similar

Lintel of Nabratein synagogue with *menorah* and wreath in center

types of buildings were constructed for centuries thereafter. Some scholars who maintain a relatively late date for the synagogue at Capernaum claim that it served a sectarian community. This is most unlikely, for all the ornamentation and capitals of the building bear distinctively Jewish themes, and there is not the slightest trace of any Christian decoration or symbol. Had this been a Judeo–Christian community at the end of the fourth century, some kind of Christian symbol would certainly have appeared. Moreover, sectarians of that time had already been rejected by the Christian church, which opposed any affiliations or associations with Judaism or the Jewish people.

Substantial concentrations of Jewish settlement apparently continued in the Galilee throughout the Byzantine period, with the central and eastern Galilean hills remaining predominantly Jewish; Christianity was unsuccessful in establishing a firm base there. Synagogues remained intact, and the "Galilean" ones are best viewed as a regional type, common in the north during the late Roman and Byzantine periods. At the same time synagogues were constructed with decorative mosaic floors, like that of the "Severus" synagogue at Tiberias.

Northern Synagogues with Mosaic Pavements

This group consists of buildings from the Byzantine period with mosaic pavements and a plan which includes two rows of columns dividing the interior into a central nave and two aisles. In some of these northern synagogues with mosaic floors there is an apse

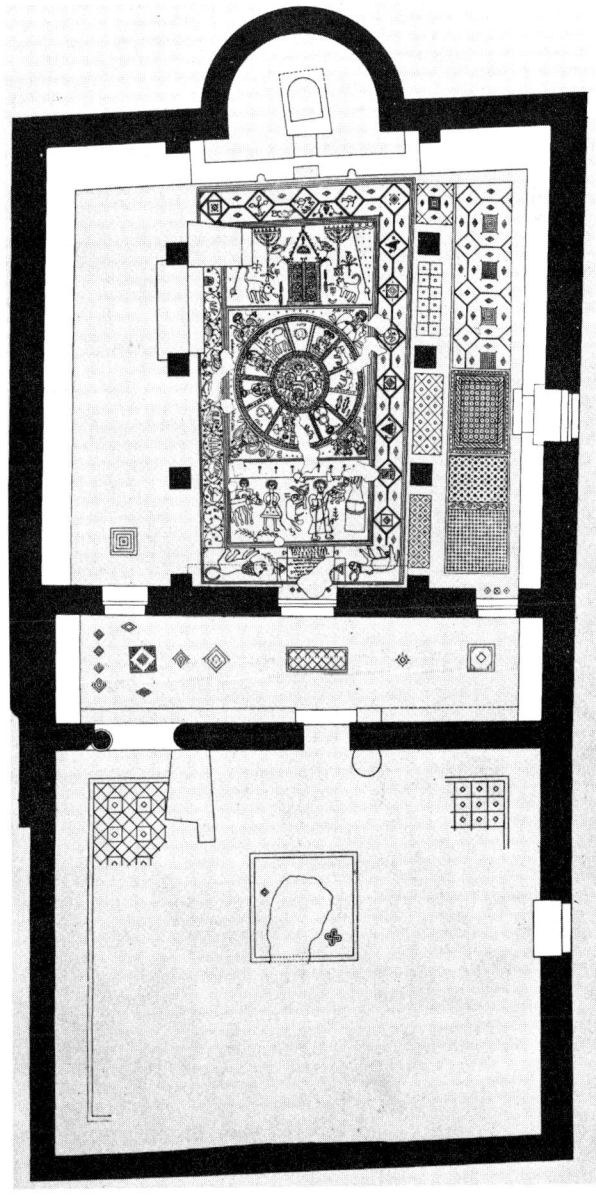

Plan of Beth Alpha synagogue

15

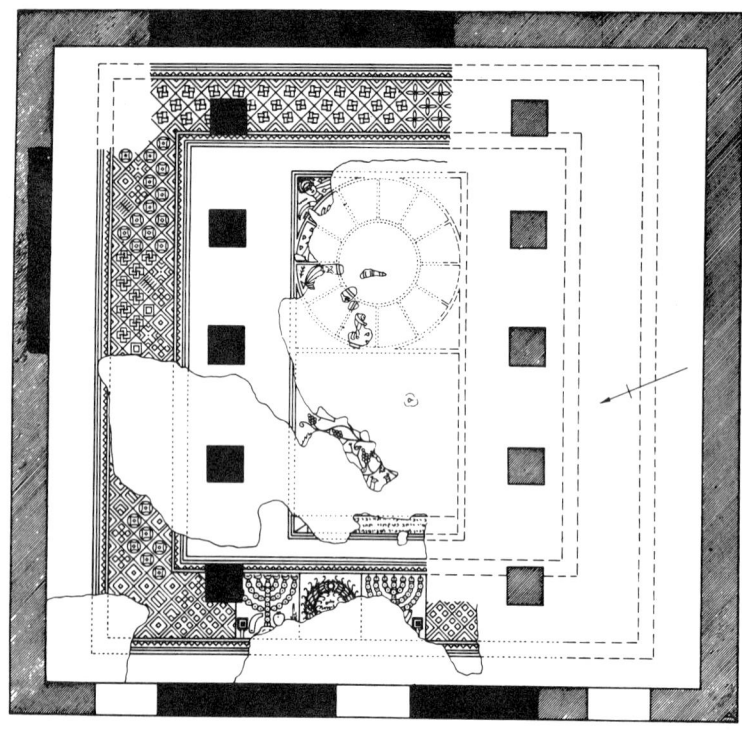

0 1 2 3 4 5 M.

Plan of Ḥusifa

in the southern wall facing Jerusalem. The study and publication of findings at Beth Alpha were of fundamental importance to the investigation of ancient synagogues. The synagogue resembles the usual Byzantine basilica. The structure consisted of a court (atrium), forecourt (narthex), and nave with an apse pointing in the direction of Jerusalem. These three sections, totaling 28 m. in length and 14 m. in width, were paved in mosaic. The floor of the nave is divided into three panels, each devoted to a single theme.

The first panel is located in front of the Torah shrine; it contains a representation of the ark, with a gabled roof, seen through an open curtain. The ark is flanked on either side by a seven-branched *menorah* with traditional religious objects nearby: *shofar, lulab, ethrog,* and incense shovel. Two lions guard the ark, one on each side. The second panel, located in the center of the floor, bears a circular depiction of the zodiac signs for the twelve months, each with its Hebrew name. In the center of the circle the sun is represented in the form of Helios, the sun-god, in a chariot with four horses (*quadriga*). The four seasons

of the year appear in the corners as winged female figures. The panel nearest the entrance depicts the sacrifice of Isaac at the moment of rescue. Abraham is about to sacrifice Isaac; above, as if out of a cloud, the palm of a hand symbolizes the angel of God, and an inscription bears the command *al tishlaḥ* ("do not send forth").

Near the entrance Greek and Aramaic inscriptions were found noting the craftsmen as well as the emperor Justin (I?), during whose reign the pavement was laid, near the beginning of the sixth century. Remains of an older floor were revealed under the pavement described above, indicating that the building itself was constructed earlier, possibly at the end of the fifth century C.E.

A plan similar to that of Beth Alpha has recently been uncovered in the ancient synagogue of Maʿoz Ḥayim. The synagogue of Ḥammath-Gader, dating from the fifth century C.E., belongs to this group. The plan of the building at Beth Yeraḥ resembles that of the synagogues of this type, as does that of the northern synagogue at Beth-Shean.

Another phenomenon existed among northern synagogues — those with the same plan, but lacking an apse. Some of these buildings had a *bema* attached to the wall facing Jerusalem. At Ḥusifa (ancient Isfiya) such a building has been found with entrances in the northwest. A similar structure exists at Reḥob. The synagogue at Ḥammath-Tiberias, paved with signs of the zodiac, had a similar plan except for one extra aisle in the east. It is reasonable to assume that the synagogues at Caesarea, Sepphoris, and Kefar Kanah, some of which have sections of mosaic pavement with inscriptions, also belong to this type. In all events, the emphasis in decoration in this group was clearly placed on their mosaics, and not on stonework of friezes, lintels, or capitals. These buildings show no trace of exterior monumental façades, and most of their ornamentation was inside. Each of these synagogues essentially represents the adaptation of a general plan to local needs. The same phenomenon also appears in southern synagogues.

Southern Synagogues with Mosaic Pavements

In southern Israel, synagogues paved in mosaic are concentrated in three geographic areas — the Jordan valley, the Judaean coastal plain and the southern Hebron hills, the latter having a particular type of building. The area of the higher Judaean-Hebron hills, including Jerusalem and Beth-el, was a stronghold of Christianity in the Byzantine period, and to date no remains of synagogues have been uncovered there. Synagogues in the south appear in peripheral settlements, where Jewish communities at that time were concentrated.

Jordan valley. Synagogues have been uncovered at Na'aran, Jericho and 'En Gedi (see pp. 116–119). All three were of the basilica type, with mosaic pavements and the direction of worship toward Jerusalem.

Judaean coastal plain. Synagogues with a similar basilical plan and mosaic pavements are also found on the coastal plain. The buildings at Ma'on and Gaza (see pp. 129–132) have been excavated. The excavator of the latter site reconstructs a building with five parallel aisles created by four rows of columns. In Ascalon and Ashdod architectural elements of synagogues have been found, but nothing is known about their plan. The mosaic pavement at Hulda, with its *shofar*, incense shovel, *ethrog*, *lulab*, and seven-branched *menorah*, is apparently not a synagogue, but rather an installation of some kind, probably a winepress.

Synagogues in the southern Hebron hills. At Susiya and Eshtemoa (see pp. 120–128) similar buildings were found, and form a separate group, presumably typical of this geographical area. These were broadhouse structures with entrances on the short eastern wall. In each of them a *bema* and niche for the Torah ark were constructed in the northern wall facing Jerusalem. They were paved in mosaic and their walls were built of ashlar. The ceilings were attached to a wooden frame covered with tiles, but no columns supported this roof. At Horvat Rimon remains of an impressive synagogue structure paved with

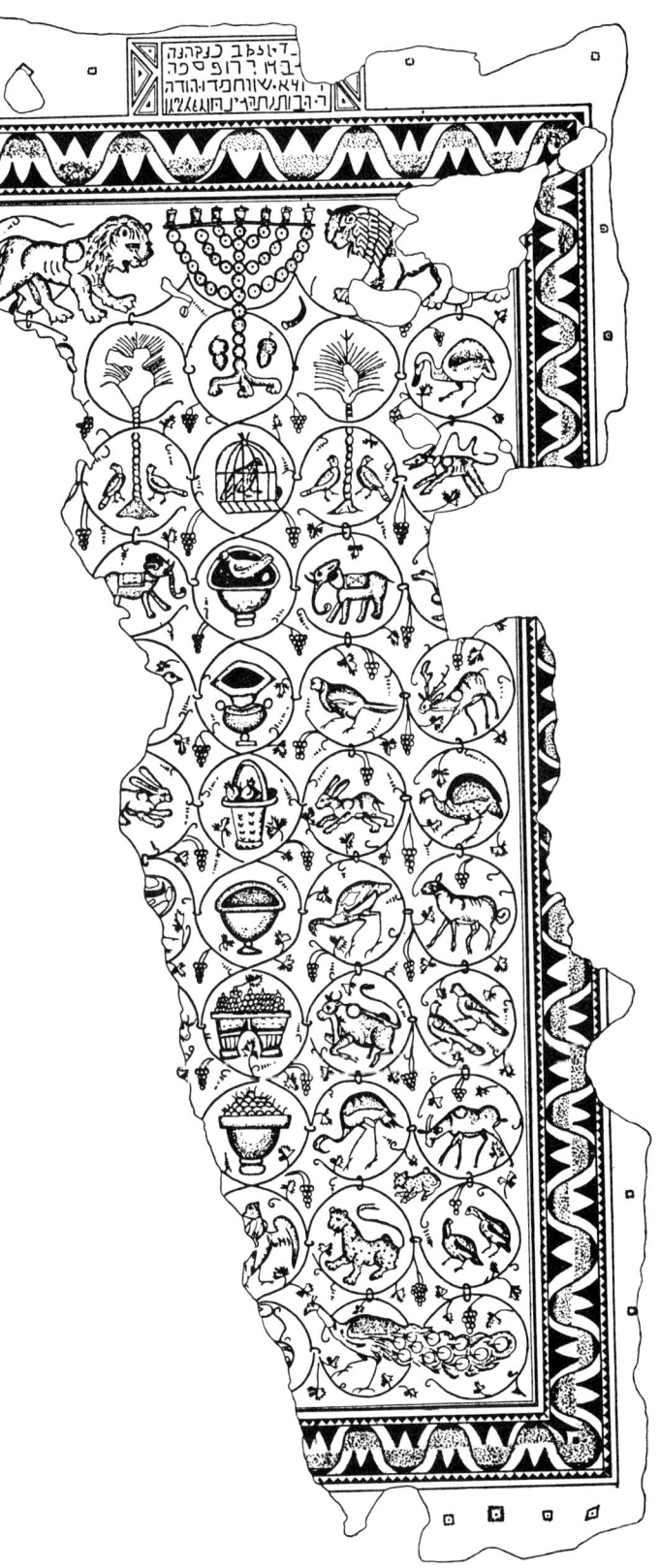

Mosaic floor of Ma'on synagogue

limestone slabs are now in the process of being excavated. We know of architectural elements of other synagogues in this area, for example, at Ḥorvat Kishor and Beth Guvrin. The synagogues in this group were first built in the third and fourth centuries C.E., and confirm what we know from literary sources about the important Jewish centers there in the period following the Bar Kokhba rebellion. Eusebius mentions seven large Jewish villages in the southern parts of both Judaea and the *Shefela.*

The regional division employed here is primarily a geographical rather than a chronological device. Each group shares certain characteristics in building plan. Some of the regional groups, such as the Galilean and south Judaean, contain elements indicating that the buildings were built in the third and fourth centuries C.E. This also holds true for several sites in the north with mosaic pavements, such as Ḥammath-Tiberias.

Scholars engaged in the study of synagogues have up to now usually delineated three chronological types of synagogue plans during the Roman and Byzantine periods. The Galilean synagogue constitutes the earliest type, dating from the second and third centuries C.E. onward. The Byzantine type, with its basilical form, mosaic pavement, and apse, represents the latest group and dates from the fifth through seventh centuries C.E. An intermediate group of synagogues, like those at Ḥammath-Tiberias, Eshtemoa, Ḥorvat Shema', and Ḥorvat Susiya, forms a transitional type. This stage was the expression of the tendency to move from a building with entrances facing Jerusalem and no permanent place for the Torah ark to one having an interior focal point in the form of a Torah ark and *bema* oriented toward Jerusalem. Its entrances were therefore on the opposite wall, facing away from Jerusalem. Such an arrangement emphasizes the functional development of these structures. The buildings of this stage have been dated to a period between the early and late groups, mostly in the fourth and fifth centuries C.E. This division was based on knowledge that had accumulated until recently.

In the past ten years several fundamental suppositions regarding the typological division and dating of synagogues have been challenged. Buildings of the "Galilean" type were also erected in the Byzantine period, as noted above. The third century witnessed the construction of both the synagogue at Ḥorvat Shema', a broadhouse structure, and, at the same time and place (a mere 600 m. away), a "Galilean-type" synagogue at Meron. While "Galilean-type" synagogues were being built, a building decorated with mosaic pavements was built by the fourth century at Ḥammath-Tiberias. A similar process occurred in the south; at 'En Gedi, and apparently at Ḥorvat Rimon, synagogues were built in the third century C.E., and shortly thereafter the type found in the Hebron hills was added.

Both standard and atypical zodiac pavements have been found at Ḥammath-Tiberias, Ḥusifa, Susiya, Beth Alpha, and Na'aran. These decorative elements appear over a wide geographical area and chronological span, from the fourth to the sixth centuries C.E. Thus, various motifs were used at considerable distances in place and time and are not attributable to the limited framework of a single architectural type or short historical period. Hopes of dating synagogues and creating a chronological typology with the aid of inscriptions have also failed to materialize, while attempts at paleographic distinctions have likewise been disappointing, since differences in the form of letters used in inscriptions have no chronological significance.

At the present stage of investigation the most fruitful method seems to be the examination of each building individually. Similar characteristics are shared by buildings in the same or neighboring regions, but there is no chronological distinction between the various regional types.

Excavation and study of synagogues have become one of the most important subjects in the archeology of Roman and Byzantine Palestine. The numerous excavations of the past decade reflected in this volume suggest that much remains to be published, and that accepted views are likely to be altered.

The Synagogue at Masada

Y. Yadin

At the very beginning of our first season of excavations, while digging in the northwestern section of the wall of Masada, we came upon a strange structure adjoining the wall, so close that it seemed part of the wall, even though it projected substantially inward and eastward, inside Masada. It was unlike any of the buildings we had excavated up to then in the casemate wall. Early in the dig we noticed what looked like benches plastered with clay protruding from the debris inside the building, next to the walls. Gradually, pillars began to appear, made in sections, and when we had finished excavating, what appeared before us was a rectangular structure with benches all round the walls, tier upon tier, all plastered

with clay. On the eastern side there was an opening. In the center were two rows of columns, three in the southern row and two in the northern. The northwestern corner of the building was a kind of cell which merged into the casemate wall, and there was an entrance to it from the south next to the western pillar of the southern row.

Even while excavating we felt that the final stage, at least of the building, and particularly of the benches, had been constructed by the Zealots. Not only did we find many coins from the period of the revolt on the floor of this room, but here and there, where the plaster on the benches had peeled, we could tell that the benches had, in fact, been made out of

Masada synagogue within casemate wall

quarried stone and broken pieces of dressed stone which had been taken from other buildings on Masada. Particularly conspicuous among these were portions of column drums and of capitals which could be identified immediately as having belonged to the lower and perhaps also to the upper terrace of the northern palace-villa. It was clear that at least these benches had been built after various parts of the palace-villa had been destroyed; and it was even clearer that this structure had the character of a communal building and was designed for public gatherings. But what was its purpose?

During the first season we already dared to suggest, albeit with considerable hesitation, that it was perhaps a synagogue. What strengthened this assumption was also the fact that the entrance faced east, and it was wholly oriented towards Jerusalem, as required by the traditional injunctions of the sages. Moreover, we found on the floor an ostracon with the inscription "priestly tithe," that is, one of the tithes that was allocated to the Levites, and another inscribed sherd which bore the name "Ḥezekiah," perhaps the name of a priest.

In one corner of the main room we found scores of soot-blackened lamps and in the rear cell the floor was covered with the remains of a powerful fire; it was evident that numerous articles of furniture and many vessels had been collected here and set alight. They included handsome vessels of glass and metal, and among them was a wash-basin.

If what we had just unearthed was indeed a synagogue, then this was a discovery of front-rank importance in the field of Jewish archeology, and certainly one of the most important finds in Masada. For up to then the very earliest synagogues discovered in Israel belonged to the end of the second or beginning of the third century C.E. There were no remains of any synagogue from the period of the Second Temple.

Because of its outstanding importance, we decided to continue our excavations of this building in the second season, and to cut sections in it and its vicinity to enable us to

examine the stages of its construction. What spurred us particularly was the fact that towards the end of the first season, while cutting a section in the upper floor-level of the rear cell, we found beneath it the base of an additional column. It was clear, however, that those who built the last floor of the building, while building this special cell in its corner, had removed that column and covered its base with the floor. It was evident, therefore, that before the Zealot stage of construction the plan of the building had been different.

The cuts made during the second season showed that there had been two clear stages of construction. The last structure with the benches was, as shown in the plan, on the right; in its earlier stage, the building had an ante-room, and the main room had columns along its southern, western, and northern sides. When the Zealots came to add the cell and the benches, they removed two of the pillars from the western row, tore down the wall dividing the ante-room from the main room to its west and set up the two pillars in its place.[1]

It is difficult to determine the function of the building in the original Herodian plan, but one may hazard the guess that even then it

[1] There can be no doubt that in its second stage this building served as a place of public assembly, and as such it resembles the *ecclesiasteria* known to us from the Hellenistic period onwards. That the building was used as a synagogue is suggested by such details as the fact that the adaptations in this stage were the work of the Zealots; the nature of the finds (the back room appears to have served as some kind of *genizah*); the cistern built north of the building; the silver sheqels found in its vicinity and the fragments of scrolls and Scriptures found nearby, and the other finds made south of it. Moreover, the fact that its back wall was orientated exactly in the direction of Jerusalem (this was facilitated by the fortuitous planning of the original building) also strengthens this supposition. We do not possess any data which could help us to establish the usual plan for a synagogue from the time of the Second Temple, but we may assume that at this stage it served first and foremost as a place of assembly and preaching; it is possible, therefore, that such synagogues were built on the model of the assembly buildings of the type mentioned above, i.e., resembling a kind of theatre, roofed-over and square in shape. If this hypothesis is correct, then we have here not only the earliest synagogue ever discovered, but also the only one dating from the time of the Second Temple (first published in *IEJ*, 1965 — ed.).

served as a synagogue. The theory may be backed by the following assumptions. First, it seems most unlikely that Herod would have denied a place of worship for the Jewish members of his court. Second, the architectural plan with its pillars is very reminiscent of the plan of several early synagogues discovered in Galilee. And third, there exists a strong conservative tradition in the siting of houses of worship, and it would be in keeping with this tradition that the Zealots, when deciding on their synagogue, specifically chose this place, in the knowledge that it had previously served as a synagogue. This would explain, too, why even the original building had been oriented toward Jerusalem. It is possible that in the period between Herod and the Zealots, when Masada was occupied by the Roman garrison, the building may have served as a stable, for between the two floors, the original and the later one, we found many layers of animal dung.

I turn now to a most interesting find which, I believe, enables us to state with greater certainty that this building was indeed a synagogue. While making the exploratory cuts in the rear cell, the two architects of our expedition, Dunayevsky and Netzer, measured the distance between the bases of the two columns we found there, and examined the filling between the two floors. In so doing they extended the area of the cut, and came upon a piece of a rolled scroll. (It was the first time, incidentally, that an architect at Masada had the fortune to find a scroll!) How had it got there, and why beneath the upper floor? When we studied the area of the cut more carefully, we found that a pit had once been dug at this spot, from the upper floor. The scroll was found at the bottom of this pit which had later been filled with earth and stones. This had therefore been a kind of *genizah*, where observant Jews buried — since they would not destroy — documents in the holy language, Hebrew. This was traditionally done to Hebrew documents which had gone out of use, either because they were old and tattered or because they contained mistakes. This scroll may have been buried while the

Ostraca from Masada

Zealots lived here because it was no longer usable, or it may have been hidden by them just before they ended their lives. Whichever it was, we were spurred by the find to excavate the whole of the upper floor in the rear cell to see if there were any other such pits.

Chief Petty Officer Moshe Cohen, from the Israeli Navy, was assigned the delicate task of clearing and sifting through the earth above the upper floor. After several days' work, he discovered a portion of the floor missing in the southern section of the cell, and beneath it a pit full of stamped down earth. At the very moment of his discovery, an urgent telegram arrived recalling him to his job in the Navy for three days. He begged us to hold up the clearance work until his return, and though it was not easy to restrain our eagerness, we agreed to the delay. When he returned, he immediately resumed excavating the pit, while we all stood by, tense with excitement. Within a few hours he had reached almost to the bottom of the pit and there his groping hands found the remains of a scroll. Though the parchment was badly gnawed, we could immediately identify the writing as chapters from the *Book of Ezekiel;* and the parts that were better preserved than others, and which we could easily read, contained extracts from Chapter 37 — the vision of the dry bones.

As for the rolled scroll discovered in the first pit, it was found on opening — which had to be done with great care in the laboratory in Jerusalem — to contain parts of the two final chapters of the *Book of Deuteronomy*. But the tightly rolled core of the scroll, on which we had pinned much hope, turned out, to our dismay, to be simply the blank end "sheets" of the scroll. They had been sewn to the written "sheets" to facilitate rolling and unrolling.

It need hardly be added at this stage that these two scrolls, too, are virtually identical with the traditional biblical texts. There are only a few slight changes in the *Ezekiel* scroll.

These two scrolls are important in themselves. They also lend support, as we have indicated, to the probability that this building was indeed a synagogue. But there is another aspect of high importance to the discovery of these two scrolls: they are the only ones found not on the floor of a room, but in a *genizah* beneath the floor laid by the Zealots. This means that the date of the scrolls cannot possibly be later than 74 C.E. and not even the most skeptical of scholars can challenge this.

All in all, we discovered at Masada portions of fourteen scrolls, biblical, sectarian and apocryphal. From the point of view of scroll research and a study of the literature of the Second Temple period, these were the most important discoveries of our Masada excavations.

Apart from scrolls, other important inscriptions were found. These were the ostraca, inscribed pieces of pottery, which was the common writing material for everyday use. Papyrus and parchment were too costly for such a purpose. Altogether we discovered almost 700 inscriptions on pottery. Where such inscriptions had been written on complete vessels, they are short, simply recording the name of the owner. The names we found were Jewish names, written in Hebrew, and most of them are familiar. Where the owner was a male, the inscription would contain both his and his father's names; where it was a woman, she would appear as the wife or the daughter of so-and-so. The inscription on one jug is worth mentioning. It read *Kahana Raba 'Aqavia*, the literal translation of which is "Great Priest 'Aqavia." What it meant was that the owner of the vessel was 'Aqavia, and he was *of the family* of High Priests.

We also found jars belonging to the Herodian period. They were almost all broken vessels, and it is possible that the Zealots forebore from using them. From the archeological point of view, these sherds were of great importance, enabling us to observe with ease the differences in the shapes and makes of pottery vessels that had developed from the period of Herod to that of the Zealots, only a brief — in archeological terms — seventy years. In this sphere, we were extremely lucky to find sherds of wine jars which bore an exact date — a very rare and always hoped for occurrence at an archeological dig. The dating on these jars followed the standard Roman system of date recording — by noting the name of the consul of that particular year. In our case, all jars bore the name of the Roman consul for the year 19 B.C.E., C. Sentius Saturninus. These jars had contained wine which had been specially sent from Italy to Herod. We know this from the last line of the inscription, which read: "To King Herod of Judaea." This was the first time we had discovered an inscription with the name of Herod.

Among the various ostraca were quite a number with a specific type of inscription — a name accompanied by a special sign. There were three groups of this type of ostraca. On the sherds of the first group appeared the name *Yehohanan* (John), written literally in the handwriting of the man — his signature, in fact. Below it, to the left, was the letter *alpha* (A), and to the right the letter *yod* (Y) in the Paleo-Hebrew script. The second group bore the name *Shimeon* (Simon), below it the letter *gimel* (G) and to its left the letter *dalet* (D) or perhaps *resh* (R), also in the Paleo-Hebrew script. Here, too, *Shimeon* appeared as a signature. The third group of sherds contained the name *Yehuda* (Judah), and below it the letter *samekh* (S) in Paleo-Hebrew, and the Greek letter *beta*, written from right to left instead of from left to right.

What were these ostraca? Were they some kind of coupon or chit? And for what were they used? The combination of name and symbol suggests a conventional sign or perhaps an esoteric code. For what purpose? Could it be that John, Simon and Judah were the names of commanders, or of brigades, and that the troops of the particular unit were given these "chits" to draw their rations? Or perhaps they were "passes" to enable them to enter the Masada stronghold? Or was this whole system of "chits" associated with the distribution of the special rations for priests and Levites? We can only speculate; we have no definitive answer.

There were some 275 ostraca of another type, where each sherd bore a single letter, two letters or three; again we have no way of knowing what this meant. The lettering, I may say, is done in a very beautiful script. We found ostraca with such markings as the Hebrew for "Z," "ZZ," "ZZZ," "QA," "GT," and indeed almost all the letters of the Hebrew alphabet are represented. Most of these sherds were found near the storehouses, so perhaps they had something to do with the rationing system of the Zealots during the siege.

It is clear that the writing on the ostraca was done by experienced scribes, and these inscriptions fill gaps in our knowledge of writing during the period of the Second Temple. Though very short, these inscriptions are of great paleographic value and shed much light on the history of Hebrew script. In the case of the scrolls, we were aided by the archeological and historical data in determining that they

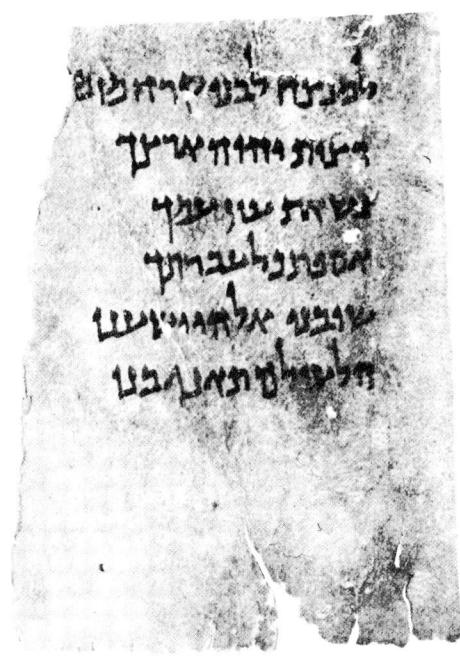

Fragment of scroll of *Psalms* (85:1ff.) found at Masada

could not be later than 74 C.E., but we could not know exactly when they had actually been copied, for each scroll may have been in the possession of its owner for decades. With the ostraca, however, it was possible to be accurate to within eight years, and to determine with absolute certainty that those with the Hebrew inscriptions were written between 66 and 74 C.E., namely, the period when Masada was occupied by the Zealots.

The Synagogues at Masada and Herodium*

G. Foerster

The existence of numerous synagogues in the period of the Second Temple is a fact long known from literary sources. Josephus, the New Testament, and rabbinic literature all mention synagogues at many sites.[1] The only archeological evidence, however, until quite recently, was a single inscription from a synagogue in Jerusalem.[2]

In the extensive excavations conducted in Herod's fortress–palaces at Masada and Herodium,[3] assembly-halls were uncovered which, in the opinion of the excavators, were synagogues. These two halls are almost identical in dimensions: at Masada, 12 × 15 m.; at Herodium, 10.5 × 15 m. They were undoubtedly constructed along with the other structures at these sites, though significant modifications were made in both of them during the First Revolt against Rome, when these buildings fell into the hands of the insurgents.

The structure at Masada in its initial Herodian phase was divided into two elements: a vestibule and a hall. During the Revolt, the partition between the two chambers was removed and a smaller room was built in the northern corner. Along the walls of this expanded hall, three rows of stone benches were constructed, built of ashlars taken from Herod's palace structures (see pp. 19–20).

At Herodium, a similar process is evident. The oblong hall, originally a triclinium, received four new columns and rows of benches along its walls.[4] The bases and drums of the columns were apparently taken from the western colonnade of the grand peristyle. The benches, too, were built in part of architectural fragments taken from other parts of Herod's palace, most likely during the First Revolt.

The architectural conception of this second phase in both structures is essentially identical: an oblong hall lined with benches and with supporting columns in the space of the hall proper. Both halls are quite plain, with no ornamentation. At Masada, the walls and benches were plastered over with a clay-like plaster tempered with straw, like the other Zealot constructions on the site; at Herodium, the walls were plastered with stucco — apparently original — while no traces of plaster have survived on the stone benches. In neither hall has a fixed place been found for the Torah shrine. At Masada the smaller room

* Abridged from *Eretz-Israel*, 11 (1973), 224–228 (Hebrew).

[1] Jerusalem: T *Sukka* 4, 5 mentions a synagogue on the Temple Mount, and according to B *Ketubot* 105a, Titus destroyed 394 synagogues here (480 synagogues according to J *Megilla*, III, 1, 73d); Caesarea: cf. Josephus, *War*, II, 285–290; Dor: Josephus, *Ant.* XIX, 300; Nazareth: e.g., *Mark* 6:2; Tiberias: Josephus, *Life*, 277; Capernaum: e.g., *Mark* 1:21.

[2] See, e.g., *Inscriptions Reveal, Documents from the Time of the Bible, the Mishna and the Talmud* (Israel Museum Cat. No. 100), (Jerusalem, 1973), No. 182 on p. 83 of the English section; ill. on p. 183 of the Hebrew, and p. 11 above.

[3] Y. Yadin, *Masada, Herod's Fortress and the Zealots' Last Stand* (London, 1966), pp. 181–191 (cf. above, pp. 19–23); *idem, IEJ*, 15 (1965), 76–79, Pl. 17; V.C. Corbo: "L'Herodion di Giabal Fureidis," *Jerusalem Through the Ages* (Jerusalem, 1968), 42*–47*, Pl. V:1. See also M. Avi-Yonah and E. Stern (eds.), *Encyclopedia of Archaeological Excavations in the Holy Land* (Jerusalem, 1975–) s.v.

[4] In contrast to Corbo's conclusions, the present author, in his clearance work on the site in 1969, found that the bases of the four columns were not founded upon stylobates but merely rested upon a layer of earth, 10 cm. thick, beneath which were traces of the original floor of the chamber. See *IEJ*, 19 (1969), 123–124.

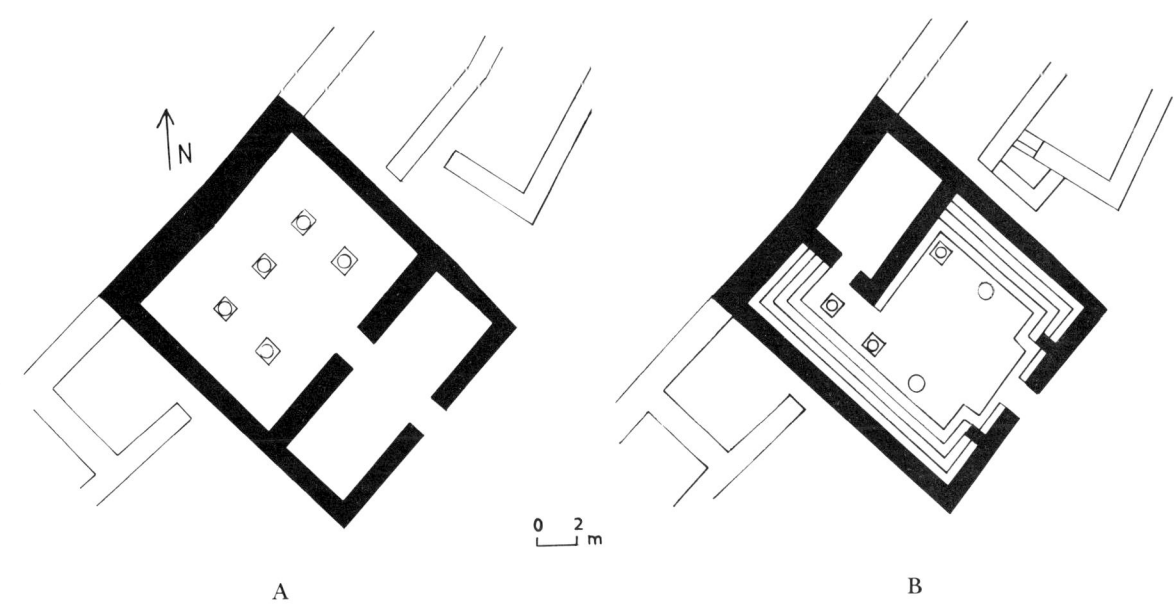

Herodium: the synagogue area, looking southwest

The two stages of the synagogue at Masada. A: the original Herodian stage; B: the synagogue of the insurgents

A

B

0 2
⊢⊢ m

N

may have functioned as a repository, since scroll fragments were discovered there. At Herodium, one of the smaller rooms flanking the hall may have served this purpose.

It should be noted that, adjacent to both of these halls, there were *miqvaot* (ritual baths). At Herodium the ritual bath actually abutted the eastern wall of the synagogue, while at Masada it was in a structure close by.

To these two buildings under discussion dating from the Second Temple period, we may possibly add a third, described in 1926 by J. Ory in an unpublished excavation report on the clearance of the synagogue at Chorazin; the structure in question is located some 200 m. west of the later synagogue:

> A square colonnaded building of small dimensions, of a disposition similar to the interior arrangement of the synagogue, 7 columns, 3 on each side [sic!] (the entrance was afforded through the east wall) were supporting the roof, and the whole space between the colonnade and walls on three sides was occupied with sitting benches in 5 courses.

In a recent visit to Chorazin, the present author was unable to locate this structure. Its exact date is unknown, but we can assume that it is like the halls at Masada and Herodium; if so, it would probably have been erected in the first century C.E.

Two other early synagogues, apparently of similar type, have lately been discovered in the north, the one at Magdala on the Sea of Galilee, and the other at the recently identified site of Gamla, northeast of the lake (see pp. 30–41). These finds attest to the existence of a group of northern synagogues from late Second Temple times.

All these structures are characterized by stone benches along three walls and two or three rows of columns. They were clearly intended as assembly-halls. It should be noted that in all the buildings but one, the entrance was from the east.

Y. Yadin and N. Avigad have proposed different solutions for the origin of the synagogue plans at Masada and Herodium (see pp. 20, 44). Yadin compares the plan of the Masada synagogue with that of an *ecclesiasterion* at Priene, and similar buildings intended for assembly at other sites in Asia Minor. However, this comparison is weakened by considerable differences in dating and in the dimensions of the buildings involved.[5] Avigad, in contrast, regards the Masada synagogue as the "local archetype of the Galilean synagogue plan." He holds that the Masada plan is based on that of a basilica, on which he considers the plan of the "Galilean" synagogues also to be based. Avigad points out that the orientation of the Masada synagogue differs from that of the "Galilean" synagogues, although all of them are oriented toward Jerusalem. At Masada the worshippers faced Jerusalem immediately upon entering the building, whereas in Galilee the worshippers had to turn around in order to pray toward the Holy City, for the entrances there were on the Jerusalem side. Even so, Avigad regards the synagogue at Masada as the missing link in the development which led to the "Galilean" synagogue plan of the third century C.E.[6] The absence of such a link was noted already by Kohl and Watzinger in their monumental study of the "Galilean" synagogues, published over 60 years ago.[7] These early scholars discerned that the decoration of the "Galilean" synagogues derived from the classical style so common in Syria and Asia Minor, whereas the plan of the structures had no clear parallels in our region.

Avigad appears to be correct in relating the plan of the synagogue at Masada to that of the "Galilean" synagogues; however, it seems that this plan should not be regarded as basilical, for it differs in too many elements from the basic form.[8] In our opinion, the synagogues

[5] Yadin: *IEJ*, 15 (1965), 78–79.

[6] N. Avigad, "On the Form of Ancient Synagogues," *Kol Eretz Naphtali* (Jerusalem, 1967), pp. 91–100 (Hebrew).

[7] H. Kohl and C. Watzinger, *Antike Synagogen in Galilaea* (Leipzig, 1916), pp. 147 ff.

[8] The basilical plan, of western origin, is of much grander proportions; the principal feature is four or, occasionally, two rows of columns. Each such structure had a focal point in the form of a raised tribunal, often located within an apse. Such buildings had no benches along their walls.

Air-photo of Herodium, looking southeast. The synagogue is visible on the southwest, between the two semi-circular towers

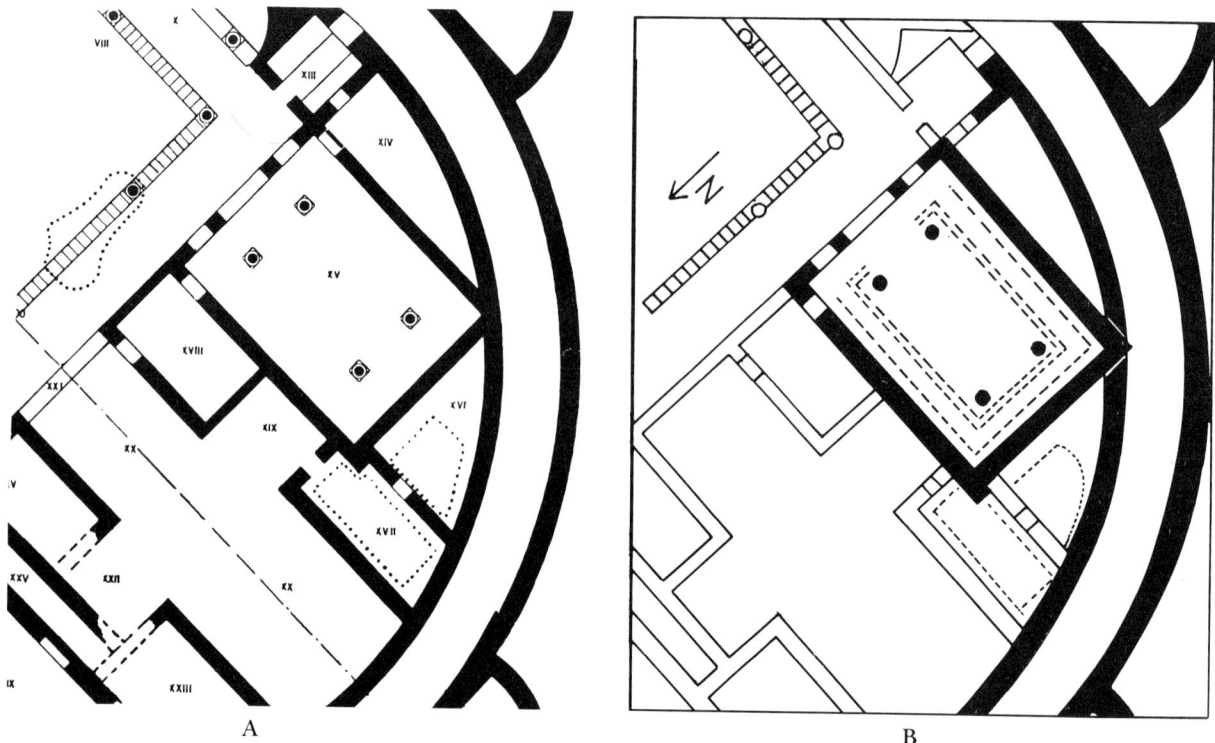

The two stages of the building at Herodium. A: the original Herodian triclinium; B: the synagogue of the First Rebellion, 66–74 C.E.

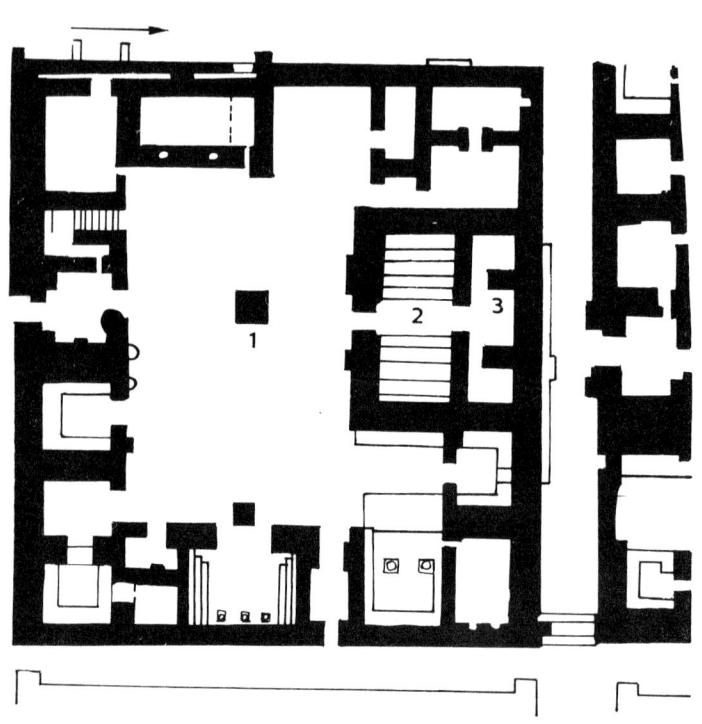

Temple of Atargatis at Dura: 1. Courtyard; 2. Pronaos with benches; 3. Naos.

under discussion should be compared not with structures whose geographical remoteness makes doubtful any architectural connection with Israel, but rather with a less distant group of halls which has not hitherto been considered in this context. In these halls, benches are arranged in a horseshoe around the walls, and the general plan resembles a very small theater or *odeon*; they may be either covered or open. The foremost examples are the assembly halls found at Dura Europos — the *pronaoi* of the temples of Atargatis, Artemis, and Tyche. Cumont denoted them "salles aux gradins," stepped halls, on the basis of their internal form. There, the benches along two or three walls are also plastered, and dedicatory inscriptions on several of them date these structures to the first half of the first century C.E. These halls served for the assembly of worshippers who were barred from entering the temples proper. Here, a ritual was held culminating with the introduction of a statue of the god of the temple.

There is thus a great resemblance both in plan and in function between the halls at Dura Europos and those at Masada, Herodium, and Chorazin.

The most characteristic feature of the assembly halls at Masada, Herodium, and Chorazin is their uniform orientation; in all three, entrance is from the east, as in the Temple in Jerusalem. This uniformity cannot be regarded as coincidental, but must be seriously considered in any discussion of the function and date of these structures. A uniform orientation is a constant feature of structures intended for worship. The conformity to the orientation of the Temple in Jerusalem would indicate that these buildings were planned consistent with the most sacred Jewish site at a time when it still stood in all its glory. This is confirmed by one of the few halakhot in talmudic literature treating synagogues in general, and our problem in particular: T *Megillah* III, 22 states: "One should only place the entrance to synagogues in the east, for we find that in the Temple the entrance faced the east." This passage has always raised difficulties in interpretation, for it is in decided contrast with the orientation of most of the ancient synagogues known till recently, all dating from the third–seventh centuries C.E. We may now regard this statement as referring to synagogues in the final period of the Second Temple, and in accord with recent archeological finds.[9]

---

[9] Though from a later period, three other synagogues, all in Judaea and stemming from the fourth century C.E., can be added to this group as far as their plan is concerned: the structure of "David's Tomb" on Mount Zion in Jerusalem (see Y. Yadin [ed.], *Jerusalem Revealed* [Jerusalem, 1975], pp. 116–117, and J. Pinkerfeld, *Bulletin of the Louis M. Rabinowitz Fund...* 3. [1960], 42–43, Fig. 1); the synagogue at Eshtemoa (see pp. 120–122); and that at Ḥorvat Susiya (see pp. 123–128). In all three the entrance is on the east, while the apse is on the north. These are "broadhouses," apparently a hybrid plan incorporating both the eastern entrance and the orientation of worship toward Jerusalem.

The Synagogue at Gamla

S. Gutman

During the First Revolt against Rome, one of the earliest Jewish defeats in 67 C.E. occurred in the siege of Gamla, east of the Sea of Galilee. Gamla was, in Josephus' words:

> a city over against Tarichaea, but on the other side of the lake (of Galilee) ... [part] of Gaulanitis ... Gamla did not submit to the Romans, but relied upon the difficulty of the place ... for it was situated upon a rough ridge of a high mountain, with a kind of neck in the middle: when it begins to ascend, it lengthens itself, and declines as much downward before as behind, insomuch that it is like a camel [Aramaic: *gamla*] in figure, from whence it is so named ... There are abrupt parts divided from the rest, and ending in vast deep valleys; yet there are parts behind, where they are joined to the mountain ...; but then the people belonging to the place have cut an oblique ditch there ... On its acclivity, which is straight, houses are built, and those very thick and close to one another ... and its southern mount ... was in the nature of a citadel ... (*War* IV, 1 ff.).

The Roman siege was lengthy and costly, requiring heavy siege machinery, ballistae and catapults, shooting huge stones and giant arrows. Eventually, Roman sappers undermined one of the towers of the town-wall, and the city was stormed. Jewish resistance was fierce but futile. As at Masada — the final tragic focus of this same revolt — only two women survived the month-long siege.

In the course of archeological surveys after the 1967 war, Yitzhaq Gal, dissatisfied with the traditional identification of Gamla with el-Ahdab, some miles to the southeast, suggested that the site actually lies on a spur between the two branches of Naḥal Daliot, west of the village of Deir Qeruḥ. The present author followed up this suggestion in a three-day survey,[1] and found that the spot was visible from Tarichaea, that the topographical factors matched Josephus' description, and that the southern slopes bore archeological remains, precisely where Josephus describes them. We also found the remains of buildings, a town-wall blocking the spur on the east, and pottery from the two historical periods in which Josephus mentions Gamla. The area of excavations is located on the southern flank of the spur, in a region of exposed ruins of about 45 acres in extent.[2] The site included part of the town-wall, running across the spur close to the saddle. The wall itself could be traced even prior to excavation, and it was assumed that a gate was to be found here. Near the western face of the wall we noticed several architectural fragments, hinting at the possibility of a

[1] Together with Y. Gal and D. and F. Sela (the latter from the Golan Field School). Gamla was long considered to be at Jamlieh some 15 km. southeast of the present site. Josephus' description, hardly suited to Jamlieh, perfectly fits the peculiar topography of our site. This mistaken identity stemmed from the misidentification of Tarichaea by Pliny (*Nat. Hist.* V, 15), but several decades ago it was properly placed at Magdala (the home town of Mary Magdalene), on the northwestern shore of the Sea of Galilee.

[2] The excavations were conducted by the author on behalf of the Department of Antiquities and Museums. Kibbutz volunteers were organized by the Geography Department of the Kibbutz Movement; material assistance was received from the Jewish National Fund and from the local settlements, especially the recently-founded Gamla as well as Keshet Yonatan Field School. The Gitlin family of Mexico made a significant financial contribution, through the good services of Mr. M. Yavnai. The surveyors were headed by M. Feist of the Department of Antiquities and Museums.

View of Gamla, looking westward

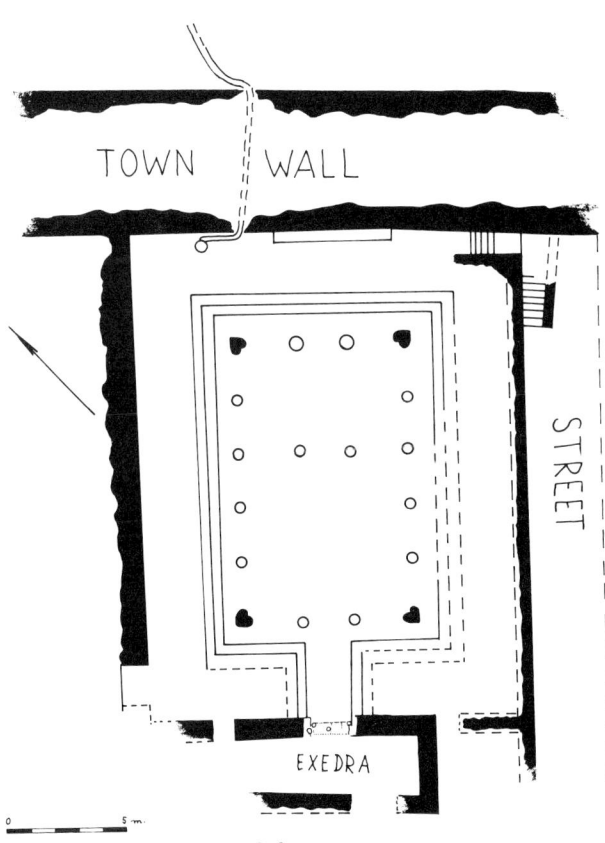

Plan of the synagogue

public structure there. Our hopes were not disappointed, for we have uncovered in this area the town-wall, a gate, and a public building — apparently the main synagogue of Gamla.

West of the wall, within the town, we concentrated on an area stretching some 23 m. inward from the wall and 19 m. along it. This area, part of the southern slope, is quite steep and is covered with rubble that has tumbled from above. The heaps of debris included ashlars, smashed drums of columns, and a few Roman ballista stones.

Working conditions were very difficult, for the steepness of the slope precluded the usual technique of excavation by strata. Two building levels were revealed. In the upper level a structure abutted the town-wall, measuring ca. 16×20 m. West of this building, an exedra was uncovered, 3 m. wide, with two openings giving access to the interior. At a level 3 m. lower than that of the building, a narrow street was partially revealed, running from near the town-wall westward along the southern wall of the building. Steps led up from it to an opening at the eastern corner of the building. On these steps numerous ballista stones were found, together with a few arrowheads.

The structure is a large, elongated hall with the principal entrance on the west. The

31

View of northeastern benches of synagogue with piles of ballista stones

eastern wall is actually the western face of the town-wall; the northern, long wall is also the supporting wall of the terrace spreading to the north. The southern wall has collapsed almost entirely down the slope; its foundations, however, border the street.

The northern floor is 20 m. long, running the entire length of the building and meeting the eastern and western floors at either end. From the northern wall to the edge of the upper bench (see below), the floor is 2.40 m. wide. It is unpaved and bears traces of hearths, apparently used by refugees for cooking during the siege. Parallel to the northern wall, and bordering the southern edge of the floor, were three rows of benches built of well-dressed basalt ashlars. Each bench was about 50 cm. high and was attached to counterparts on the east and west. At the foot of the lowermost bench was a row of well-dressed basalt flagstones, on the lower, central floor-level.

The eastern floor, abutting the town-wall, is also 2.40 m. wide, from the wall to the edge of the upper bench, and is paved in part with well-dressed basalt flagstones. There is a bench along the eastern wall, standing on this pavement. In the northern, unpaved part of this floor, a water channel penetrates through the town-wall from the north; a small depression caught the water. This channel branches off from an aqueduct, parts of which have been uncovered east of the town-wall. From this floor down to the floor of the hall proper, there are four rows of benches, joining up with those on the north and south. South of the paved area is a pit.

The southern floor is equal in length to the northern floor, though its width is not known, for the southern wall is entirely destroyed. On the basis of the southern supporting wall, built along the street below, it can be assumed that it was of the same width as that on the north. Here, too, there were three rows of benches, mostly destroyed.

The western floor, along the western wall, is divided into three parts. From the western wall to the edge of the upper bench, the floor is 2.10 m. wide. The benches join up with those on the north and south. The lower part leading in from the exedra to the hall is 3.20 m. long and 1.50 m. wide at floor-level, and is flanked by two extant rows of benches which join up with those of the western floor on either side.

The exedra is 3 m. in width and, from north to south, in the part so far cleared, 8.70 m. long. The area south of the exedra has not yet been completely cleared. The area to the west contains several rooms, including a *miqveh* or ritual bath. In the northern part of the exedra, where the floor-level is somewhat raised, a water channel runs from the doorway to the *miqveh* on the west.

The floor of the central hall, surrounded on all four sides by the stepped benches (except at the main entrance), is 13.40 m. long from east to west, and 9.30 m. wide from north to south, and is about 0.95 m. lower than the surrounding floors. A row of basalt flagstones borders this lower level, and just within is another row of stones, only partially pre-

Section of the synagogue looking east

served, resembling a stylobate for columns. The rest of the floor area seems to have been unpaved (there is no evidence of stone looting here). The inner space of the hall is divided into two parts by a row of flagstones, apparently also a stylobate for two missing columns, running across the hall. Thus, it was divided into two spaces — the western one a square of about 7.00 × 6.50 m. which may have been open to the sky, and the eastern one measuring about 4.00 × 6.50 m.

Amongst the smaller finds from the building, several are noteworthy. Iron nails were found scattered about the floor, in the rubble overlying it and on the benches. In the northeastern corner of the hall, a concentration of nails was found in a burnt layer. Such nails may have been from the rafters of the building. Fragments of pottery oil-lamps were found throughout the excavations, all of the Herodian type (used, for example, by the Zealots at Masada during the First Revolt against Rome). These date the destruction of the building to some time during 66-67 C.E., that is, during the revolt.

Though the pottery is still being studied, certain conclusions may already be drawn. Most of the material is of the period spanning the first centuries B.C.E. and C.E. In the area excavated, no material later than this period has come to light. No intact vessels were found, except for a small bowl from the northern floor, near the niche (see plan), and a small juglet from the main entrance.

Most of the coins found at Gamla were picked up on the surface during our surveys. In the excavations, only a few coins came to light, mostly encrusted and as yet unidentified. The identifiable ones are of the Hellenistic and early Roman periods, mostly minted under Alexander Jannaeus, though a few are earlier.

Arrowheads and ballista stones were found in relatively large numbers within and around the building. Most of the arrowheads were found concentrated on the eastern benches and on the adjacent floors. Some were also found near the main doorway, on the west. All were found lying directly on the floor, on benches, or within the layer immediately overlying them; and most seemed to be pointing east–west, their probable direction of flight. Most of the points were bent from impact, and all are heavily corroded. They are of various sizes, ranging from 3 cm. to 14 cm. in length; the shafts, of course, have not been preserved. Ballista stones were noted on the surface during the surveys; during excavations, extremely large numbers of them came to light. Such stones were found within the layer immediately overlying, and directly on the floors and benches. This quantity, more

Arrowheads found in vicinity of synagogue

than 350 stones, is indicative of the heavy bombardment of the adjacent town-wall and this major building, which is 320 sq. m. in area. Scores more were found east of the town-wall, opposite the building and especially near the gate. This is the first time in the history of archeological excavations in Israel that direct traces of such fierce fighting have come to light, and the discoveries are in full accord with Josephus' account of the siege. All the ballista stones are of basalt, indicating their local origin. They range in diameter from 37 to 48 cm.; some very large rounded fieldstones were also used as missiles.

Identification of the Building as a Synagogue

The interior layout of this building clearly indicates that it was intended for public assembly. The benches and the surrounding floors obviously served some public function. The arrangement of the benches, especially on the east, together with the layout of the main entrance, is noteworthy in this respect.

Another notable feature in the plan of the hall is the several entrances — relating to the separate floors — and the main doorway onto the central floor of the hall. This would seem to have a direct bearing upon the nature of the function of the building.

At present, we can note that there are no pagan motifs or traces of pagan cult within the building; such remains are usually evident even in secular 'council houses'. The separate entrances may reflect the separation of female congregants from the male, a feature sometimes associated with ancient synagogues. The arrangement of the benches may also reflect a focus toward the southwest, on the axis of the structure; this orientation — toward Jerusalem — is a prominent, universal feature of ancient synagogues. Certain architectural features also typify the style of synagogues, even in later periods: the heart-sectioned corner columns (three were found *in situ*); the carvings on the broken lintel found near the main doorway, and the large niche at the western corner of the building.

In the second and third seasons of excavations on the site, probes were made at several spots beneath the level of the Roman period. In the eastern corner of the central floor, near the heart-shaped column, virgin soil was reached, and coins of Alexander Jannaeus were found beneath the floor-level. Within the thick town-wall, just north of the eastern corner of the building, a casemate-like room was discovered, with two successive floor-levels; on the upper floor were coins of John Hyrcanus II (63–40 B.C.E.), while on the lower one were coins of Alexander Jannaeus (103–76 B.C.E.). This, in brief, points to a major change here in the days of Hyrcanus II, and it is in this connection that we may posit the erection of the adjacent synagogue.

Thus, assuming that our interpretation is correct (and despite the lack of any conclusive evidence), Gamla would be the earliest known synagogue uncovered so far in Roman Palestine.

Rosetta incised on architectural fragment
from Gamla synagogue

The Synagogue of Gamla and the Typology of Second-Temple Synagogues

Z. Ma'oz

In comparison with our extensive knowledge of the synagogues of the late Roman–Byzantine period, the available evidence on the synagogues of the Second Temple period is insignificant. The reason for the paucity of synagogue remains from this period appears to be fourfold: (1) fewer excavations have been carried out at sites from this period; (2) later, massive building activities have destroyed strata from the Hellenistic–early Roman periods; (3) the lack of exact definitions of the architectural plan or decorative symbols which could identify a building with certainty as a synagogue; and (4) some of the early synagogues may have been housed in large unadorned rooms and no traces of their appurtenances — the seats and the Torah shrine — have survived, since they were probably made of wood.

Prior to the excavations at Gamla, only two synagogues antedating the destruction of the Second Temple were known. Both these structures were found in Herodian fortress-palaces, one at Masada and the other at Herodium (see pp. 19–29). They were discovered in buildings which were originally reception and ceremonial halls and were hastily improvised into houses of worship during the First Revolt. The Herodian triclinia were converted into religious halls of assembly by the introduction of acts of worship — scriptural readings and prayers — and the sole architectural expression of their new function was the addition of benches along the walls.

Because of this paucity of evidence, the discovery of a synagogue from this period at Gamla in the Golan (see pp. 30–34) took on even greater importance. This is the only building known from the Second Temple period which, from the start, was designed and built as a synagogue for use by an urban congregation. The examination of its plan is therefore of great value for understanding the architectural beginnings of the Palestinian synagogue. Fortunately, it was well preserved and its various components can be clearly observed.

After examining the Gamla building as an independent architectural–functional unit, we shall compare it with those of Masada and Herodium, and attempt to identify the common architectural features shared by synagogues of the period. Finally, we shall consider such problems as the origin of the plan of the buildings, the development of the ritual in the synagogues, and the relationship between the synagogues of the Second Temple period and the "Galilean" synagogues of the late Roman period.

Date of the Gamla Synagogue

There is no doubt that the Gamla synagogue dates to the Second Temple period, since the city was razed by the Romans in November, 67 C.E. during the First Revolt against Rome and was never resettled (Josephus, *War*, IV, 83). Gutman assigns its construction to the end of the Hasmonean period, during the days of John Hyrcanus II (63–40 B.C.E.), on the basis of coins of Alexander Jannaeus and Hyrcanus II discovered in the dirt fill beneath the synagogue (see above, p. 34). It would appear, however, that the building is of later date and was erected sometime between 23 B.C.E. and 41 C.E., as seems to be indicated by the stratigraphy of the excavations and the literary evidence.

35

Fragment of capital from Gamla

The synagogue was located at the eastern end of the city, in the area farthest from the presumed Hellenistic nucleus — the acropolis — which stood on the high western end of the ridge. In the excavations, three clear strata of building were uncovered in the area of the synagogue. Of the earliest stratum, only the foundations were preserved. This stratum was uncovered in places where the succeeding stratum was built on a different plan, and did not utilize the earlier remains. Buildings of the earliest stratum seem to have been completely dismantled during the construction of the following one, though the later builders did utilize the terraces, the same general plan, and even a number of the earlier walls as foundations. Though it is difficult to assess the character of the building and the extent of its area on the basis of the few remaining walls, it is nevertheless apparent that the houses of the earliest stratum correspond to those of the succeeding one in both nature and quality of construction.

The remains of the second stratum were the best preserved, since it continued in existence down to the fall of the city. Some of its houses still stood to the height of the roofs, though only the lower walls of others had survived. In one of the rooms, on the west side of the terrace on which the synagogue stood, a coin of Herod was found in the fill of the foundations, and a coin of Agrippa I lay on the floor.

The last stratum belongs to the period of the Jewish revolt against Rome. Here, the eastern walls of the houses on the outskirts of the city were widened and incorporated within a new wall which protected the approaches to the city. As we shall see below, the synagogue was demolished at this time.

The pottery uncovered in this excavation area — most of it unstratified from fills and eroded debris of the destroyed city — dates from the first century B.C.E. through the first century C.E. Since no pottery was found here from the second century B.C.E., it seems that all three strata belong to the time span between the first century B.C.E. to 67 C.E.

Gamla is first mentioned in the literary sources in connection with Alexander Jannaeus' conquest of the Golan between the years 83–81 B.C.E. (Josephus, *Ant.,* XV, 394; *War,* I, 93). Jannaeus captured the Hellenistic fortress here, which was ruled by the tyrant Demetrius. This stronghold, which was later turned into the acropolis of the city, has not yet been excavated and there is, therefore, no architectural or ceramic evidence as to the date of its construction. The earliest stratum in the eastern part of the city, quite a distance from the Hellenistic center, was built only during the time of Alexander Jannaeus, following the conquest of Gamla and its incorporation into the Hasmonean kingdom as a defensive and administrative center of the Golan. The eastern part of the city underwent a period of development and expansion. The events behind the reconstruction of the eastern flank in the second stratum are related to the annexation of the Golan by Herod and its incorporation into Gaulanitis in 23 B.C.E. (*Ant.,* XV, 343). Herod's reign was marked by ambitious building projects throughout the country, which included not only royal edifices, but also the large-scale construction of new private urban dwellings of high technological standard. Such structures have been found in the excavations of the Jewish quarter of the Old City of Jerusalem, in Samaria and Caesarea, and in other sites. Thus, the attribution of the second stratum of building on the east side of Gamla to the time of Herod after the year 23 B.C.E. also conforms to the general situation in Roman Palestine, as well as to the stratigraphic evidence uncovered from this stratum.

From an architectural standpoint, the synagogue at Gamla belongs to the buildings of this second stratum. This points to a date for its construction between the last part of the first century B.C.E. and the first half of the first century C.E.

Observations on the Orientation and Plan of the Synagogue

As noted above, the synagogue was erected on the extreme eastern side of the unfortified city on a broad terrace which supported the massive southern wall of the synagogue. The building was oriented on a northeast– southwest axis, with the entrance in the short southwest side. Though the building and the entrance are directed towards Jerusalem, its orientation seems to have been dictated by the exigencies of the topography. Since the synagogue was constructed on an artificial terrace with a sharp incline to the north and south, there was no approach from these sides. Thus, the architects had no alternative in choosing on which side the doorway would be located. The most convenient sides for the entrances are the two short walls to the west and east. Here, however, there was only one possible choice, since the east side led outside the city, and only the west side opened into its interior. In addition, the axis of the building could not be deflected, for it was determined by the contour of the terrace, and a deviation would necessitate great efforts in quarrying or filling in. Thus, the orientation of the building and the location of the entrance are not to be interpreted on ideological or religious grounds, but were rather due to the difficulties of erecting a building on a steep slope.

The main sanctuary of the synagogue (19.60 × 15.10 m.) was divided by four rows of columns into a central nave (9.30 × 13.40 m.)

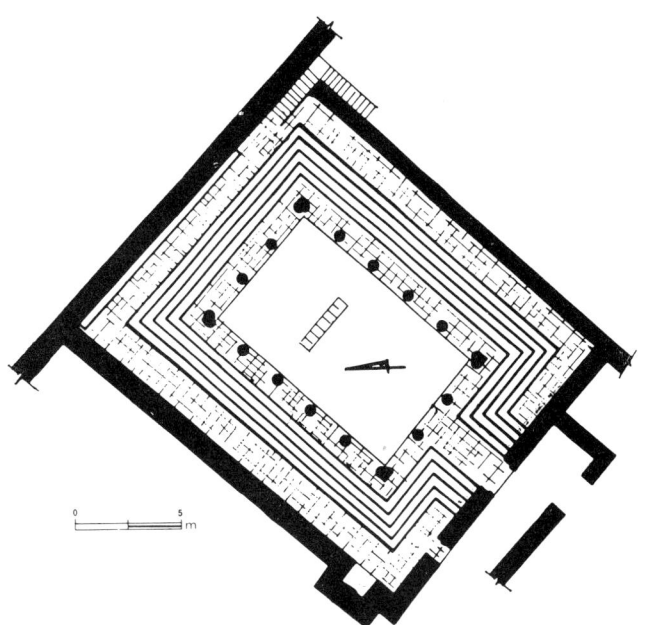

Reconstructed plan of Gamla synagogue

surrounded by four aisles, one on each side. On the west, north, and south sides, the aisles were 4.10 m. wide; on the east side the aisle was 4.50 m. wide. These aisles were used for seating the congregation. In the eastern aisle, which was preserved almost in its entirety, were found four stepped benches made of well-hewn basalt. The areas above and at the foot of the benches were paved with stone. (The lower area was 1.10 m. wide, the upper area ca. 2 m. wide.) The benches and upper areas were not completely preserved on the other sides. Erosion had washed the southern side down the slope; the other sides had not suffered from the elements but were probably damaged when parts of the synagogue were dismantled during the war with Rome. As at Masada and in the private dwellings in Jerusalem, the arrival of a large group of refugees (*War*, IV, 10; *Life*, 58) led to the requisition of public and private property and their division into improvised dwellings to house the refugees. Traces of cooking fires and other remains of these hastily-erected dwellings were visible in the area of the northern portico. Part of the eastern portico was removed and a small round plastered basin and water channel were installed.

The porticos should probably be reconstructed according to the plan of the eastern one. According to our restoration, the synagogue contained four porticos, each of which contained four stepped benches and adjoining paved areas, a higher one running between the upper bench and the walls. The eastern portico had an additional bench along the wall. These porticos were an important part of the synagogue, and provided comfortable accommodation for a large group of worshippers around the focus of the religious services. The paved areas served as landings which allowed easy approach to the upper and lower tiers of seats, as in Greco-Roman theaters.

The central area — the nucleus of the building — was enclosed within the four rows of columns. Its level floor was made of earth and not stone; this seems to have been its original design, and not the result of dismantling or destruction. Judging from the remains, the paving of the lower landing terminated in a straight line with smooth edges at the row of columns on the west and east sides and at the stylobate on the south side. On the north side, on the other hand, the line is not straight and a row of stone slabs seems to have been removed. At first glance it seems strange that the center of the hall lacked paving, thus presenting a shabby appearance in comparison with the surrounding paved and ashlar-built porticos.

However, was this really the case? What, in fact, was the function of stone pavements in that period? If we examine the stone floors in the Herodian buildings at Masada, Jericho, and other sites, and especially the public and private houses in Jerusalem, we find that the most important rooms of the buildings had not stone, but earthen floors. Stone pavements are restricted to the streets and courts of the houses, while in the rooms, mats or elaborately-worked woven rugs, none of which, of course, has been preserved, were laid on the dirt floor (for this reason we find mosaic pavements — waterproof stone carpets — in the bathrooms). Open areas called for sturdy floors which could withstand rain and

the wear and tear of pedestrian traffic. Moreover, even rough household chores, such as drawing water and washing clothes, were carried out in the courts. Use of stone pavements in this period was therefore dictated by their practicality and strength, and was not a sign of importance or the desire for ornamentation.

This also appears to have been the case in the synagogue at Gamla, since the congregation was seated in the porticos and a sturdy pavement was therefore necessary on the landings along which the worshippers reached their places. The center of the hall, in contrast, could have been adorned with colorful woven rugs, which lent an air of splendor and beauty to this area. It is also possible that only synagogue functionaries, priests, and perhaps some important worshippers were permitted to enter this area, and were thus the only ones to walk on the rugs. For this reason we cannot accept the excavator's view that part of the central hall — the unpaved area — may not have been roofed; in our opinion, the entire hall was covered.

A strip of stone paving preserved along the width of the central area may have been either the base for additional columns, part of the construction supporting the roof (the strip is in line with the third column from the east), or perhaps the base of a podium where the Scriptures were read. During the services, the Torah scroll may have been brought into the center of the hall from its storage place, a recess in the wall raised slightly above the floor near the northwest corner of the hall.

The functional division of the hall into two parts — central and side areas — is also confirmed by the position of the entrances. There were two entrances in the western façade. A wide main entrance (1.50 m. wide) was located in the center, with its threshold flush with the floor of the hall. This entrance led through a passageway between the benches to the lower landing and the center of the hall. The other doorway was a narrower side entrance near the northwest corner (0.90 m. wide), with the threshold one meter higher than that of the main entrance. There was no attempt to create a symmetrical façade, either in the number of entrances or their heights. The side entrance led directly onto the upper landing with which it was level. Another side entrance was located in the opposite southeastern corner of the hall. It, too, led to the upper landing and was approached by way of a staircase on a lower terrace south of the synagogue. The congregation's entrance into the synagogue was thus directed from outside the building, with some worshippers entering through the main doorway to the lower landing and bottom benches, and others through the side doorways to the upper seats. This arrangement recalls the movement of the audience into the theater, which was an efficient and convenient system to prevent crowding.

In our opinion, there is no connection between the position of the entrances or the landings and the isolation of the women into a special gallery. The view that synagogues of this period did not contain a women's gallery is supported by the synagogue at Gamla where no traces of any separation are found.

The synagogue at Gamla was richly adorned with various architectonic ornaments. The surviving fragments of the lintel of the main entrance show that it was decorated in the center with a six-petalled rosette and flanked by date palms (only their tips have been preserved; they were restored by analogy with another complete lintel, identical in shape, uncovered at the site). The rosette is a common motif in Jewish art of the Second Temple period. It appears on reliefs found in the Jerusalem Temple area, on the façades of rock-hewn tombs, on sarcophagi, as well as on stone tables and jewelry boxes. Its significance is a subject of controversy, but its discovery as the main motif on a synagogue lintel of the Second Temple period strengthens the view that its symbolism was of a religious nature. The date palm is less prevalent in Jewish art, though it occurs on Hasmonaean and Herodian coins, as well as on the Judaea Capta coin series struck by the Romans to commemorate their victory over Judaea. This motif appar-

View of synagogue remains, looking northwards

ently symbolized Judaea and the Jewish people in general. The appearance of these two decorative symbols on the entrance to a synagogue attests to their importance, and may provide a clue to identify synagogues of this period.

The stone columns supporting the roof of the hall were constructed of basalt drums of excellent workmanship. At the end of the rows, in the corners, were columns with heart-shaped sections, composed of two half-columns, each pointing in the direction of a different row, and square pilasters. The column capitals were of a Hellenistic-type Doric order (bearing affinity with its classical model) and show a high standard of craftsmanship. Capitals and columns with identical profiles also appear in the first-century nympheum excavated by the Franciscans at Magdala, on the western shore of the Sea of Galilee, north of Tiberias. The similarity in the architectural details attests to a firmly established and uniform architectural tradition in this period and region.

Columns should perhaps be restored along the entrance as a propyleum or in the center of the hall as a podium for scriptural readings. Since no columns or capitals of smaller diameter were found, it seems that the

39

synagogue was of a single story without a gallery, and the roof rested on a wooden construction. It was nonetheless an impressive building of outstanding splendor and plan. Its components point to an advanced architecture with proficiency in Hellenistic building techniques and the ability to adapt the various parts of the building to specific functions.

In comparing the synagogue of Gamla with those of Masada and Herodium, we have seen that the last two were transformed from triclinia into synagogues by the addition of benches; this is their only point of resemblance with the Gamla synagogue. In both of them stepped benches were built along *all four walls* of the halls and terminate only at the main entrances. (At Masada benches were even built around an additional room which probably held the scrolls and ritual vessels.) At Herodium not all the columns were found, but, in our opinion, the plan of the synagogue was very close to that of Gamla: a large hall surrounded by columns with porticos between the columns and the walls where the congregation was seated, the division of the seats by upper and lower landings, and additional seats along the walls. The synagogues at the three sites of Gamla, Masada, and Herodium share two basic architectural principles: (1) the major part of the hall is occupied by seats, i.e., the entire area of the porticos; (2) the benches extend around the four walls of the hall and face a focal architectural and ritual point *in the center of the hall.* These two principles, in our opinion, provide the key to understanding the synagogue plan and religious services in this period (see below).

Foerster attributed considerable importance to the fact that at Masada and Herodium the entrances were located on the eastern side, and he related this to the halakha in T *Megilla* III, 22: "One should only place the entrance to synagogues in the east..." The synagogue at Gamla, however, does not conform with this law, and moreover, seems to indicate that the location of the entrances was determined not by the halakha, but by the topography of the site. Was this also the case at Masada and Herodium? Avigad has already pointed out

that the builders of the synagogue at Masada had no alternative but to place the entrance in the east because the building was incorporated in the western wall of the fortress. At Herodium no new entrances were added to the synagogue by the Zealots, who continued to use the doorways of the Herodian structure. These were situated on the east side because of the position of the villa on the summit and of the court into which they gave access. The focal point of worship at Herodium faced north or north–northwest, i.e., it was at a right angle to the entrance, directed towards the long wall. It thus seems that the location of the entrances at all three of these Second Temple period sites was not determined by halakhic considerations, but was rather a continuation of the usage of the earlier phases of the buildings.

We have shown that only two architectural features are, in fact, shared by these synagogues: a spacious area for seating the congregation and a central focal point. According to Avigad, this plan was derived from the Hellenistic basilica. Following Kohl and Watzinger, who were the first serious researchers of the origins of the "Galilean" synagogues, Avigad considered their principal architectural feature to be the columns in the hall, which, he maintained, were inspired by the large Hellenistic roofed and columned halls serving judicial, commercial, and cultural purposes. Foerster rightly opposed this view on the grounds that the basilica was a Roman building which was restricted to the west and did not appear in the east prior to the second century C.E.; it also lacked benches like its predecessor, the Hellenistic portico, which was open on all sides. Neither the Hellenistic portico nor the Roman basilica contains an architectural focus. The tribunal of the basilica was a subsidiary feature which occurred only sporadically, and, when present, was situated in the apse or a small side chamber. If our contention that the seats constituted an essential component of the synagogue plan is accepted, none of the above proposals is plausible, despite a certain similarity between the buildings resulting from the presence of columns in the two groups. In this period it was, of course, impossible to roof a large building without the use of columns.

Furthermore, we reject Foerster's suggestion which seeks the source of inspiration for the synagogue plan in the eastern pagan *pronaos* halls of assembly, such as those found in the temples at Dura Europos (see pp. 26–28). The ritual–architectural focus of all these buildings was located in one of the short sides of the hall or chamber, and not in the center as in contemporary synagogues. For this reason the seats of the congregation extended only along two or three sides of the hall, or in a semicircle, leaving the side where the ritual was conducted without benches. Furthermore, these halls of assembly date from the first century C.E., whereas the synagogue at Gamla shows a highly developed architectural form already at the end of the first century B.C.E., and apparently represents the culmination of a series of less sophisticated architectural experiments, as yet not discovered. Thus, from the chronological standpoint as well, the pagan halls of assembly of Dura Europos could not have provided the inspiration for the synagogue plan.

It is the author's opinion that the proposal made by Yadin, following his excavation of the synagogue at Masada, should be accepted, namely, that the plan was derived from the Hellenistic secular halls of assembly (see above, p. 20, n. 1). Unfortunately there is a dearth of Hellenistic *ecclesiasteria* and *bouleteria*, and none of the types known exactly duplicate the synagogue. Nevertheless, if we examine the *ecclesiasterion* at Priene, the *bouleteria* at Heraclea and Notium or the *telesterion* at Eleusis, we can observe signs of the Hellenistic practice of constructing halls for a seated assembly (see pp. 45–48). The hall was occupied in large part by stepped benches and its plan reflects the main purpose of this institution — to allow free discussion among the seated public and enable them to hear

speeches delivered from the center of the hall and the lowest tier of seats. This explains why the seats lined three or four sides of the hall and the focal point was in the center; in the pagan temples it was set at a distance so that the statue of the deity was isolated from the congregation. In these Hellenistic buildings the emphasis was on the *public* — the active participants in the proceedings — and not on an external power who was but remotely visible to the congregation of the faithful. In this Hellenistic model the architects of the synagogue found the architectural conception which filled the requirements of the synagogue ritual. Here, the most important element was the *congregation,* which assembled to worship, listen to the scriptural readings, and participate in instruction and prayer. Thus, from among the buildings of this type known in the Hellenistic world in a number of variants they selected the plan most suitable for gathering a large seated assembly and invested it with Jewish religious significance. At the same time they also adopted the general physical appearance of the Hellenistic buildings: columns, rendering of the architectural details and placing of the seats with landings between them, and several entrances. In all these features the synagogue at Gamla displayed a typical Hellenistic appearance.[1]

---

[1] Avigad's assessment of the synagogues of the Second Temple period — as the likely prototypes of the "Galilean-type" synagogues of the late Roman period — should also be considered. In our opinion, no architectural connection exists between the two groups of buildings. The "Galilean" synagogues represent a different and new ideological, religious and architectural conception. Their characteristic features are expressed in the symmetrical façade lavishly decorated on the exterior, a two-story interior, a central area enclosed by porticos and galleries, and the emphasis on the internal façade wall facing Jerusalem by the installation of the Torah shrine and the orientation of the seats towards this architectural focal point. All these elements are lacking in the synagogues of the earlier period, in which the relative importance of the seats stands in sharp contrast to their insignificance in the vast monumental hall of the "Galilean" synagogues.

The "Galilean" Synagogue and its Predecessors*

N. Avigad

The ancient synagogues of Galilee, though few in number, are a continuing source of interest for investigators. These monumental structures, with their elaborate ornamentation, shed light on the artistic trends of the period, the esthetic tastes of their builders and the interplay of foreign influence and indigenous traditions within Jewish art. The synagogues point to the existence of a firmly established Jewish community in a period characterized by both spiritual and economic advancement as well as political security. Their decoration has led to a re-examination of the Jewish laws regarding the plastic and representational arts and regarding idolatry, while the inscriptions contained in these synagogues provide important information on the development of writing, orthography, and language in this period.

H. Kohl and C. Watzinger, the pioneers in the investigation of the "Galilean" synagogues at the beginning of the twentieth century, were struck by the similarity between the architectural style and decoration common to these synagogues and those occurring on buildings of the second–third centuries C.E. Since Syro-Roman architecture was renowned in that period for its variety and innovative forms and styles, subsequently spreading throughout the Roman Empire and reaching Rome itself, it can be conjectured that this school of building also served as a source of inspiration for the "Galilean" synagogues.

* The following article was originally part of an address, "On the Form of Ancient Synagogues in the Galilee," delivered at the archeological convention of the Israel Exploration Society, 1966, and first published in the volume entitled *Kol Eretz Naphtali*.

This is particularly true with regard to various architectural elements and ornamental details, such as the façade with the so-called Syrian gable, three entrances, friezes bearing architectural and floral motifs, carved figures of animals, and other themes derived from pagan art. At the same time it should be noted that there are some noticeable differences between the Syrian and Palestinian friezes and lintels, due to the fact that they were produced by different artisans.

The synagogues at Capernaum and Chorazin were initially attributed to the first century C.E. and identified as the synagogues in which Jesus preached to the congregations, as described in the New Testament. However, the date of the construction of the "Galilean" synagogues has been lowered to the end of the second and the third centuries C.E. on the basis of the architectural evidence alone. This supposition also conforms with the political

View of reconstructed façade of Capernaum synagogue

situation in Palestine; at that time large numbers of Jews had migrated from Judaea to Galilee in the wake of the Bar-Kokhba revolt. In this period the Galilee contained a dense chain of prosperous settlements. In the political sphere this was an age of security and peaceful relations with the Roman authorities, which were fostered by the spiritual leaders of the Jews; the seat of the Sanhedrin was located in the Galilee. It seems very likely that these magnificent structures dedicated to prayer and study belong to this phase of Jewish history.

Kohl and Watzinger found it difficult to believe that these buildings were erected by Jews because of what they viewed as ornamental motifs which included forbidden images taken from the world of idolatry. Instead, they proposed that the synagogues were built for the Galilean settlements by the Roman authorities as a gesture of good-will. This peculiar suggestion was conclusively refuted long ago by the archeological evidence uncovered in numerous excavations. It is now certain beyond doubt that the Jews themselves, under the influence of their gentile neighbors and the fashion of the times, adorned their houses of worship for their own esthetic enjoyment. Furthermore, they found some rabbinical authorization for this ornamentation, since a number of rabbis had reconciled themselves to the prevailing situation, interpreting the biblical injunction against the making of images in a tolerant manner.

Since Kohl and Watzinger recognized the influence of Syrian architecture on the building style of the synagogues, and since they surmised that they were built by order of the Roman emperors as a gift to the Jews, they arrived at the logical conclusion that the actual work of construction was executed by Syrian builders. These investigators, however, failed to resolve a number of issues, including the question of the origin of the basilical plan. As they correctly concluded, this plan was derived from the secular Hellenistic basilicas which served judicial, commercial, and cultural purposes. The rows of columns were

Aerial view of Capernaum synagogue environs. Note synagogue remains in foreground and Byzantine church in background

basically utilitarian and allowed the construction of large spacious halls combining the functional and the elaborate. The synagogue was apparently the first structure to be built according to the basilical plan explicitly for religious purposes. It thus antedates the Christian basilica, and may have even had a direct influence on it. Since there is a considerable time gap between the pagan and secular basilicas outside Palestine and the synagogue basilicas of the Galilee, the question remains: how did this plan come to be adopted by the architects of these synagogues? Though the basilical plan may also have been derived from Syrian architecture, it is surprising to observe that none of the secular or pagan–religious buildings known prior to the synagogues followed the basilical plan. Kohl and Watzinger therefore suggested that the builders of the synagogues were apparently influenced by earlier synagogues from Palestine or elsewhere, which have not yet been uncovered, but which preceded the Galilean examples. This, however, conflicts with their view that the "Galilean" synagogues were the work of Syrian architects!

In the fifty years following the publication of Kohl's and Watzinger's study, the "missing link" between the Hellenistic prototype and the basilica of the "Galilean" synagogues had not been found, despite the fact that references to early Palestinian synagogues are contained in literary and epigraphic sources. Only in recent years has a synagogue of this type been uncovered, at a wholly unexpected site — Masada.

The synagogue at Masada is considered to have belonged to the fortress. Two phases of construction were distinguished in the building: an upper phase dating to the time of the Zealots and an earlier phase from the time of Herod. In both phases the synagogue was built on the basilica plan with rows of columns, as in the majority of the "Galilean" synagogues. This early example apparently represents a local prototype of the "Galilean"

synagogues, and since its original plan also shows the influence of Hellenistic architecture, the "Galilean" synagogues seem to have evolved from the traditional plan of earlier synagogues in Palestine itself. It can be assumed that remains of these early synagogues will be exposed in the Galilee in the future.

The Masada synagogue is similar to the "Galilean" synagogues not only in plan but also in its orientation toward Jerusalem. It faced northwest, while the entrance was in the southeast side. Thus, worshippers faced in the right direction, toward Jerusalem, on entering. In the "Galilean" synagogues, on the other hand, the entrances were located in the southern walls facing Jerusalem and the congregation, after entering the hall, had to turn around to pray. In this respect the synagogue at Masada resembles the later Byzantine synagogues in which the wall of the apse containing the Torah ark was in the direction of Jerusalem.

It can be assumed that it was due to the topography of the site that the entrance at Masada was located in the southeast, since the synagogue stood at the very edge of the cliff and the northwest wall was incorporated into the main wall. However, it is also possible that the synagogues in the Second Temple period were oriented differently from the "Galilean" synagogues of later date because of changing conceptions of the direction of the synagogue in relation to Jerusalem.

Architectural Models of the Greco-Roman Period and the Origin of the "Galilean" Synagogue*

G. Foerster

The problem facing the architects of the "Galilean" synagogues was that of constructing a roofed building with a spacious interior area sufficient for the entire congregation for the purpose of public worship. A varied selection of public buildings was available which might have served as models. These included secular buildings, such as stoas and council halls, *bouleteria, ecclesiasteria*, the *curia* and basilicas. Temples, designed to house the deities, might also accommodate a large congregation.

Let us begin by examining assembly halls found throughout the Greek world. The first organized places of assembly known to us come from the Creto-Mycenaean culture and are found mainly at Knossos and Phaistos. They date from the middle of the second millennium B.C.E. Open areas with rows of seats on one or more sides, they represent the simplest way of gathering a large number of persons around a single focus. In Athens, the *ecclesia* (legislative assembly) met in the area of the sanctuary of Dionysus in the fifth century B.C.E. Later, the theater became the main place of assembly, though meetings were also held on the Pnyx. Similar meeting places are also known from other cities, such as Corinth, Delos, Ephesus, Herakleia, Messene, Miletus, and Rhodes.

The *ecclesiasterion* at Priene, erected at the beginning of the second century B.C.E., is the only roofed structure known so far in which all the citizens could assemble, in contrast to the *bouleterion* where the city councillors alone

met. The *ecclesiasterion* was almost square in shape (21.60 × 20.25 m.) and had rows of seats along three of its walls. The columns were situated behind the seats so that the view of the center of the hall would not be obstructed. An outstanding feature of this building is the façade, which had two entrances flanking a large arched window.

Buildings similar in plan from the Hellenistic period are also encountered on other sites of the west coast of Asia Minor. Their dimensions are more or less identical, and are probably determined by the technical limita-

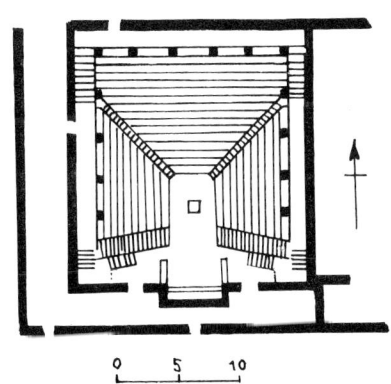

Plan of Priene *ecclesiasterion*

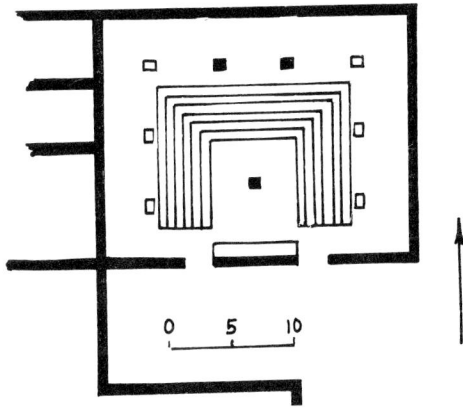

Plan of Herakleia *bouleterion*

* This article is an abridgement of a chapter from the author's doctoral thesis, *Galilean Synagogues and Their Relation to Hellenistic and Roman Art and Architecture* (Hebrew University, 1972) (in Hebrew), pp. 56–80, due to be published shortly.

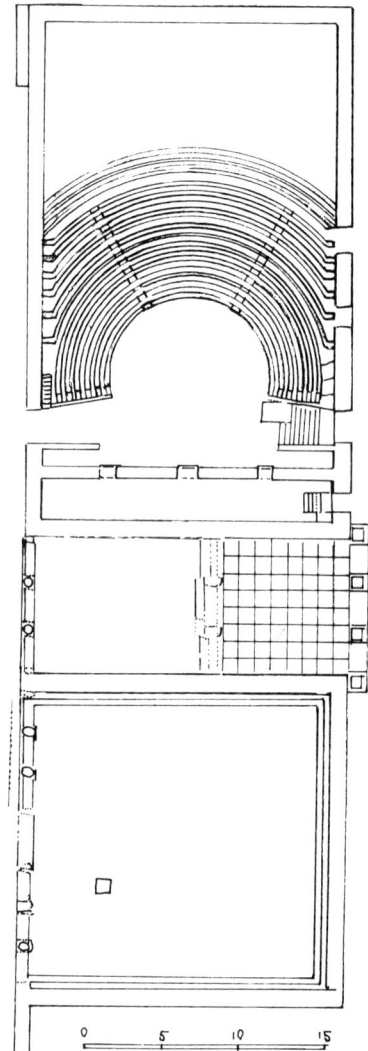

Plan of Messene council building and odeum

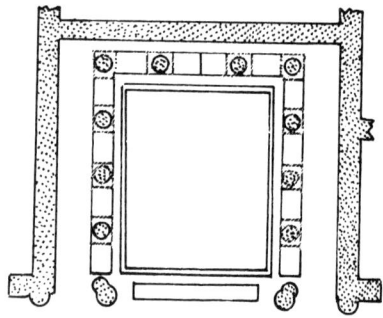

Plan of a reception hall in Pompeii

located on the fourth side. These structures provided a very simple functional solution to the problem of accommodating a large group of persons around a focus in a roofed building, but differ from the synagogues in the arrangement of the columns and the internal division of the halls. This group of buildings contains a large number of variants. The council building at Messene contained an odeum and an inner chamber measuring 21.60×20.80 m., and had a row of stone benches along three walls. Traces of columns indicate that the building was roofed. The entrance façade contained five doorways. These remains apparently date from the beginning of the third century B.C.E. Though the plan of this structure somewhat resembles that of the "Galilean" synagogues, the possibility of a direct influence is precluded by the chronological and geographical gap, as well as the greater simplicity and utilitarian character of these Hellenistic buildings.

The arrangement of the columns in rows along three of the walls in the sanctuary of the "Galilean" synagogues also has analogies in reception and assembly halls in villas and palaces. A number of examples appear in houses from Pompeii. These houses were assigned a Hellenistic origin and have been compared to the "Galilean" synagogues. Nevertheless, despite a certain general resemblance, the plan of the synagogue does not seem to have been derived from this source. In recent excavations and surveys, on the other hand, a number of reception halls with dimensions similar to those of the synagogues have been uncovered in Palestine itself (cf. below, pp. 49–51) and in neighboring lands, and a possibility exists that such halls influenced the plan of the synagogues.

A new type of reception hall evolved in the latter half of the first century C.E. These halls, found in the palaces of the Roman emperors, were divided by two rows of columns into three aisles. Their most characteristic feature was the apse. Two typical examples of these halls are the basilica in the Domus Flavia in the palace of Domitian and the basilica in the "Villa Hadriana" in Tivoli. Various scholars

tion of the span which could be roofed. The only analogies between the plans of these buildings and those of the "Galilean" synagogues are the fixed seating arrangements of stone benches running along three sides of the buildings and the doorways

have rightly argued that these reception halls may have served as a model for the basilical plan of the church adopted by the architects of Constantine the Great in Jerusalem, Rome and elsewhere at the beginning of the fourth century C.E. However, while a connection between the imperial reception halls and the Christian basilica is likely, not only from architectural but also from political and cultural considerations, no such links with the "Galilean" synagogues can be postulated.

The civic basilica was the most common type of assembly hall in the Roman world. Though it does not appear in the East in its final highly developed style found in Rome prior to the end of the second century C.E., nevertheless, the theory that the plan of the "Galilean" synagogues was derived from the basilica has been almost unanimously accepted. This theory was already proposed in the nineteenth century and was followed by Watzinger, Krauss, Krautheimer, Sukenik, Goodenough, Avigad, Avi-Yonah, and others.

Nothing is known of the basilical plans in the Greek or Hellenistic world. The literary and epigraphic evidence, as well as archeological finds from the West, on the other hand, contain a wealth of information on the basilica as early as the period of the Republic. A wide range of private and public buildings, both secular and religious, were known as basilicas.

Before the rise of Christianity, the most common feature of the basilica seems to have been four rows of columns which surrounded a central area and which supported galleries and the roof. The focal point (tribunal) could have been in the center of the long or short side. This plan evolved in Italy in the period of the Republic and soon thereafter spread throughout the Empire. A second type must have evolved from the stoa and is the one represented in royal reception halls, or the "Kaisareia" of Alexandria, Antioch and elsewhere. This type of basilica is always a 'long' hall divided into aisles with a focal point on one of its short sides, generally represented by an apse. It attained its most highly developed form in the East and was adopted as the standard church plan.

Plan of basilica of Domitian in Domus Flavia

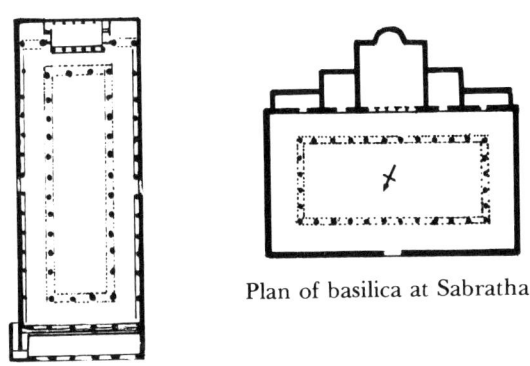

Plan of basilica at Sabratha

Plan of basilica in Pompeii

Among the basic elements of the basilica, only the columns (though in a different arrangement from the basilica) and the galleries (known also in buildings of other types, e.g. stoas) occur in the "Galilean" synagogue. Despite these common features, the basilica and the synagogues cannot be linked with certainty; other basic features of the basilica are absent in these synagogues.

The "Galilean" synagogue plan can also be compared to a variety of religious buildings found mainly in the East, in which the whole congregation took part in the rituals (e.g., the Mysteries of Eleusis and Samotrace), or rooms which were intended for the sacred meals (Dura Europos, Petra). These 'dining rooms' are related in plan and function to what is the nearest parallel to the plan of the "Galilean" synagogues, namely the partly-roofed forecourts of some Nabatean temples.

47

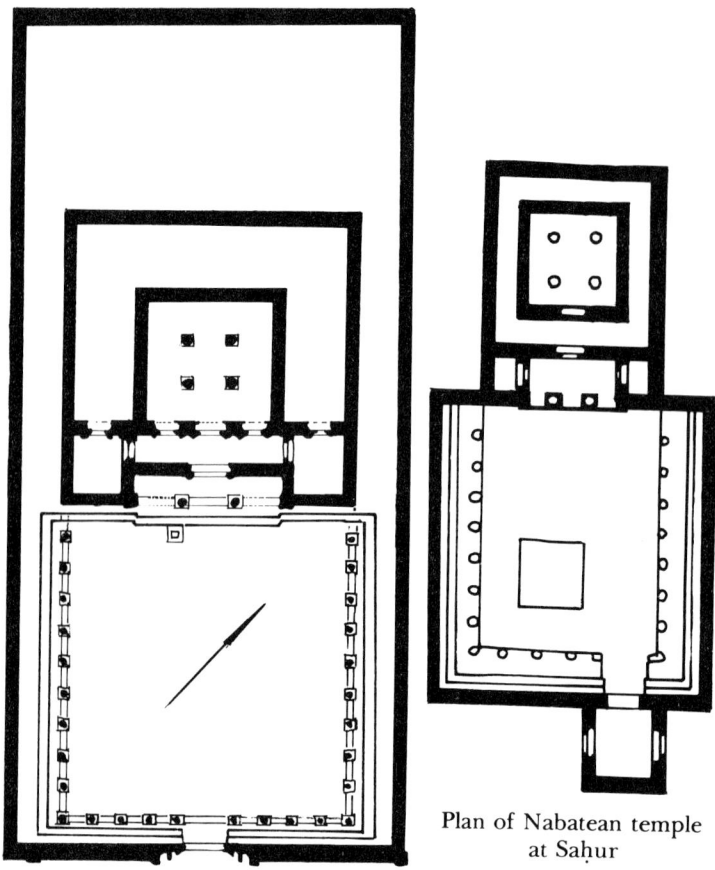

Plan of Nabatean temple
at Saḥur

Plan of temple of Baal Shamin at Sia

Dura Europos, the "Galilean" synagogues, in our opinion, drew their inspiration from a similar group of halls, or more specifically, from temple courts with rows of covered stone seats. This group of Nabatean temple forecourts is found northeast of Roman Palestine, as well as to the south. Underlying this plan was the need to enable a congregation of the faithful to witness and participate in the ritual. These arrangements were also required by the Jewish congregation, and in spite of some differences from the forecourts of the Nabatean temples — all of the basic features of the Nabatean plan are readily apparent in the "Galilean" synagogues. The stone benches along the walls, the arrangement of the columns in front of the benches, the splendor of the entrance to the court, the excellence of the stone construction, the architectural decorations, as well as the stone-slab pavements of the court are features which closely link these courts with the "Galilean" synagogues. The location of the Nabatean temple, attached as it was to the forecourt, is probably to be paralleled in the "Galilean" synagogues by the *aediculae* — the Torah shrine — which was conceived as a miniature temple, an imitation of the Temple in Jerusalem. The parallel is further indicated by the direction of worship.[1] The tie between the Nabatean forecourts and the "Galilean" synagogue gains further support from the geographic propinquity of these structures. Moreover, southern Syria also served as the main source for the decorative art found in the "Galilean" synagogues. Finally, our suggestion seems preferable to the "basilical" one, since the local Galilean planners were certainly more familiar with Nabatean and Syrian architecture than with the western basilica, and thus preferred this "local" plan, though making some modifications.

The classic example of such a temple is that of Baal Shamin at Ṣia in the Ḥoran in southern Syria. Access to the forecourt is through a monumental entrance, and there were two rows of benches along three walls. In front of the benches were three colonnades supporting the roof over the benches. These were built along each of the walls except for the entrance wall. The enclosed area measures 21 × 25 m. This type of forecourt is found also at Sûr, Saḥur in the Ḥoran, and at Petra as well as Ḥ. Tannur further south. Most of these temples were probably already built in the first century B.C.E. and continued in use to the second and third century C.E.

As we have shown (see pp. 24–29), the plan of the synagogue at Masada is not derived from the basilica but probably from a group of similar halls with benches. While parallels for the synagogues at Masada and Herodium may well be found in some small square halls at

---

[1] The differences between the two types of buildings stem mainly from the fact that the architects of the "Galilean" synagogues continued to develop the Nabatean plan. They roofed the entire structure (not only the area above the benches), erected galleries, and added courts to some of the buildings.

The Herodian Triclinia — A Prototype for the "Galilean-Type" Synagogue

E. Netzer

One of the many problems raised by the "Galilean" synagogue is the question of the origin of its plan. H. Kohl and C. Watzinger offered the suggestion that the Roman triclinia might have served as a prototype, but they then rejected the idea.[1] However, an analysis of triclinia built by Herod and his descendants indicates that the subject should be reconsidered, especially following recent discoveries at Jericho. Here, in Herod's elaborate winter palace, built on both sides of Wadi Qelt, a huge triclinium (29 × 19 m.) was exposed.[2] This hall had three rows of columns around the inside, parallel to three of its walls, and a wide entrance (5.5 m.) in the center of the southern wall. This door afforded a "picture-window" view of the landscape.

Nearby, another triclinium, nearly identical in plan but little more than half the size of the first (18.5 × 12.6 m.), was found in 1951 by J.B. Pritchard.[3] It formed part of a complex which was interpreted by the excavator as a gymnasium, but was no doubt Herod's earlier winter palace. This triclinium was oriented towards a central courtyard, the "picture window" entrance giving a view of the courtyard, undoubtedly full of greenery.

Larger and even more luxurious triclinia probably existed in Herod's central palace in Jerusalem. There is great similarity between the two halls in Jerusalem, as described by Josephus, and the two triclinia uncovered in Jericho. The halls in Jerusalem were paved with colored stones: "... the variety of the stones (for species rare in every other country were here collected in abundance)" (*War* V, 177–183); at Jericho we have evidence of imported marble incorporated into the opus sectile floor. Josephus mentions large ceiling beams in the Jerusalem palace: "... ceilings wonderful both for the length of the beams and the splendor of their surface decoration" (*ibid.*); in the building in Jericho the large span between the two rows of columns (13.5 m.) is a testimony to the use of huge beams here. One of the two buildings in Jericho was oriented towards the open landscape, and the other towards a central court.

The Herodian hall at Jericho looking south, with Wadi Qelt in the background

[1] *Antike Synagogen in Galilaea* (Leipzig, 1916), pp. 176-178.

[2] See E. Netzer, "The Hasmonean and Herodian Winter Palaces at Jericho," *IEJ*, 25 (1975), 94-95; *idem*, "The Winter Palaces of the Judean Kings at Jericho at the End of the Second Temple," *BASOR*, 228 (1977), 8–10.

[3] "The Excavation at Herodian Jericho 1951," *AASOR*, 32–33 (1958), 6–7, 56–58, room 33, misinterpreted by Pritchard as a courtyard.

In Jerusalem, although the palace was encircled by walls, it included "open courts all of greensward; there were groves of various trees ..." (*ibid.*) We assume that the triclinia enjoyed views of the courts. The two buildings in Jerusalem were named for Caesar Augustus and Marcus Agrippa. This in itself testifies to the importance of the buildings. The palace in Jericho is barely mentioned by Josephus, but he does tell us that it was also named for Caesar and Agrippa: "At Jericho ... the king constructed new buildings, finer and more commodious for the reception of guests, and named them after the same friends" (*War* I, 407). Taking all of the above into consideration, we have no doubt that the triclinium excavated in Jericho was named after one of these Roman rulers.

The two Herodian triclinia of Jericho were separated by an interval of 15–20 years, and were located in two separate palaces built in totally different architectural styles. The first one was a rectangular structure, built around a central courtyard, with no direct view to the surrounding countryside. In contrast, the second one was a complex of buildings generally open to the landscape. Both palaces included a triclinium built on the same plan, indicative of the popularity of this plan during the period. We assume, therefore, that triclinia with a similar plan also existed in other palaces, including the one at Jerusalem.

An important architectural feature of the two halls in Jericho is their orientation towards a focal point outside the buildings themselves. Both lack an interior focal point such as a niche or an altar, as existed in the Roman basilica or the large triclinia (for example, the Domus Augustana in the Palatine), halls which many scholars interpret as prototypes for the early churches.[4] A vivid demonstration of the function of the entrance door serving as a "picture window," with the architectural focal point outside, is given in Josephus' description of an event concerning a triclinium built by Agrippa II in Jerusalem, shortly before the destruction of the Second

Temple: "About this time King Agrippa built a chamber of unusual size in his palace at Jerusalem .... The palace ... afforded a most delightful view to any who chose to survey the city from it. The King was enamored of this view and used to gaze, as he reclined at meals there, on everything that went on in the Temple" (*Ant.* XX, 189–190). Here we can see that the tradition of Herod's triclinia continued in the days of his descendants.

The huge triclinia built by Herod were among the major achievements of his building program. We have no doubt that their fame spread far and wide in those days. It is important to note here that many of Herod's palaces were still standing nearly intact, till the destruction of the Second Temple, such as those at Masada and Herodium, where we have archeological proof, and the palace at Jerusalem, about which we learn from Josephus (*War* V, 178–183). The impression they made probably lasted for many years.

This brings us to the question of the "Galilean-type" synagogue. The similarity in plan and architectural conception between these triclinia (as known to us principally from Jericho) and that of most of the "Galilean" synagogues is striking, and probably not accidental. In both cases they served as assembly halls for the people: the one for entertainment, the other for scriptural readings and prayer. In both cases the orientation of the hall is toward the outside, rather than toward a focal point inside the building. The triclinia were oriented towards a real landscape, and the synagogue towards a spiritual landscape — i.e., towards Jerusalem. The orientation towards Jerusalem may have had symbolic meaning, but it may also have been practical, enabling prayer (at least in part) with the doors open while facing the holy city.

This resemblance indicates that the architects who built the large synagogues may have seen Herod's triclinia. An important point to be considered is the size of the buildings. The larger triclinium in Jericho is bigger than any of the known "Galilean-type" synagogues, and the triclinia in Jerusalem may have been even larger.

[4] See J.B. Ward-Perkins, "Constantine and the Origin of the Christian Basilica," *PBSR*, 22 (1954), 69–89.

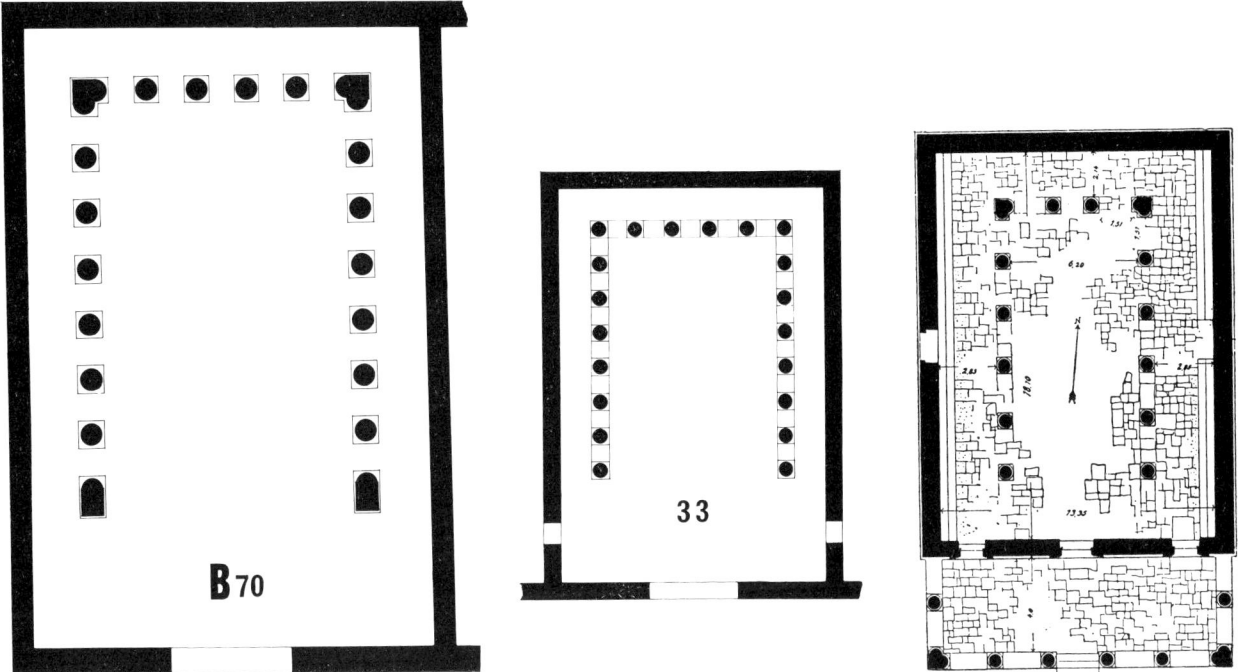

Comparative plans of Herodian triclinia (B70, 33) and the "Galilean-type" sunagogue at Bar'am

How do the synagogues found in Masada and Herodium fit into this picture? It is true that in the case of Herodium the synagogue was actually built into a triclinium, but this was probably accidental, the triclinium simply meeting the needs of the revolutionaries. The adaptation represents an improvisation, not an intentional architectural concept. The location of the hall's entrance on the east could have been the reason for its choice, but may be a coincidence. On the other hand, the hall at Herodium was not oriented toward Jerusalem.

At Masada we have another case in which an existing hall was converted into a synagogue. It is an open question whether this building served as a synagogue in Herod's time. So far there is no proof for any synagogue being included in Herod's building projects. The building at Masada could have originally served a totally different purpose, such as a stable.[5] But even if the building at Masada was

originally a synagogue, it is quite different from the "Galilean" type. It is a broadhouse, with a kind of entrance hall, and was not orientated toward Jerusalem. Its later phase, as a synagogue built by the Sicarii, reflects an improvisation, as the case in Herodium. The most significant feature of the synagogues at Herodium and Masada is the benches, enabling the community to gather together in the halls. Such benches were not needed in Herod's triclinia, but became a frequent feature in the later synagogues.

It is true that there is a chronological gap between the date of Herod's triclinia and the building of the earliest "Galilean-type" synagogues. As Kohl and Watzinger have already suggested, we may assume that synagogues were built during this hiatus which would predate those built in Galilee, and which represent the architectural tradition followed by the "Galilean" ones. As yet, however, no synagogue dated to this time has been found, even though a large Jewish community existed in the country throughout these years. Hopefully synagogues of this period will be uncovered and will provide the missing link between the "Galilean-type" synagogue and their proposed prototype, the Herodian triclinia.

[5] If orientation toward the east were an important consideration for the builders, they could easily have found another building to serve their purpose, for example the western palace. The orientation toward Jerusalem may well be accidental. In any case, we must not forget that since these synagogues were built before the destruction of the Temple, the orientation of the building was probably unimportant.

The Late Chronology of the Synagogue of Capernaum

S. Loffreda

Most archeologists consider the synagogue of Capernaum to be the best example of a group of synagogues which flourished in Galilee in the second–third centuries C.E. This consensus is based on architectural, stylistic, and historical considerations. It is now challenged by two Franciscan archeologists, Fr. V. Corbo and the writer, on the basis of data gathered during eight seasons of excavations at Capernaum (1968–1972). We claim that the synagogue was built from the last decade of the fourth to the mid-fifth century C.E.[1]

Even before our excavations, some prominent Israeli scholars had noticed several elements which were hard to explain according to the traditional chronology. Professor E.L. Sukenik identified the Aramaic inscription of our synagogue as undoubtedly Byzantine, i.e., fourth century C.E. or later.[2] Professor M. Avi-Yonah went further, suggesting a date in the Byzantine period for the capitals used in this class of synagogues. He writes: "The capitals are mostly of the Corinthian type, but they deviate strongly from the classical type, especially owing to the usual absence of the chalices and the inner spirals. The formation of the acanthus leaves on these Corinthian capitals is of particular interest for the history of Jewish art, because they antedate by at least two centuries the

typical Byzantine capitals; in fact, if we did not know the approximate date of these synagogues, we would assign them, on the basis of their architectural decoration, to the Byzantine period."[3]

The decipherment by Professor N. Avigad of an inscription from the synagogue of Nabratein provided another stumbling block; the inscription tells us that the synagogue was built in 564 C.E.[4]

Finally, a late date for the synagogue of Chorazin was suggested by a passage of Eusebius, telling us that the town of Chorazin was still in ruins in the early fourth century C.E.[5] Since the synagogue there was in use at least until the early seventh century C.E.,[6] Eusebius' statement should be taken as a *terminus post quem* for its construction.

These observations alone would disprove the assumption that the traditional chronology is firmly established. They show dramatically the shaky ground upon which the consensus of archeologists is based. We strongly believe that only archeological data, collected through systematic excavations, can overcome the problems which have beset the study of ancient synagogues for almost a century. For this reason we have excavated for several months, both inside and around the synagogue of Capernaum, in order to analyze

---

[1] V. Corbo, S. Loffreda and A. Spijkerman, *La Sinagoga di Cafarnao dopo gli scavi del* 1969 (Jerusalem, 1970); S. Loffreda, "The Synagogue of Capharnaum. Archaeological Evidence for its Late Chronology," *Liber Annuus*, 22 (1972), 5-29; V. Corbo, "La Sinagoga di Cafarnao dopo gli scavi del 1972," *Liber Annuus*, 22 (1972), 204-235; *idem, Cafarnao* I (Jerusalem, 1975), pp. 113-169.

[2] E.L. Sukenik, *Ancient Synagogues in Palestine and Greece* (London, 1934), p. 72.

[3] M. Avi-Yonah in C. Roth (ed.), *Jewish Art* (Tel-Aviv, 1961), p. 165.

[4] N. Avigad, "A Dated Lintel-Inscription from the Ancient Synagogue of Nabratein," *Bulletin of the L.M. Rabinowitz Fund for the Exploration of Ancient Synagogues*, 3 (1960), 49–56.

[5] D. Baldi, *Enchiridion Locorum Sanctorum* (Jerusalem, 1955), p. 305.

[6] G. Kloetzli, "Coins from Chorazin," *Liber Annuus*, 20 (1970), 359–369.

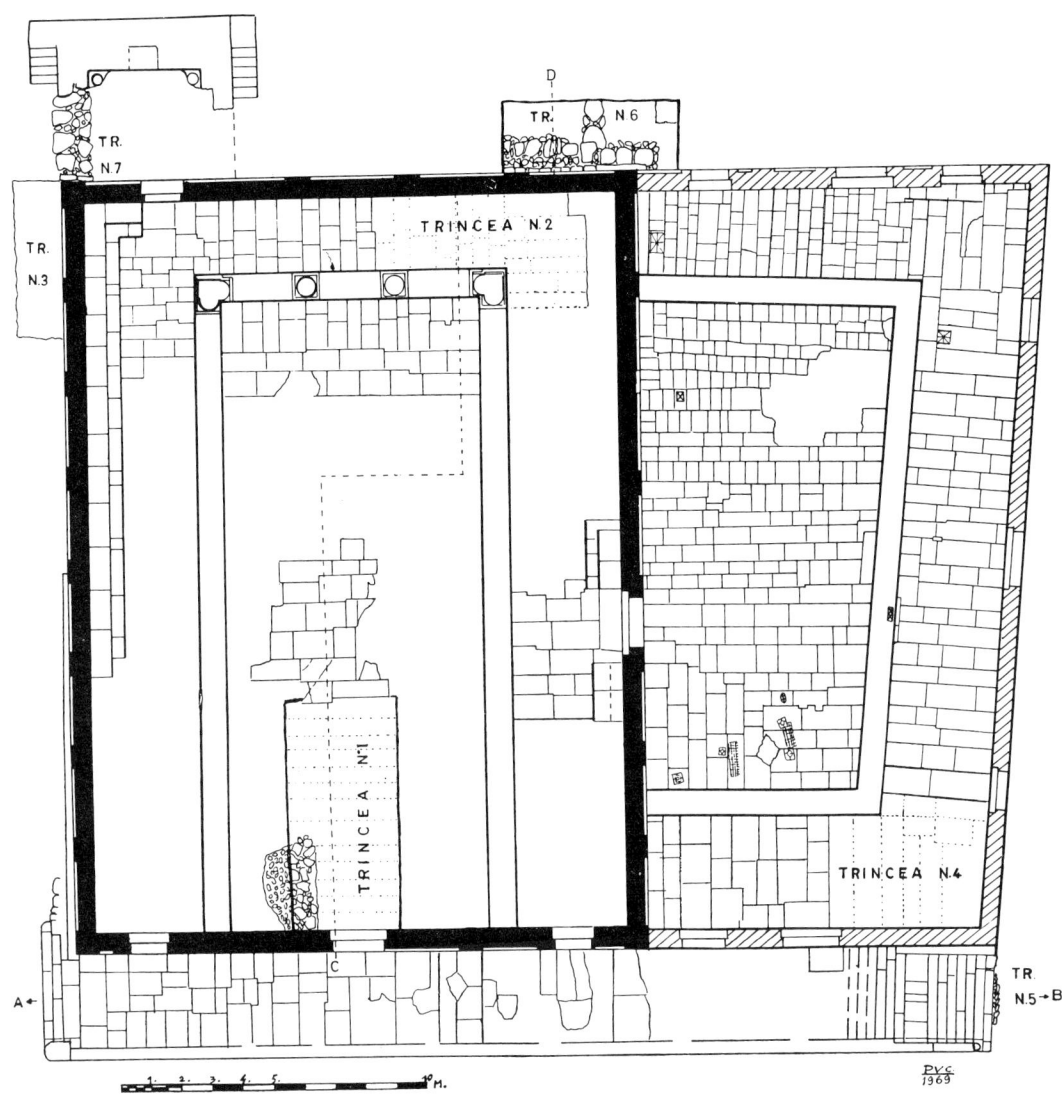

Plan of Capernaum synagogue, indicating the location of major trenches

the stratigraphic context of the building and to collect any bit of archeological evidence which might provide a more solid foundation for the solution of this problem.[7]

The plan shows the location of the trenches dug so far in the prayer hall, courtyard, and porch. In addition, we have uncovered the entire quarter of the city located along the building's south side and a large area along its eastern and northern sides. As a result, the synagogue of Capernaum can now be studied in the general context of the town.

[7] More trenches will be dug inside the synagogue in the forthcoming seasons of excavations.

Four broad streets running parallel to the four sides of the synagogue linked the building to the rest of the town; the edifice rose upon an artificial platform reached by means of three stairways. Two of these, already known in the past, led to the southern porch; a third one was located in 1971 at the northeastern corner of the courtyard.

The first important discovery was that the synagogue was built on an occupational level of the town (stratum A), not on virgin soil. By digging trenches and exposing extensive areas, we encountered basalt stone pavements, walls, and a drainage system which antedate the construction of the synagogue. In trench

No. 1, at a depth of 1.8 m., we found a stone pavement which continues southward under the foundations of the façade. A much better preserved stone pavement was found in trench No. 2 at a depth of 1–1.25 m. The foundations of the northern wall and the northern stylobate rest upon this pavement, which is the last of two superimposed basalt stone pavements of a private house. The same pavement continues eastwards under the foundations of the prayer hall and appears again along the whole length of trench No. 11. Another stone pavement, upon which the western wall of the synagogue was partly built, was found in trench No. 3. A pavement was also traced in trench No. 7 some 0.9 m. below the foundations of a structure, which is believed to lead to the upper "matroneum."

Several walls were found, also belonging to stratum A. After tracing the street which links the southeastern and southwestern stairways, we cut trench No. 9 starting from the foundations of the porch. A wall was encountered in a north–south direction, originating from a group of private houses on the south side of the synagogue and continuing under the foundations of the porch. In trench No. 6 we found that the northeastern corner of the prayer hall stands on a row of basalt stones belonging, most probably, to the same house whose pavements were traced in trench No. 2. A very long wall ran parallel to the northern face of the prayer hall and was found to continue under the steps of the structure believed to lead to the "matroneum." In 1972, a well-constructed drain was traced for several meters under the northern street. The construction of the synagogue obviously put the drain out of use; in fact, the northeastern stairway blocked it entirely. A branch of the same drain continues under the courtyard and was followed in trench No. 12. This branch was also blocked by the foundations of the courtyard.

Two additional facts help clarify the relationship between the stratigraphy of the synagogue and the urban areas which have been uncovered. First, the street between the porch and a group of private houses to the south blocked a corridor in one of these houses (room 66). Since the street level was some 0.8 m. higher than the upper pavement of room 66, two steps were needed to reach the street from this room, after the passage was blocked. Secondly, the northeastern stairway was built against a wall of a private house.

As we have said, the synagogue and the courtyard were built on an artificial platform; the platform was devised not only to stress the monumentality of the building, but also for practical purposes. There were slopes from north to south and from west to east. The fill of the platform constitutes our stratum B; it was 3 m. deep on the south side and was composed of undressed basalt stones, earth, ashes, and many broken vessels. The presence of many stone chips of the limestone used for building the synagogue is significant; these chips were found mainly in trenches No. 1 and No. 11. From the sections and from the findings it is quite clear that the fill was made in one single period.

The fill of stratum B was hermetically sealed by a layer of white mortar with an average thickness of 30 cm. This layer (our stratum C) was preserved perfectly both in the prayer hall and in the courtyard. We were able to trace the main outlines of the missing stones in the synagogue and in the courtyard by cleaning the top face of the mortar. It is quite obvious, therefore, that the stone pavement was laid while the mortar was still soft. Durable limestone slabs up to 55 cm. thick were used for the pavement. We found no hint anywhere that the stone pavement was rebuilt; one claiming that such rebuilding took place would have to prove his theory.

We will now turn to the findings, concentrating on the numismatic evidence. Of course, only the latest coins coming from sealed levels can determine the date of the synagogue.

The private houses of stratum A were in use until the second half of the fourth century C.E. In trench No. 9 three coins, dated to the very end of the fourth century C.E., were found ca. 40 cm. below the foundations of the porch. This date is perfectly in line with the changes which took place in room 66, blocked by the street. In trench No. 2, a coin dated to 341–346 C.E. was found in the occupational level of a house; the stone pavement of this house continues under the foundations of the prayer hall. Another coin, dated to the end of the fourth or the beginning of the fifth century C.E., was found in the stone pavement of a house in trench No. 11; in this case, however, the coin might belong to the fill. It was, in fact, difficult to make a clear distinction between the end of stratum B and the beginning of stratum A.

The fill of stratum B provided coins dating from the Hellenistic period onwards. Here again the latest coins date to the second half of the fourth century C.E. A coin dated to 352–360 C.E. was found in the fill of trench No. 1. This was the first coin found in a sealed level at the beginning of our 1969 excavations inside the synagogue. At the time, both Fr. Corbo and I were completely upset by its late date; in fact, we were unprepared for such a late chronology for the synagogue. For this reason we suggested that the coin *might* have slipped down to this level during our excavation. In trench No. 4, however, all doubt was dispelled when two coins were found at a depth of 1.25 m. below the stone pavement of the courtyard. The first was issued in honor of Constantine I after his death and was dated to 341–346 C.E.; the other belonged to Constantius II and was dated to 352–360 C.E. Another Late Roman coin was rescued from the fill of trench No. 11, and in trench No. 8, a coin from the fill was dated to 383–395 C.E.

The coins from stratum C can be counted by the thousands. A hoard of 2,920 coins was uncovered just inside the southern entrance to the western aisle, and a hoard of more than 6,000 coins turned up in trench No. 12. The study of these coins is still under way; the latest coins identified so far bring us to the middle of the fifth century C.E. The hoard from trench No. 12 was sealed by the stone pavement still *in situ*. The coins coming from level C of the prayer hall were found where the stone pavement was missing. It must be stressed that several of these Late Roman

coins were still firmly imbedded in the thick layer of mortar, making their chronological significance unquestionable.

Late Roman coins were also found in the foundations of the side benches of the prayer hall. Of the 67 bronze coins, only six were clearly imbedded in the mortar; they belong to Constantine I, Constantius II, Honorius, and Arcadius.

We would like to mention only two significant groups of coins coming from outside the synagogue. In trench No. 5, dug in 1969 against the southeastern stairway, we collected 45 bronze coins; all of them range from Constantius II to Theodosius II. It must be noted that 11 Late Roman coins were found under the foundation of the lowest step. Their state of preservation was unfortunately very bad. In 1971 we found 20 bronze coins in trench No. 10, in the first few centimeters at the bottom of the foundations of the courtyard. All of them belong to the fourth century C.E.

Due to a lack of space, we cannot review the great quantity of pottery, but we can mention the presence of highly fired jars with white paint on dark surfaces, cooking bowls with bevelled rims and raised horizontal handles, pieces of *pseudo-terra sigillata* bowls of the Late D class, etc. These finds come both from sealed levels and from several pieces of stucco belonging to the synagogue.

On the basis of these archeological data, coming from different stratigraphic contexts and yet pointing consistently to the same conclusion, it appears to us a matter of course to date the synagogue at Capernaum to the late fourth–early fifth century C.E.

The results of our excavations have aroused interest both in Israel and abroad. A fresh impetus was given to the systematic study of ancient synagogues soon after our work in Capernaum. It is not by chance that the synagogue of Chorazin was re-excavated only a few months after our third season (1969). We would like to call attention to the many pieces of broken jars still imbedded in the plaster of that synagogue; they are to be dated, in our opinion, from the fourth century C.E. onwards. Two other synagogues were uncovered in the following years at Horvat Shema' near Meron and at Susiya near Hebron; their fourth century chronology is in line with our results.[8]

In the meantime, Dr. G. Foerster has published a review article[9] in which he asserts that the second–third century chronology of the early type of "Galilean" synagogues is "firmly established," and "therefore, Corbo's conclusions are in contradiction to the accepted dates (see pp. 57–59)." It is our impression that Foerster overlooked or altered several archeological findings which might have disturbed him. For instance, according to him, "the fill (of trench No. 1) contained Hellenistic and Roman pottery, the latest being of the second–third centuries C.E.;" we dated the latest types of vessels to the fourth century C.E. Nor does Foerster mention the fourth century coin found in the same fill. As for trench No. 2, he does not note the crucial fact that many fourth century coins rescued "in the impressions left by the floor slabs" were clearly imbedded in the mortar.

Consequently, his conclusion that "it is impossible to tell *where* the coins were left" is contradicted by fact. Foerster also states that "only one fourth century coin is clearly attributed to the fill below the sealed floor." As a matter of fact, the coin was found in the occupational level of a house destroyed before the construction of the synagogue, and does not belong to the fill at all. According to Foerster, "in this trench scanty remains of two floors, the purpose and date of which are not clear, were distinguished below the fill." In fact, the pavements were preserved perfectly along the entire length of trench No. 2; we attributed them to a private house in use until the fourth century C.E. Finally, Foerster states, "further trenches cut outside the synagogue did not produce any conclusive evidence concerning the chronological problems of the synagogue." In our opinion, the Late Roman coins and potsherds from trench No. 5 are not to be overlooked.

We warmly subscribe to Foerster's suggestion that our "sweeping conclusions should be carefully scrutinized" and that "one must hope for further excavations in the Capernaum synagogue." Indeed, the excavations carried on since 1969 have provided a tremendous amount of archeological data supporting a late chronology for the synagogue of Capernaum.

[8] E. Meyers, "Archaeology and Rabbinical Tradition at Khirbet Shema'," *Biblical Archeologist*, 35 (1972), 2–31. See below, pp. 70–74, 123–128.

[9] G. Foerster, "Notes on Recent Excavations at Capernaum (Review Article)," *IEJ*, 21 (1971), 207–211.

Notes on Recent Excavations at Capernaum

G. Foerster

The synagogue at Capernaum, partly restored in the twenties of this century, serves as the best surviving example of the "Galilean-type" synagogue. Excavations at the site were started in 1905 by the Deutsche Orient Gesellschaft, directed by H. Kohl and C. Watzinger.[1] The Franciscan Custody of the Holy Land continued the excavation of the synagogue and of the area south of it since 1907.[2] Most scholars have dated it to the late second or third centuries C.E.[3] This date is firmly established on architectural, stylistic, and historical grounds. After half a century, the Franciscan Custody of the Holy Land resumed the excavations at Capernaum. Fathers V. Corbo, O.F.M. and S. Loffreda, O.F.M. were in charge of the excavations since 1968. They extended the excavations to the south of the synagogue in the area of the Byzantine octagonal structure, discovered by G. Orfali.[4]

The Synagogue
Though only preliminary reports have been published to date, and the excavations have been continued since, it seems worthwhile to discuss the additional information because of the serious problems it has raised.*

The late second or third century C.E. dating is founded on architectural and stylistic parallels in contemporary Roman art and architecture in Syria and Asia Minor. The synagogue at Capernaum is in harmony with the classical architectural concept that stresses the outer appearance of a building. In contrast, Byzantine architecture concentrates on the interior (e.g., the lavish mosaic pavement of the synagogue of Ḥammath-Tiberias, which dates from the first half of the fourth century C.E.). Though in some remote areas in Syria and Asia Minor classical concepts of the exteriors of buildings seem to continue even into the Byzantine period, the architectural details are non-classical.[5] At Capernaum, however, the capitals, friezes, cornices, and other architectural details belong to types well-established in the late second and third centuries C.E.

Historical considerations are also in line with the date suggested above. In the second century, the Jewish authorities, together with a large number of Jews, left Judaea and settled in the Galilee after two wars against the Romans. The prosperous condition of the Jewish communities, as a result of their political, economic and, not least, spiritual strength was the proper background for unusual building activity, of which the Capernaum synagogue can serve as one example.[6]

Corbo states, in the preface of the preliminary report, that the date of the synagogue is based on historical and stylistic considerations

---

[1] H. Kohl and C. Watzinger, *Antike Synagogen in Galilaea* (Leipzig, 1916), pp. 4-40, 219.

[2] G. Orfali, *Caphernaüm et ses ruines* (Paris, 1922).

[3] Most recently, N. Avigad, *Encyclopaedia of Archaeological Excavations in the Holy Land,* I (Jerusalem, 1975), pp. 288-290.

[4] V. Corbo, S. Loffreda, A. Spijkerman, *La Synagoga di Cafarnao dopo gli scavi del* 1969 (Jerusalem, 1970) — (Publications of the Studium Biblicum Franciscanum, collectio minor, 9); cf. also *Liber Annuus,* 20 (1970), 7-117.

* [Although written in 1971, the views expressed here continue to be espoused by the author — ed.]

[5] R. Krautheimer, *Early Christian and Byzantine Architecture* (Harmondsworth, 1965), e.g., p. 43 and pp. 105-116.

[6] G. Alon, *A History of the Jews in Erez-Israel During the Period of the Mishna and Talmud* (Tel Aviv, 1953), I, 18; II, 128-158, *passim* (Hebrew).

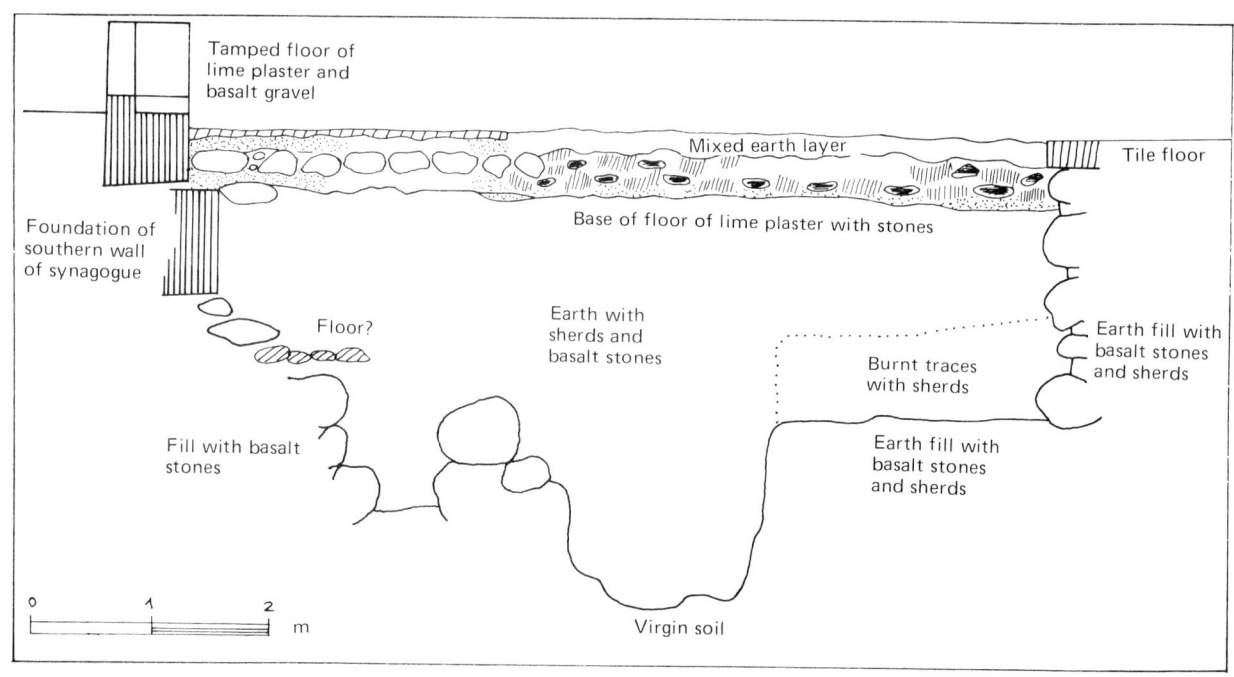

View of interior of partially reconstructed Capernaum synagogue, looking towards northwest

Tamped floor of
lime plaster and
basalt gravel

Mixed earth layer

Tile floor

Foundation of
southern wall
of synagogue

Base of floor of lime plaster with stones

Floor?

Earth with
sherds and
basalt stones

Burnt traces
with sherds

Earth fill with
basalt stones
and sherds

Fill with basalt
stones

Earth fill with
basalt stones
and sherds

0   1   2
|____|____| m

Virgin soil

Section drawing of trench 1, looking west

alone; he seems to attach undue importance to the late Byzantine date suggested for the Aramaic dedicatory inscription on one of the synagogue's columns (p. 9). This is in line with the general tendency of the report, which led to the suggestion that the synagogue was built in the second half of the fourth century C.E.

The report is divided into three chapters: "New Excavations at the Capernaum Synagogue" (pp. 13–60) by V. Corbo; "The Pottery" (pp. 61–123) by S. Loffreda; and "The Coins" (pp. 126–140) by A. Spijkermann.

Seven trenches were laid out, two of them in the synagogue hall and one in the courtyard (the "Beth Hamidrash" according to Corbo[7]). The other four trenches were cut outside the synagogue structure, but were carried to its walls. The trench in the southern part of the synagogue nave cut through the floor level and below it, at a spot where the floor slabs were missing. The floor foundation consisted of rubble reinforced with mortar. Below the floor there is a packed fill of rubble and brown earth. The fill contained Hellenistic and Roman pottery, the latest being of the second–third centuries C.E. The latest coins found in this trench are from the same period.

The second trench was cut in the northeastern part of the synagogue, again at a spot where the floor slabs were missing. Corbo attaches great importance to some seventy coins of the fourth century (the latest of 364–375 C.E.), found in the impressions left by the floor slabs. Since the floor slabs were missing, it is impossible to tell *when* the coins were left (except as a *terminus post quem*). Consequently, these coins bear no relation to the foundation date of the synagogue. Only one fourth century C.E. coin is clearly attributed to the fill below the sealed floor. The pottery found at this point is typical of a fill, the latest being dated by Loffreda to the fourth century C.E. In this trench scanty remains of two floors, the purpose and date of which are not clear, were distinguished below the fill. The trench at the southeastern corner

of the synagogue court was also cut in an area where the floor slabs were missing. Two fourth century C.E. coins were found in the fill, which contained pottery dated by Loffreda to the fifth century C.E. Further trenches cut outside the synagogue did not produce any conclusive evidence concerning the chronological problems of the synagogue.

Two thousand sherds were found (glass is not mentioned in the report) and 170 coins, of which only three fourth century C.E. coins were attributed by the excavators to the fill below the sealed floor. To accept the excavators' date of the second half of the fourth century C.E. for the synagogue and the first half of the fifth century C.E. for the courtyard would mean that this synagogue was founded not at one of the most prosperous periods of Judaism in the Galilee, but under Byzantine rule. It would be a strange example of anachronism in Roman provincial art and architecture of the fourth and fifth centuries C.E. for a style to appear simultaneously with Byzantine church architecture and synagogues in the style of Ḥammath-Tiberias.

It seems, therefore, that Corbo's conclusions are in contradiction to the accepted dates for the architectural style and decoration of the early group of "Galilean" synagogues on the one hand, and the historical situation on the other. Such sweeping conclusions should therefore be carefully scrutinized.

The three fourth-century coins found in the fill under the sealed floor level, as well as some of the pottery found there and attributed by the excavators to the fourth century C.E., suggest that the fill should be dated to the late fourth century C.E. This may, then, be either the foundation date of the synagogue or, what seems to us more probable, a result of repairs and renovations. The latter explanation is possibly supported by the fact that in the three trenches laid out in the synagogue, the floor slabs were missing. This possibility is, however, rejected outright by Corbo without any explanation. The difficulties which would arise from accepting Corbo's dating clearly outweigh any other possible interpretation.

---

[7] It is difficult to accept this interpretation since this space is open to the elements, in particular to winter rains.

Some Comments on the Capernaum Excavations

M. Avi-Yonah

The "late chronology" proposed by Fr. Loffreda for the Capernaum synagogue has caused a great deal of discussion. We are therefore grateful to the excavators for having supplied the wider public with a reasoned statement of their case. It would seem proper, however, to point out the existence of other interpretations of the archeological evidence, so ably presented by Fr. Loffreda, and to note some of the consequences of his proposals for the history of Jewish art and archeology in the Galilee in the talmudic period.

Fr. Loffreda has honored two eminent Israeli archeologists, the late Prof. E. L. Sukenik and Prof. N. Avigad — as well as the present writer — by calling them as witnesses for the soundness of his assumptions. However, even if Sukenik's late date for the Aramaic inscription at Capernaum were generally accepted (which is by no means the case), some consideration should be given to the Greek dedicatory inscription on another column, reading "Herod the son of Mokimos donated this column." This text is certainly not Byzantine, neither in the form of the script nor in the names of the donor and of his father. Avigad's reading of the Nabratein inscription does indeed include the date 494 (i.e., 564 C.E.) and the statement that the house was "built" at that time, but the author assumed that the inscription was added to a much earlier lintel. As regards the quotations from an article by the present writer, the "Byzantine" features noticed at Chorazin were included in an argument concerning an entirely different matter, namely the "survival" of an Orientalizing under-current in Palestine in the Roman period and its subsequent re-emergence in

Byzantine times. In all three cases above, the authors held fast to the early chronology of the "Galilean" synagogues, and their *obiter dicta* do not indicate any doubts as to its correctness.

It would be discourteous to refuse to accept the facts as stated by the excavator and the dating of the coins by his eminent confrère, Fr. Spijkerman. One may take the liberty, however, of interpreting the same facts in another way. For instance, Fr. Loffreda assumes that the lower basalt pavement in trench 2 and the wall in trench 6 belonged to a private house. This would be a much larger and better paved structure than any other private dwelling in Capernaum. Indeed, would it not be possible to conclude that these were the remnants of a *public* building (preferably a synagogue) which existed before the present one? There was surely a synagogue at Capernaum in the New Testament period; several others could have been erected later on in the same place.

The problems of the fill (stratum B) and the layer of mortar (stratum C) are by no means easily solved. Fr. Loffreda does not note the relation of the fill to the walls of the synagogue; assuming that a pavement was to be *re*laid, a fill could have been spread inside the building and a layer of mortar placed over it. Moreover, the overly confident use of the term "hermetically sealed" arouses some doubts. No sealing in an ancient site was ever "hermetic" in the physical sense.

Coming now to the numismatic evidence, we must note with regret that it is used only too often to draw far-reaching conclusions from what is, at best, rather slender proof. Coins, if legible — and sometimes even if not —

are easily dated and hence are favored by archeologists over almost any other type of material. Yet it must be remembered that coins are small and slippery objects. In our opinion, there are three different circumstances under which coins can provide the archeologist with information: (a) They are deliberately placed under the foundations as an offering, in which case the date of the foundation is well and truly established; (b) They are lost, slipping between the stones of a pavement or between a bench and a wall. In this case they can only serve as an approximate date for the use of the structure; (c) They are deliberately cached to secure them for later recovery. In such a case the latest coin of the hoard can serve as a *terminus post quem* for the destruction of the building, but certainly not for the *terminus ante quem* of its construction. The most glaring example of the misuse of numismatic evidence is supplied by Fr. Loffreda's reliance on the finds of Chorazin to prove that the synagogue there was in use "at least until the early seventh century." The list to which he refers is a selection of 71 coins out of a total of 550 *surface* finds. *Two* out of 550 coins belong to the seventh century. Does this prove that the synagogue was still in use, or that some pilgrims had holes in their pockets or money bags?

In order to be truly impressive, numismatic evidence must be sufficient in quantity; we should be wary of drawing too hasty conclusions from finding one coin here, two coins there, and so on. Fr. Loffreda's dating is based on *four* stray coins. Would he date a level because of four potsherds? Far more important are the finds of the two hoards of 2920 and 6000 coins. These hoards show that the synagogue officials (for such hoards were most probably not private) were afraid of attack and ruin. To anyone familiar with Jewish history in fifth-century Palestine, such fears were only too well-founded. The fact that the caches were never recovered is clear evidence that all those who knew of their location either perished or were driven away. The *earliest* of the stray coins mentioned is dated 341, which would give the synagogue barely one century of existence if built then.

We must definitely take issue with Fr. Loffreda on one point of his argument, his statement that for dating we should use *only* archeological evidence. This might be true in the case of prehistoric research, where the only evidence available is from excavations. In the later periods we should certainly take into account *all* the relevant material, including written sources and stylistic parallels. We should avoid staring, as if hypnotized, at the five-meter squares of a locus and basing all our arguments on the finds in such a small area. This method, favored by many of the younger and less experienced archeologists — and even some older ones — has led only too often to hasty conclusions, which later must be revised when the excavation area is enlarged.

Let us now consider three possible ramifications of accepting the late dating proposed by Fr. Loffreda. First (as G. Foerster has already pointed out), the Capernaum synagogue would have been built at one end of the Sea of Galilee — a solid stone structure, with its façade pointing to Jerusalem, and with a stone pavement and architectural details resembling those of 3rd century Roman buildings in Syria. At the same time the synagogue at Hammath-Tiberias would be erected, barely twenty km. away, with a niche in its back wall facing Jerusalem, a mosaic pavement with figurative mosaics, and quite a different architectural character. The dating of the Hammath-Tiberias pavement is certainly no later than the middle of the fourth century. If we consider all we know of the development of architectural styles, we would probably find this to be the only case of such astounding architectural diversity within so small an area.

The second point is a historical one; a date in the middle of the fourth century would mean that one of the most magnificent of "Galilean" synagogues was built during the reign of emperor Constantine or his son, Constantius II, neither of them friendly toward the Jews or Judaism. The reign of Julian, the only one among the emperors of the Constantinian dynasty to be friendly to the Hebrews, was too short for the erection of such a sumptuous structure.

Thirdly, there existed, according to Fathers Corbo and Loffreda, a Christian place of worship barely some tens of meters from the synagogue, the "House of St. Peter" transformed into a church. Such a state of affairs might be conceivable in our ecumenical age, but it seems almost impossible to imagine that it would have been allowed by the Byzantine authorities of the fourth century.

It is true that the later synagogues of the Byzantine period were erected despite the laws prohibiting the building of new places of worship for the Jews — most likely a result of efficient bribery. However, these late synagogues are entirely different in architectural character from the Capernaum synagogue, which proclaims its purpose boldly for all to see. All the splendors of the Byzantine synagogues were saved for the interior; from the outside they could hardly be distinguished from the private dwellings surrounding them.

It is true that the recent discoveries of those synagogues at Ḥorvat Susiya, 'En-Gedi, and Shema' have upset our previous theories on the development of the synagogue plan and we must reconsider. However, it is still too early to accept the proposed "late chronology" for the synagogue of Capernaum. Perhaps we ought to await further developments at Capernaum and elsewhere.

The Synagogue at Ḥammath-Tiberias

M. Dothan

The remains of Ḥammath-Tiberias extend from the hot springs (al-Ḥammam) to the southern boundary of ancient Tiberias. In the Talmud, the place is identified with Ḥammath (Josh. 19:35), a fortified city of the tribe of Naphtali: "Ḥammath-Ḥammatha" (J *Megilla* I, 70a). This identification is not certain, however, since the excavations and the survey of the Ḥammath area uncovered no remains earlier than the Hellenistic period. Ḥammath is mentioned many times in the Mishnah. Tiberias and Ḥammath were originally two separate cities, each surrounded by a wall of its own ("R. Jeremiah said ... from Ḥammath to Tiberias — a mile" [B *Megilla* 2b]) but they were subsequently united into a single city, apparently in the first or second century C.E.: "Now the inhabitants of Tiberias and the inhabitants of Ḥammath again became one city" (T *'Erubin* V, 2). Tiberias was known as Maziah, after the priestly order that had settled in Ḥammath (Tiberias was forbidden to the priests because it contained a cemetery). The suburb of Ḥammath shared the prominence of Tiberias. When the latter became the seat of the Patriarchate and of the main Palestinian rabbinical academy in the third century C.E., it served as the spiritual center of the Jews of Palestine and the Diaspora. With the demise of the Patriarchate in 429 C.E., Ḥammath began to decline, but it continued to exist as a city, supporting itself by its profitable hot springs. The Jewish community remained in the city throughout the Arab period until its decline in the Middle Ages.

Toward the end of 1961, the author received word of extensive development projects on the western shore of the lake, on the slopes of Ḥammath-Tiberias. The site had been known since a survey in 1947 revealed the existence of ruins, and rumors were rife in Tiberias of the discovery of a church or synagogue. On a visit to the site late in 1961, it was found to be overgrown with vegetation; on the southeast there was a crescent-shaped mound, which we assumed was the site of the apse.

Several weeks later, excavations commenced on the site.[1] From the outset, building stones were noted at two levels, raising the possibility of early structures below. After some two weeks, at a depth of 1 m. below the level of the upper remains, a polychrome mosaic floor was revealed, bearing part of an inscription and a depiction of one of the seasons of the year. These were clearly the remains of a synagogue; it later became evident that the upper level, too, had served as a synagogue.

An area of approximately 1.200 sq. m. was excavated near the hot springs, about 150 m. west of the Sea of Galilee. The ancient remains had been erected on an artificial terrace running parallel to the seashore from southeast to northwest, closely following the contours of the terrain. Beyond the southern limit of the main excavation area were uncovered the remains of the city wall and one of its towers. These were found to date not earlier than the Byzantine period, although they appear to rest on the remains of walls of an earlier city. Three main construction levels of the synagogue were discovered.

---

[1] The excavations were carried out on behalf of the Department of Antiquities and Museums, and directed by the author.

General view of the synagogue during excavations, looking west

Level III. The numismatic evidence showed that remains from the first century B.C.E. lay beneath Level III. The main building in Level III dates from the first century or first half of the second century C.E. This building (60 × 40 m.), only half of which was excavated, consists of a central court with halls and rooms along at least three of its sides. Two entrances to the building were found on the south side. Its plan resembles that of a public building, such as a gymnasium, and it may have already been a synagogue in that early period; furthermore, all the later structures above the building (except perhaps those of Intermediate Phase III–II) were synagogues. Noteworthy among the meager finds in this building is a unique glass goblet in the shape of a centaur, silvered on the inside and outside and decorated with floral reliefs below the rim.

Level III seems to have been destroyed in the middle of the second century, and the few remains above it (Intermediate Phase III–II) do not apparently belong to a public building.

Level II B. The synagogue of Level II B was erected on the ruins of Level III, and stood apart from the buildings around it. In form it was a basilica, oriented on a southeast–northwest axis; it measured 13 × 15 m. The basilica was divided into four halls by three rows of columns (three columns in each row). The principal and widest hall (the second from the west) served as the nave. A corridor on the south, giving access to the nave, was paved in white mosaics with a black, linear border, and was entered from the east; this appears to have been the main entrance to the building. In the floor of the nave, north of the doorway, a fragment of a polychrome mosaic pavement is preserved, bearing geometric motifs. A room adjoining the northern side of the building may have contained a stairway leading up to the roof or to an upper story. The earliest finds of Level II are from the first

64

half of the third century C.E., and this was apparently the period in which the synagogue was built.

In comparing the plan of this building with the "Galilean" synagogues, the "broadhouse" character of our building is immediately apparent; that is, the entrance is situated in one of the long walls. These proportions are created by the additional row of columns and aisle on the east; our building stands in contrast to the traditional long basilica with a nave flanked by single aisles. The additional eastern aisle here may have been intended for women worshippers; nevertheless, there was no trace of a wall or other division between this aisle and the remainder of the hall, though there may have been some temporary partition (such as a curtain) between the columns.

The characteristic features of the two main synagogue types of Israel — the early type, which flourished mainly in the Galilee in the second–third centuries C.E., and the later type, primarily of the fifth–sixth centuries C.E. — have been reviewed above (see pp. 11–18). We see that in the synagogue of Level IIB, the worshippers entered from the side facing Jerusalem; there was no permanent location for the Torah shrine and few decorative elements were discovered (though a section of mosaic pavement was found). On the basis of these facts, this synagogue can be regarded as largely continuing the tradition of the early synagogue group, though it already displays some of the characteristics of the later synagogues. Thus, we can ascribe it to an early phase of the transitional period between these two types.

Level IIA. The earlier synagogue of Level IIB was at least partially destroyed toward the end of the third or in the early part of the fourth century C.E. The founders of the new synagogue, whose names are known from the mosaic inscriptions, reutilized the plan of the earlier structure, but modified it, apparently following a newer fashion. This new synagogue, in its final form, was the most sophisticated of the synagogues on the site. Like its predecessor, the building was a

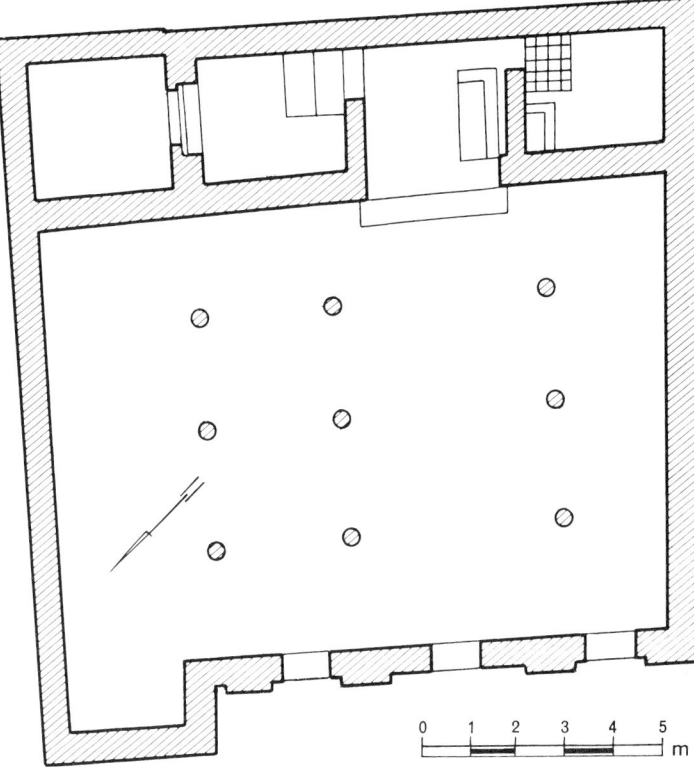

Plan of the synagogue of Severus (Level IIA)

basilica measuring 13 × 15 m., and was divided into four spaces by three rows of columns (each row of three columns); the widest space, the second from the west, served as the nave. However, in Level IIA several innovations were introduced, among them the entrance corridor opening onto the nave was now divided into cells, thus cancelling its use as a thoroughfare, and entrance to the synagogue was now from the north. Despite the destruction of the thresholds, there is no doubt concerning the position of the doorways, for three recesses in the northern wall indicate the openings into the nave and the two aisles immediately flanking it. From the southern end of the nave, steps led up into a raised cell (part of the former corridor). This apparently became the permanent location for the Torah shrine, for which there was no provision in the earlier synagogue. The staircase on the north was no longer used, and access to the roof (or a second story, if there was one) was by way of a small room at the southeastern corner of the former corridor.

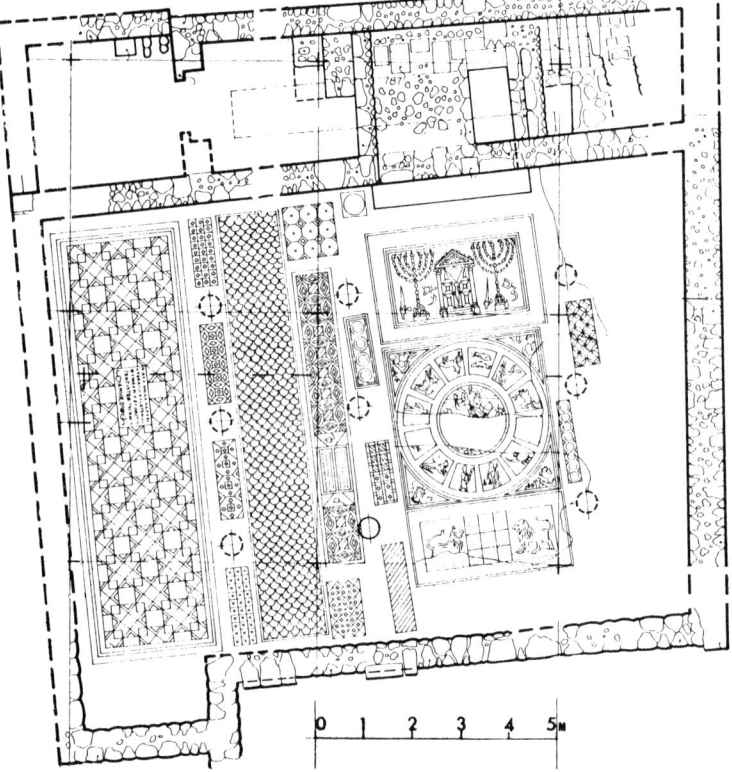

Plan of the synagogue of Severus, showing the position of the mosaic pavements. See above, p. 8.

The walls of the hall were ornamented with polychrome frescoes, traces of which were discovered within the debris on the floor.

The tradition of the mosaic pavement continued from the earlier synagogue, and herein lay a major surprise. The hall was paved with a well-preserved mosaic floor, executed in some thirty colors. The nave contained the most important part of the mosaic, divided into three panels: at the center of the southern panel, closest to the chamber for the Torah shrine, is a depiction of a Torah shrine flanked by *menorot*. In the field are a *lulab, ethrog, shofar* and an incense shovel. The middle panel contains a zodiac circle, at the center of which is Helios, the sun-god, riding in his chariot. (In Level I, the chariot was obliterated by the construction of a wall across it.) At the corners of this central panel, the busts of four female figures represent the four seasons of the year, with their names inscribed in Hebrew beside them.

The significance of the figure of Helios (or

Sol Invictus, "Invincible Sun," the Roman title by which he was known in the third–fourth centuries C.E.) here at Ḥammath is indicated by the fact that this depiction is a century or two earlier than the representations of Helios in the synagogues at Naʿaran, Beth-Alpha and Ḥusifa. The god is depicted here as riding in the chariot of the heavens, above the sea. Though the chariot is destroyed, it can readily be reconstructed on the basis of parallel depictions and upon the remaining traces. The god is portrayed frontally, with his head turned to the right; upon his head of curly hair is a rayed crown surrounded by a halo. His right arm is raised in a gesture of might and blessing, and his left hand holds the orb of the universe — emblem of sovereignty. He is wrapped in a red *paludamentum*, the cloak of the Caesars, with a long-sleeved, girdled tunic beneath. This depiction of Sol Invictus, with all the attributes of a Roman emperor, is typical of the third–fourth centuries C.E. It was popular in cults throughout the Empire — particularly Mithraism, where Sol was the principal god alongside Mithra, and was sometimes even identified with him. The figure of Sol is known, too, in the liturgy and symbolism of Christianity. In a mosaic discovered in the mausoleum of Julius, beneath St. Peter's in Rome, Sol Invictus is seen riding in the sun-chariot, crowned by a halo with seven rays, bearing a close resemblance to the halo of Sol at Ḥammath; he wears a *paludamentum* over a girdled tunic and holds an orb in his left hand. His right arm was apparently raised in a gesture similar to that of Sol at Ḥammath. This figure of Sol has been identified with Jesus Kosmokrator, and the mosaic has been dated to 250–300 C.E.

The significance of Helios in the mosaic at Ḥammath-Tiberias is indicated by the fact that he is clearly the central figure in the panel with the zodiac circle and the seasons of the year. Two different interpretations may be given to the appearance of the figure. If the architects or planners of the pavement were not Jews (as is quite possible), the image of Sol Invictus was none other than that of the emperor. However, if the image was regarded

Aramaic inscription in the mosaic pavement of the synagogue

as a neutral figure, it would have been intended simply as a personification of the sun, the center of the universe. To the congregation of this synagogue at Hammath-Tiberias there was no basic difference between the image of Sol and the representation of the zodiac. Just as the stars were personified, Helios was merely the personification of the sun. Thus, the "four seasons," the zodiac representing the year, and the figure of the sun controlling the cycle from the center, probably signified the annual calendar, so sacred in Jewish life.

Three different languages, in two scripts, are represented in the inscriptions of this synagogue. The legends of the seasons of the year and the zodiac circle are entirely in Hebrew, as is the single word *shalom* ("pcacc") within one of the Greek inscriptions. In the northern panel of the nave, a Greek inscription is flanked by two lions; it mentions the names of the founders of the synagogue. In the two eastern aisles, among the geometric motifs in the pavement, are three inscriptions, one in Aramaic and two in Greek. These latter inscriptions are most interesting, in both content and language. According to the Greek inscriptions, foremost among the founders was one Severus, denoted "the pupil of the illustrious Patriarchs," perhaps a person educated in the court of the Patriarch at Tiberias and included amongst his associates. This Severus "completed (the construction), praise unto him and unto Julius the *pronotes* (?)." The

other Greek inscription, which ends in the Hebrew word *shalom*, mentions a man named Profuturos, who built one of the aisles.

The Aramaic inscription is in the lower section of a *tabula ansata* panel, above one of the Greek inscriptions. When first discovered, the lower part of this panel was missing; this was surprising, for the surrounding mosaic was well preserved. Some time later the explanation became apparent; it seems that part of the mosaic here had been removed prior to when our excavations had commenced. When the missing part was returned, it was replaced and now the panel is complete. The inscription reads as follows:

יהי שלמה על כל מן דעבד מצותה בהדן
אתרה קדישה ודעתיד מעבד מצותה
תהי לה ברכתה אמן אמן סלה ולי אמן

Peace be upon everyone who has fulfilled the commandment in this holy place, and who will fulfill the commandment.
May the blessing be his. Amen. Amen. Selah. And unto me. Amen.

This is a new version in Aramaic of a blessing for donors to a synagogue. The language is the Galilean Aramaic of the third–fourth centuries C.E.

Interestingly, Hebrew was used within the synagogue only for defining the astronomical symbols; Aramaic was used principally for matters of halakha; and Greek was the principal language in honoring donors.

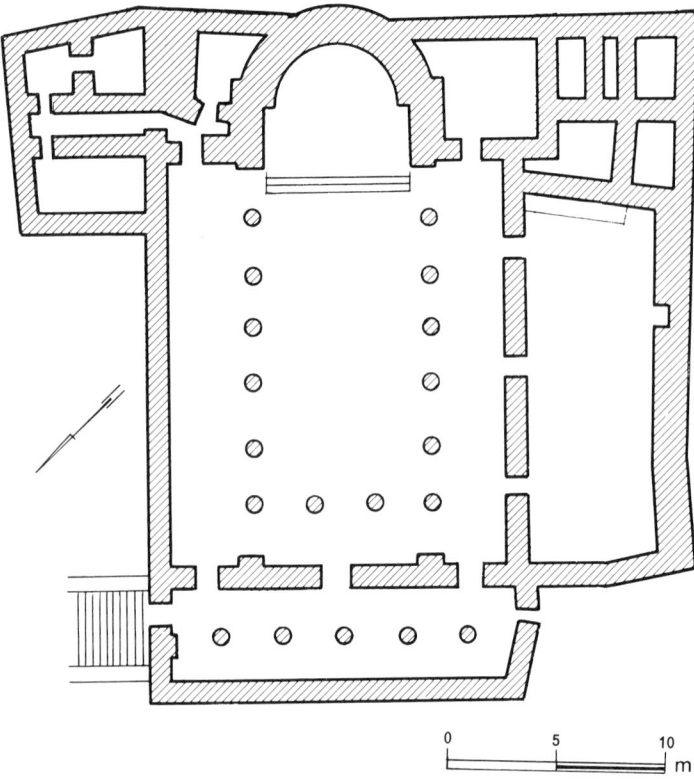

Plan of the synagogue in the 7th–8th centuries
(Level I A)

The few objects found on the floors, including the coins and lamps, assist in ascribing the synagogue of Level II A to the fourth century C.E. This is also suggested by the style of building and the plan. The building style differs from all that is known of second–third century C.E. synagogues, as well as of those of the fifth and sixth centuries C.E.; yet we find here typical third century characteristics (such as the absence of an apse), as well as features dating from the fifth century onwards (such as the situation of the entrance, facing Jerusalem, and a specific location for the Torah shrine).

The artistic level of the mosaics surpasses all that has so far been uncovered in the early synagogues in Israel. In the individual treatment of the figures, they strongly resemble the Constantinian mosaics at Antioch. Evident here is the strong influence exerted by Hellenistic-Roman art of the beginning of the fourth century C.E. on the Jewish capital at Tiberias (the sages of Tiberias permitted the

representation of images in mosaic, as is attested by the written sources). The free artistic expression displayed in the nude representation of the signs of the zodiac, the frequent use of Greek, as well as the various finds, all accord with the spirit that prevailed in the period when leading Palestinian sages flourished in Tiberias, and confirm a date in the first half of the fourth century C.E. for the construction of synagogue II A. The synagogue was apparently destroyed in the fifth century C.E., either by official order or as the result of a natural disaster (Tiberias has been frequently ravaged by earthquakes and floods). After its destruction, a thick layer of silt, borne down from the hills to the west, covered the synagogue entirely.

Level I B. The synagogue of this period was erected at a much higher level, but its builders sank their foundations to a great depth, damaging the remains of the earlier synagogue, especially its mosaic floor. The new synagogue differed radically from the previous synagogues. Apart from differences in plan (which will be discussed below), another basic difference is apparent; whereas the earlier synagogues had stood isolated, the synagogue of Level I was incorporated (in both its phases) within the general plan of the quarter. To the north were buildings representing a single unit, to the west was a street leading from the southern town-gate, and to the south was the town-wall. The orientation of the new synagogue was as in the earlier structures. This building, too, was basilical, as is usual in Byzantine synagogues of the fifth and sixth centuries C.E. All the foundations were preserved, as were the stylobates and the pavement. The building (including the narthex) measured about 24×31 m. Two rows of columns (none found *in situ*) divided the building into a nave and two aisles. A third row of columns formed a transverse row on the north, thus creating a *pronaos*. A narthex was attached to the northern end of the building, enclosing the three main entrances.

From the southern end of the nave, three steps led up to an inscribed apse built within the external wall of the building. East of the apse was a room containing steps which led up to a second story. In one of the rooms west of the apse, the strong-box of the synagogue was set into the floor. From the western aisle, three doorways opened onto a stone-paved courtyard, whose walls were preserved to a substantial height; the western wall of the courtyard bordered upon the street. At the southern end of the courtyard was a small apse; beyond it were plastered chambers which served as cisterns. The floor of the interior of the synagogue was paved in polychrome mosaics, of which little remains; the main surviving fragment indicates that animals and floral patterns were depicted, as was often the case in mosaic pavements of the fifth–sixth centuries C.E. The town-wall, some 3 m. thick, passed north of the synagogue. From the twin-towered gate, a paved street at a higher level than the synagogue led into the town. The synagogue seems to have been partly destroyed in the first half of the seventh century C.E., perhaps with the Byzantine reconquest in 628 C.E.

Level I A. The synagogue of this period, the last on the site, was apparently built at the beginning of the Umayyad dynasty; it reflects no significant change from the plan of its predecessor. The small apse in the courtyard was done away with, and the courtyard itself was partly roofed over, with the addition of a column to support the roof-beams. The room thus formed, with a bench at the southern end (previously one of the steps leading up to the small apse), may possibly have been the *beth-midrash*. The building was paved with a new mosaic floor, mainly of geometric patterns. In the part opposite the central entrance, a depiction of a *menorah* was found, apparently one of a pair. The schematic form of the *menorah* resembles that in the contemporary synagogue at Jericho. Among other changes in the synagogue, we may note the conversion of the cisterns west of the apse into dwelling chambers. Structures were also appended on the north. Beside the street leading from the town-gate, along the western flank of the synagogue, shops were found, where

pottery and glass vessels were sold. To their east, a group of small rooms was revealed, presumably a hostel attached to the synagogue (an institution well known from talmudic literature). In the strong-room of the synagogue, and in the store-room flanking the apse, pottery typical of the seventh–eighth centuries C.E. was found, along with numerous lamps, some of them ornamented and one bearing an Arabic inscription. A long Aramaic inscription was found on a jug, parts of which have been deciphered; the jug apparently contained a gift of oil from the town of Sepphoris. The pottery and coins show that the synagogue buildings were destroyed early in the Abbasid period, in the mid-eighth century C.E.

Summary

1) At Ḥammath a number of superimposed synagogue buildings were found, and beneath them was a public building whose function is not clear. The construction of the synagogue went through four phases, beginning in the third century and terminating in the middle of the eighth century C.E.

2) A new type of synagogue was uncovered here, a "broadhouse" type of four rooms (II A. B), with the entrance on the side facing Jerusalem (II B) and having a permanent place for the Torah shrine. This was a rectangular room which preceded the apse in Palestinian synagogues (II B).

3) The mosaic pavement in synagogue II B is constructed in the spirit of the Hellenistic–Roman art of the fourth century C.E. The zodiac depicted in the mosaic is the earliest found in the country.

4) The Greek inscriptions of the builders of this synagogue are the first to mention the Patriarchs, and contribute greatly to the knowledge of Judaism of the fourth century C.E. in Tiberias.

5) The uppermost synagogue (I A) is an instructive example of Jewish architecture at the beginning of Arab rule in Palestine and sheds light on a number of customs practiced in synagogues in those days.

The Synagogue at Ḥorvat Shema'

E. M. Meyers

Ḥorvat Shema' lies near the foot of Mount Meiron, some 300 m. south of the ancient synagogue of Meiron, on a spur on the opposite slope of Naḥal Meiron. The site has long been venerated by Jews, certainly since

Restored prayer hall, looking southwest

Northern entrance; the lintel with *menorah* relief had stood upon the door-jambs here

medieval times, as the burial place of Shammai. The three seasons of excavations there (1970–1972)[1] have revealed that this was no more than a late tradition.[2]

The excavations did uncover a prosperous Jewish village of the fourth–sixth centuries C.E. Beside the extensive clearing operations in the ruins of the settlement, a public building was discovered. While a number of medieval travelers and modern explorers had noted the substantial ruins on the site,[3] none had identified the structure as a synagogue. By the end of our 1970 season of excavations, it was apparent that the rectangular structure was, in fact, the first "broadhouse" synagogue to be uncovered in the Galilee and, further, that it was quite different from its closest parallels in the south — Ḥorvat Susiya and Eshtemoa (see pp. 120–128).

Sealed deposits within the synagogue itself and in the building to the north (possibly a *beth-midrash*) have enabled the dating of the complex. These data fit well with the chronological indications from the rest of the site, placing the synagogue (in both its phases) within the heyday of this Galilean community, spanning the late third to the early fifth centuries C.E. (Strata II–IV of the site). The proposed dating is in accord with both the

[1] The excavations were carried out under the auspices of the American Schools of Oriental Research and the W.F. Albright Institute of Archaeological Research, and directed by the author. The final results are published in E.M. Meyers, A.T. Kraabel, & J.F. Strange, *Ancient Synagogue Excavations at Khirbet Shema', Upper Galilee, Israel, 1970–1972* (*AASOR* 42), (Durham, N.C., 1976).

[2] The identification of the site with the Galilean Tekoa, as suggested by S. Klein, was also shown to be without foundation.

[3] Of special interest is the note of R.A.S. Macalister, *PEFQST*, 11 (1909), 195–200.

Lintel bearing *menorah* relief

numismatic evidence and that of the pottery; the latter has been cross-checked with sealed and dated material from trial excavations at nearby Meiron.

The earlier synagogue (Stratum III; 284–306 C.E.). In general outline, the two phases of the synagogue were very similar in plan, orientation, and size. Almost all the architectural members were found on the floors. The building, measuring 18 × 9 m., was erected on a basilical plan, with two rows of columns, each of four columns, oriented on an east-west axis. The principal entrance was on the north. It had two door-jambs, a threshold and a lintel, all monoliths. The lintel bore a *menorah* carved in relief, 0.85 m. wide — the largest such depiction from an ancient synagogue. A second entrance was located at the southwestern corner, from which an internal flight of steps led down to the main floor level of the synagogue. On one of the door-jambs was a carved eagle in relief. To the north of this entrance, west of the main hall and at the level of the doorway, were the vestiges of the women's gallery; the two rooms beneath, at the level of the main hall, had apparently been utilized, one for storage and the other (the plastered walls of which bore frescoes) for the Torah shrine. Plastered benches ran along the longer walls of the hall. The columns of the southern row stood upon plinths, whereas those of the northern row rested on simple, square bases. The architects showed great versatility in adapting their plan to local topographic conditions.

From the debris recovered between the eastern, short wall of the synagogue (the same in both phases) and the stylobate, it is clear

The western entrance

71

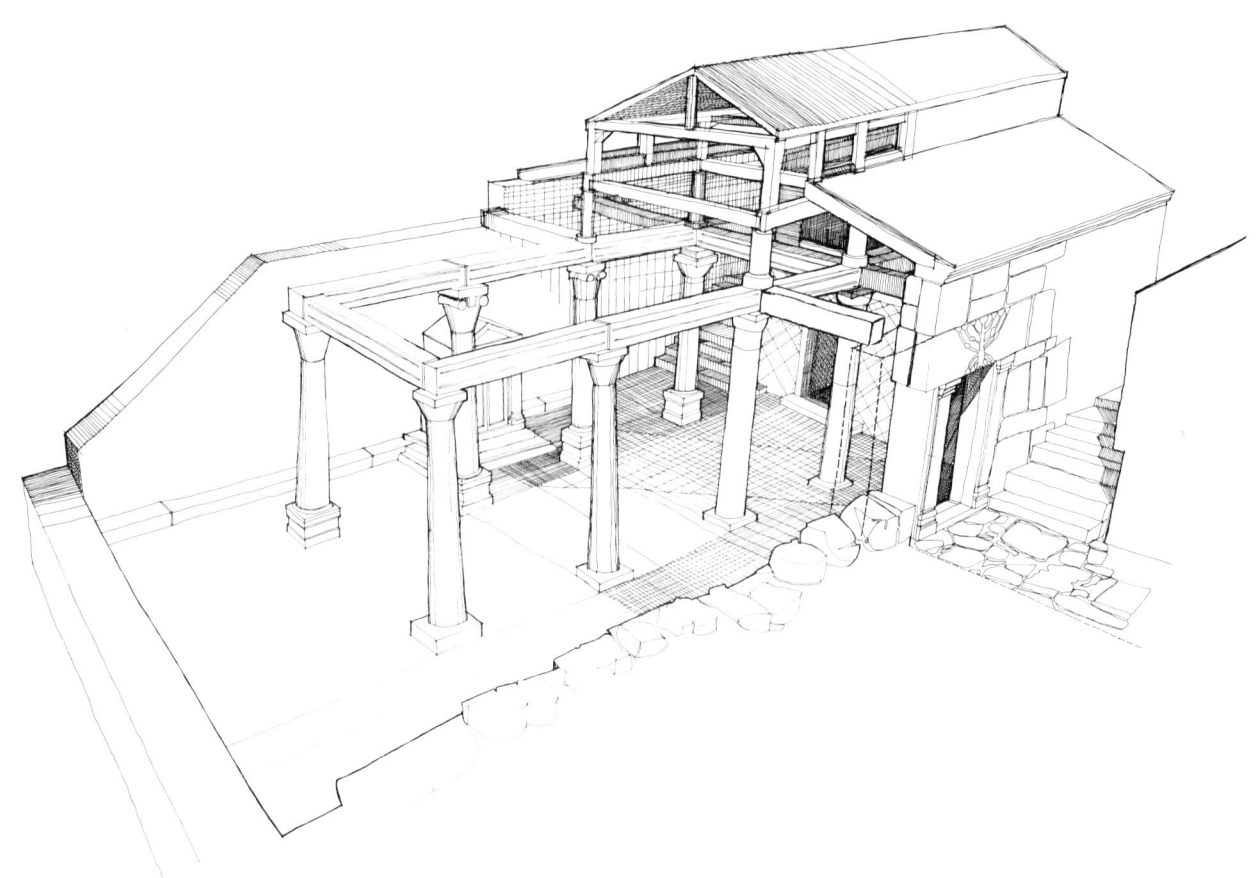

Architect's reconstruction in perspective. Note the *aedicula* on the southern wall

that the earlier synagogue was far more elaborate than the one which succeeded it. The pilasters on the four door-jambs of the two entrances are clear indicators of the high quality of workmanship. Socio-economic factors, more than anything else, seem to have caused decline in the architectural and esthetic level of the later building. The unique aspects of both structures should be emphasized: the monumental stairway (and *genizah* beneath it) on the west, the gallery attached to the western wall and entered from both the north and west, the orientation on the long, southern wall, the frescoed room beneath the gallery, and the *aedicula*, the most problematic element of all.

It was certain that there was no *bema* in the first synagogue (see below). Architectural fragments found in the rubble between the stylobate wall and the eastern wall of the synagogue included a small column base, possibly part of an *aedicula* abutting the southern wall in the earlier synagogue. If so, the *bema* replaced this in the later building.

Evidence for the destruction of the earlier synagogue by earthquake emerged dramatically in the course of excavations beneath the floor at the eastern end of the later building; here were recovered fragments of columns, capitals, and bases — all shattered so badly that they could be used only as rubble building material or fill. Virtually all that could be recovered of the details of the first building comes from these architectural discards. A precise date for the first destruction is provided by the fact that the only "strong" earthquake known in the third and fourth centuries C.E. occurred in the winter of 306 C.E., a date well in line with the pottery and coin evidence from the site.[4] The numismatic evidence provides a further piece of information on this point; although the earlier synagogue surely perished violently — and perhaps much of the rest of the village with it — the community must have remained on the

---

[4] See D.H. Kallner-Amiran, *IEJ*, 1 (1950–1951), 225; a "strong" earthquake is graded 7–8; a "major" earthquake is graded 9 and above.

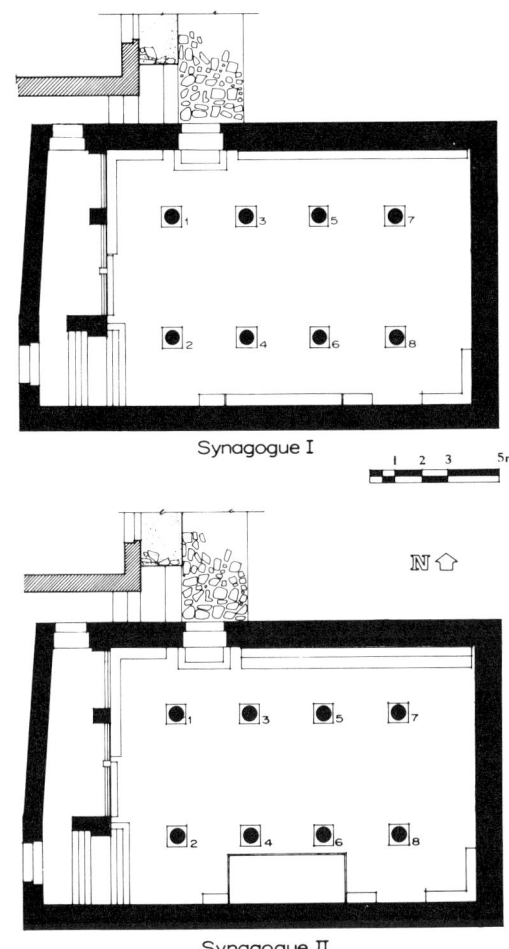

Synagogue I

1 2 3   5m

N ⇧

Synagogue II

Schematic ground plan of two phases of the synagogue at Ḥorvat Shema'. Earlier Synagogue (I) is of the 3rd century C.E.; the later synagogue (II) is from the 4th century C.E. and was destroyed in the 5th century C.E.

site and quickly decided to rebuild, for there is no break in the coin evidence from the early fourth century C.E.

The later synagogue (Stratum IV; 306–419 C.E.). Information concerning the later synagogue, which was reconstructed by the expedition in 1972, is somewhat fuller. The floor of this building was a simple mosaic. Of the thousands of tesserae recovered, nearly all were white, though there were also some gray examples; all appear to have been locally produced. The benching along the northern wall was increased, opposite the *bema*, which was installed at this stage. The *bema* clearly was built over the bench of the southern wall and

utilized part of it within its rubble core; this indicates that the *bema* was an added feature in the later synagogue. Deep in the core several coins were found, the latest being a virtually unworn coin of Constans (337–341 C.E.). The synagogue must therefore have been completed by the mid-fourth century C.E., at the latest (if the *bema* was one of the last elements to be constructed).

The addition of a stone *bema* in the later synagogue indicates a change in orientation. All four pedestals of the southern row of columns were more elaborately ornamented in this phase and stood on plinths (the best-preserved of which still stand before the *bema*). (The plinths at the eastern and western ends of this row were apparently turned upside-down after the earthquake of 306 C.E., in an attempt to strengthen this end of the building; see also below.) The northern row of bases, as in the earlier phase, consisted of simple, undecorated blocks set into the bedrock. Perhaps even in this later synagogue, an *aedicula* of sorts may have stood above the *bema*; its construction, in all probability, was wooden.

The capitals, columns, and plinths in this later structure were essentially reused from the earlier building. Their rather eclectic style reflects as much the ingenuity of the rebuilders of the synagogue as their esthetic sensibilities.

The beautiful doorway with the eagle motif in the western wall survived the destruction of the earlier synagogue, as did the northern entrance. The *genizah*, situated beneath the western stairway, yielded no significant artifacts, and the interpretation of this architectural element is entirely conjectural. It no doubt existed as a cave or tomb before the building was erected. The frescoed chamber alongside it, however, must have had a usage integral to the synagogue itself. Its entrance is exactly at the center of the western wall of the synagogue and its doors opened from within the main hall. The walls were gaily painted in red and green, but the patterns have not been reconstructed thus far.

The difficulty in interpreting this frescoed

room in both of the synagogue's phases derives from the fact that in all probability there was an *aedicula* on the southern wall in the first building and possibly one above the *bema* in the second structure. In any event, the room's importance is suggested by its elaborate decoration and by its central position in the plan of the building. It may have been a storage chamber for the actual Torah scrolls, which could have been taken out to a central place for the liturgical reading. In the earlier synagogue, however, if we can accept the presence of a fine stone *aedicula* on the southern wall, this function is less likely for the frescoed room. The introduction of the *bema* (possibly with a wooden *aedicula* on it) in the later synagogue represents a major innovation in the internal ordering of the synagogue, contrary to the more familiar pattern of the Palestinian "broadhouse" synagogue at Eshtemoa and Horvat Susiya, where the *bema* and the *aedicula* were on the same wall, the one toward Jerusalem.

The other major renovation which may have taken place during the second building phase was the cutting of a new entrance to the gallery above the frescoed room — on the north, from the staired alley separating the synagogue from the *beth-midrash*.

Evidence of the destruction of the later synagogue by an earthquake was apparent throughout the excavations. The destruction date of this synagogue can be determined with some ease, since there is a sharp break in the numismatic evidence after 408 C.E.; most of the fifth century C.E. coins are of Arcadius and Honorius (that is, very early in the century). The best explanation for such a radical break is a sudden abandonment of the site; this is corroborated by the tumbled and badly shattered debris of the later synagogue. Dating by the first "strong" earthquake after 408 C.E., it is possible to assume that the Stratum IV occupation, including the later synagogue, came to an abrupt end in the earthquake of 419 C.E. There was a "major" earthquake in 447 C.E., but it appears to be ruled out by the fact that no coins have yet been found from the period between 419 and 447 C.E.[5]

The beth-midrash and the northern entryway. The presence of a large structure (6.55 × 6.50 m.), with benching along several of its walls and an internal dividing wall, so close to the synagogue itself, led to the conclusion that it functioned as a house of study (and possibly also as a hostel). Its major entrance, on the east, was from the magnificent northern entrance path with its handsome flagstone paving, leading to and facing the *menorah* lintel and the northern entrance to the synagogue. In comparing this outside area to that on the west of the synagogue, it seems quite certain that the northern entrance was built on the major artery of the village, essentially following the main north-south contour of the hill. The street of the western entrance to the synagogue, on the other hand, gradually sloped down to an open terrace area, the industrial quarter near the mausoleum and the acropolis to the northwest.

In the synagogue of Horvat Shema' we have a novel adaptation of the basilical plan to the "broadhouse" plan. Its two major entrances on the north and west suggest that the builders were not constrained by the conventions which apparently prevailed at nearby Meiron and so many other "Galilean" synagogues. This seems to be hybrid architecture with an overwhelming concern for orientation toward Jerusalem. The two successive synagogues were not built on the highest spot of the site; indeed, from one side, one must descend stairs in order to enter the main hall. The proximity of the synagogues to a large mausoleum and other nearby tombs, and the fact that the structure was built over several declivities (some of which were surely tombs), raises further questions concerning the nature of synagogue buildings in antiquity. At the very least, it can now be said with some conviction that local traditions played a larger role in the development of synagogue plans than has hitherto been recognized.

[5] *Ibid.*

Excavations at Gush Ḥalav in Upper Galilee

E. M. Meyers

The 1977–78 excavations at the ancient site of Gush Ḥalav concentrated on the lower synagogue site in Wadi Gush Ḥalav, just east of the modern village and but a few kilometers north of Meiron.[1] While this site had attracted the notice of many earlier scholars, Guérin, Wilson, Renan and Kitchener, to mention but a few, only the German team of Kohl and Watzinger had previously done limited work there for four days in 1905. Their published plan of the synagogue has proved to be substantially incorrect.

The major surprise of the excavation, apart from the synagogue itself, has been the "hidden tell" which underlies the lower synagogue site. Ancient debris here has accumulated to a depth of more than five meters thus far, and doubtless is much deeper. Stratified remains from the following periods have been already uncovered and future excavations will probably reveal more:

Stratum I	LBII/Iron I (13th/12th c. B.C.E.)
Stratum II	Iron II (8th/7th c. B.C.E.)
Stratum III	Persian (5th/4th c. B.C.E.)
Stratum IV	Hellenistic (2nd/1st c. B.C.E.)
Stratum V	Early Roman (50 B.C.E.–135 C.E.)
Stratum VI	Late Roman (250–362 C.E.)
phase a	250–306 C.E.
phase b	306–362/5 C.E.
Stratum VII	Byzantine (362/5–551 C.E.)
phase a	362/5–447 C.E.
phase b	447–551 C.E.
Stratum VIII	Early Arab (7th/8th c. C.E.)

The chronology here is based on the study of the ceramics and the 227 coins found in the

excavation, spanning Strata III–VII, plus a hoard of 1943 specimens which are mostly from Stratum VII. The surprising number of mints from Tyre squares nicely with the evidence from Horvat Shema' and Meiron, which indicates a northern cultural orientation already hinted at in the story of John of Gush Ḥalav (Josephus, *War* II, 591–594) and represented in the so-called hoard published by Hamburger in 1954.[2]

The Synagogue

The basilical building found in Stratum VIa is a rectangular sanctuary bounded on three sides — west, north, and east — by exterior corridors or rooms. The main room is 13.75 m. × 10.6–11 m., with two stylobates running north–south and supporting two rows of columns. Overall dimensions, including corridor space, are: 17.5 m. N–S, 17.5–18 m. E–W.

The main entrance is on the southern wall, which faces Jerusalem, where an eagle is inscribed on the underside of the lintel stone.

[1] The 1977 and 1978 excavations were carried out by the American Schools of Oriental Research and supported by Duke University in Durham, North Carolina, with additional support from Garrett-Evangelical Theological Seminary at Northwestern in Evanston, Illinois.

[2] H. Hamburger, "A Hoard of Syrian Tetradrachms and Tyrian Bronze Coins from Gush Ḥalav," *IEJ*, 4 (1954), 201–226.

The synagogue remains, looking west

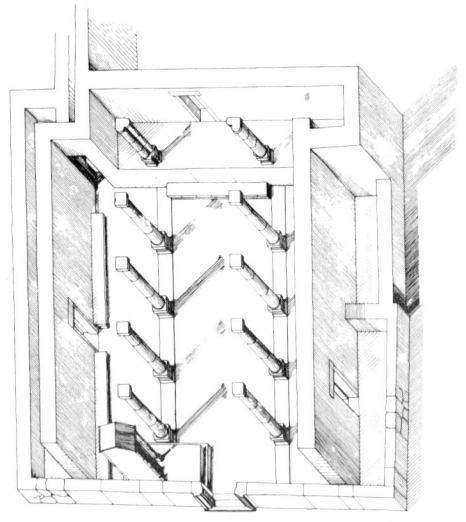

Proposed reconstruction

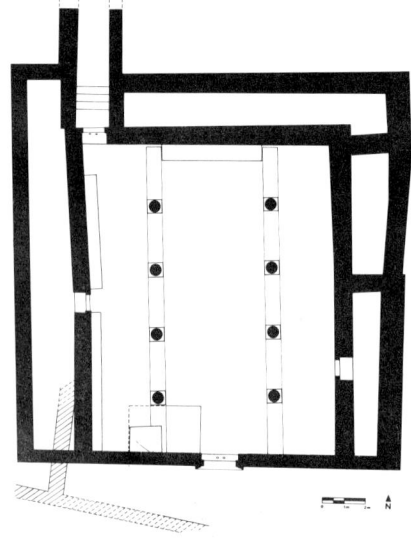

Plan of the synagogue

The entryway, 1.7 m. wide, contained a double hung door, as indicated by the post and bolt holes. It is set into an ashlar southern wall, the only wall finished in such stone. The other major entrance is located in the northwest corner of the building and is 1.15 m. in width. It leads from the synagogue interior to the space outside the building, with four well-set steps leading down and to the north. Another "possible" doorway connecting the interior space with the exterior space might be situated in the southeast quadrant.

The other main feature of the interior space is the *bema* attached to the southern façade,

Remains of synagogue building atop earlier strata

just west of the eagle doorway. The surviving small stone structure (1.46 m. × 1.17 m. × 3 m.) was partially built over the western stylobate at the beginning of Stratum VII. Another, larger rectangular stone structure, however, was found to underlie the second *bema* and extended two meters out from the southern wall and one meter eastward from the stylobate. A rectangular depression, ca. 50 × 75 cm., was built into the structure and dates to Stratum VI.

Of special interest is the long western corridor, with its doorway connecting this area to the sanctuary. Functioning as a storage area for building materials and other synagogue stores, it is bonded at its southern end into the southern façade, utilizing a pre-existent structure. In the northern end of this space the coin hoard was found, dating the final use of the complex to the mid-sixth century C.E.

On the eastern side, a series of small rooms between the exterior and interior walls was excavated, with all the cross-walls founded on much earlier walls. Quantities of painted plaster here suggest an earlier structure of some significance, probably dating to between Strata IV and VI.

The space at the northern end of the building is thought to be a gallery, suggested by the presence of several heart-shaped columns, without corresponding pedestals.

Bronze ring engraved
"Dometila"

Sherd with "Arist..."
inscription

Small *bema* built against south wall, partially covering stylobate

The gallery is slightly raised above floor level and is entered from either inside or outside, possibly by wooden stairs. The fill beneath the gallery was completely sterile.

In excavating both the interior and exterior walls, it was discovered that the synagogue builders used pre-existent walls wherever possible, some dating back to Strata III and II. In every respect, therefore, this building represents an important departure from the kind of "basilica" one might expect for this type of sacred structure.

Conclusions

The rich literary pedigree of Gush Ḥalav, when taken together with ruins of the newly-excavated lower site and previously-known remains from the upper city, suggests that this town was a major center in Upper Galilee during several periods. In proximity to a well-traveled road to the Phoenician coast, the large number of Tyrian coins found here points to a northern economic orientation.

Even though no clear link between the upper and lower sites has been established, it seems likely that the two are closely related. With the spring of Gush Ḥalav located in the wadi, and with no other water source in the immediate vicinity, it is difficult to conceive of these two localities as independent entities. It is important to note that the history of the site at Gush Ḥalav continues nearly a century and a half after the destruction by earthquake of Ḥorvat Shema' (419 C.E.) and nearly two centuries after the abandonment of Meiron (360 C.E.). While earthquake activity has greatly affected the building phases of Gush Ḥalav, apparently economic and social circumstances are adequate to sustain a very rich and important site.

Large earlier *bema* in center. At right, later *bema*; at left, original floor and southern entrance.

Coin hoard and pot found in western corridor, Stratum VII

Excavations at Ḥorvat ha-'Amudim

Lee I. Levine

The site known as Ḥorvat ha-'Amudim (lit. "Ruin of the Pillars") is located in the eastern Galilee, some 15 km. northwest of Tiberias, and is situated on a plateau at the eastern end of the Bet Netofa valley. Ruins of an ancient village are clearly visible, especially the monumental columns and capitals that once supported the roof of the synagogue. These remains, and particularly one large corner (heart-shaped) column, have given the site its present-day name.

Although noted for centuries by various travelers, the site has been investigated only once. In their survey of ancient synagogues in 1905, Kohl and Watzinger delineated the plan of the structure and, with the aid of several probes, discovered fragments of a mosaic floor.[1] The synagogue, measuring 22.55 m. × 14.06 m., was built according to a plan typical of "Galilean-type" buildings: three

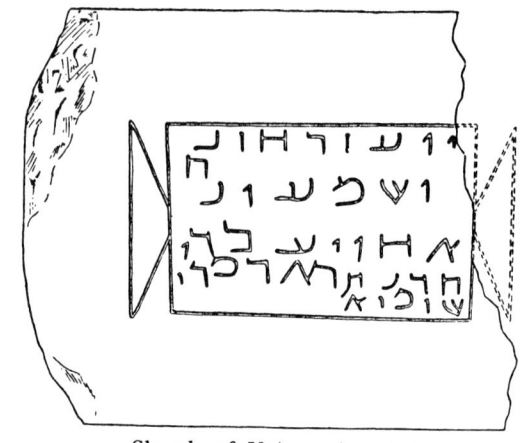

Sketch of Yo'ezer inscription

rows of columns with the open end facing south, a monumental façade (now largely dismantled and many of its fragments incorporated into a large building to the southwest) likewise facing south, three entrances, decorations carved in stone, corner (heart-shaped) columns, and benches along the sides. The nave was 7.76 m. in width and the two aisles, 3.15 m. In the 1930's a dedicatory inscription was found by Sukenik on a stone at the site and reads as follows:

1. Yo'ezer the ḥazzan
2. and Simeon
3. his brother made
4. this gate[2] of the Lord
5. of Heaven[3]

---

[1] H. Kohl, C. Watzinger, *Antike Synagogen in Galilaea* (Leipzig, 1916), pp. 71–79.

[2] For alternate interpretations of this problematic term, see J. Naveh, *On Stone and Mosaic* (Hebrew) (Jerusalem, 1978), pp. 40–42 — "ark," "chest";.F. G. Huttenmeister, "The Aramaic Inscription from the Synagogue at Ḥ. 'Ammudim," *IEJ*, 28 (1978), 109–112 — "(holy) site."

[3] N. Avigad, "An Aramaic Inscription from the Synagogue at Umm-el-'Amed in Galilee," *Bulletin of the Louis Rabinowitz Fund for the Exploration of Ancient Synagogues*, 3 (1960), 62–64.

View of standing corner column, looking northwest

78

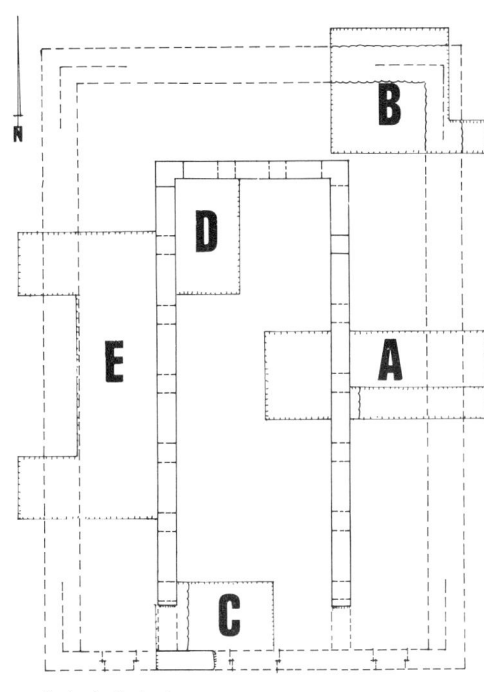

Plan of synagogue with areas excavated

View of synagogue, looking north

Area D in northwestern corner of the nave. Meterstick lies on bedrock

As part of a larger project aimed at a comprehensive study of ancient "Galilean" synagogues,[4] an excavation was undertaken at Horvat ha-'Amudim in the summer of 1979 to verify the size of the structure, and to ascertain its date of construction and the various stages of its history.[5] Trenches were made in five different parts of the building. Area A, in the middle of the eastern aisle, was excavated to bedrock, a depth of 85 cm. This area was found to be completely robbed, and bore no traces of a floor, wall or benches.

Area B, in the northeast corner of the building, was selected for the purpose of determining the size of the building. Here only foundations were discovered, but they clearly confirm earlier estimates of the size. Traces of the northern and eastern wall foundations were revealed, as well as an additional projection some 70 cm. in width.

[4] The project is being sponsored by the Institute of Archeology, Hebrew University, and is under the joint direction of the author, Dr. G. Foerster, and Dr. E. Netzer.

[5] The excavation was carried out under the auspices of the Institute of Archeology, Hebrew University, with the assistance of the Department of Antiquities, and in conjunction with the Ministry of Education's youth enrichment program under the direction of Mr. M. Cohen. Dr. E. Netzer was actively involved in the excavation itself, as well as in the evaluation of the data. Also participating in this excavation were D. Adan, Y. Hirschfeld, and D. Tritt.

This undoubtedly served as the substructure for benches which lined the interior of the building.

Area C, in the front (southern) part of the building, likewise revealed no traces of a floor. The southern ends of the stylobate were robbed, as were most of the stone blocks of the southern façade wall. A number of stones forming a square were found in the center of the southern section just inside the entrance. Whether this was the base of the Torah shrine has not been determined. More likely, it was part of an installation belonging to a later period, as were a number of secondary partitions in the southeastern section of the synagogue.

The real surprises of this excavation, however, were reserved for areas D and E. Area D

79

Fragmentary mosaic inscription from Area E

was located at the northwestern corner of the nave, next to the one standing column of the synagogue. Remains of a small section of mosaic floor were discovered, and beneath them, covering a much wider area, the foundations of that floor, consisting of small stones and mortar. This floor lay a mere 10 cm. above bedrock. A number of tentative conclusions suggest themselves. The position of the floor so close to bedrock and the absence of any traces of the large flagstones led us to the conclusion that the original floor of the building was indeed a mosaic one. This hypothesis would seem to be confirmed by the fact that here, as well as in other places (see below), the mosaic floor was higher than the stylobate, probably indicating that originally the floor had been intended to cover it.[6] The fact that the stylobate in many places was poorly hewn may further indicate that it was not intended to be seen.

[6] Only in a few places was the floor lower than the stylobate, but this may have been due to some alteration of the ground, as, for example, an earthquake or soil erosion.

No less significant a find were the pottery and coins discovered in the fill beneath this area. The pottery, although sparse, was all of a third-fourth century provenance. Four coins were found, and all dated to the latter part of the third century, from the reigns of Claudius Gothicus (268–270) and Probus (276–282), and Maximinus Heraclus (293). Thus, it seems certain that our building was constructed at the very end of the third century.

Area E contained no fewer surprises. Centering on the western part of the synagogue, most of the aisle was uncovered and a well-preserved mosaic floor revealed. The floor ends 3.15 m. from the stylobate. Clearly, there had once been a wall (and probably benches also), which was subsequently robbed. The mosaic floor, higher than the stylobate in most places, was not uniform in character. The northern part was composed of simple white tesserae. Further to the south was a series of elaborate geometric designs in several colors: black, white, red, blue, orange.

The pièce de résistance of the mosaic pavement was an Aramaic inscription found in the southern sector. Unfortunately, most of the inscription was destroyed. What remains are remnants of five lines with the word טבלה, "section of the floor" — tabula, being the most legible. A second word might be אגרא, "wages," but this is far from certain. Interestingly, the word טבלה appears in only two other synagogue inscriptions, both from Kefar Kana, some 10 km. to the southwest. The mosaic floor at Horvat ha-'Amudim was well laid, attesting to a substantial investment of time and effort. Although an altogether different medium, it is a fitting companion to the monumental lion-carved lintel which once graced the façade of the synagogue.

Also of interest in this area was the material found just above floor level. With but very few exceptions, most of the pottery was from the early Byzantine period (fourth century). It would seem, therefore, that the synagogue served the community for not much more than a century.

What, then, is the significance of these finds regarding the larger issues concerning

Relief of lion on part of the lintel of the synagogue

"Galilean-type" synagogues? First, we have rather solid evidence regarding the date of construction, i.e., around the turn of the fourth century. This would place the synagogue between the period espoused by the Franciscans (fifth century, see pp. 52–56) and that advocated by Avi-Yonah and Foerster (second–third century, see pp. 57–62). The date of our structure accords well with the results of the recently excavated synagogues at Ḥorvat Shemaʿ (see pp. 70–74), Meiron and Gush Ḥalav (see pp. 75–77) — all of which stem from the later third century.

Secondly, if the mosaic floor was original to the building, as is suggested, Ḥorvat ha-ʿAmudim would be the first "Galilean-type" synagogue with such a pavement. All others were built with large flagstone floors. Our structure would constitute one of the earliest examples of a mosaic pavement in the Galilee. Moreover, the building would serve as an excellent example of a transitional stage in the utilization of different types of art media. Both stone carvings and mosaic floors find expression here. The former was ubiquitous in an earlier period (second-third centuries), the latter in the succeeding, i.e., Byzantine, era. Furthermore, it seems certain that the Ḥorvat ha-ʿAmudim synagogue was not in use for a long period of time. As noted, most of the material above floor level was early-Byzantine. No signs of sudden destruction have been noted. It would seem as if somewhere around the turn of the fifth century the site was abandoned, a phenomenon not unknown from other Galilean locales.[7]

One final remark may be offered. There is always an urge to identify a particular archeological site with one of the places mentioned in literary sources. While little is known about specific Jewish settlements in the area of Ḥorvat ha-ʿAmudim, it has nevertheless been suggested that this site is to be identified with Kefar ʿUziel.[8] This village, mentioned in rabbinic sources, was the seat of one of the twenty-four priestly courses which had settled in the eastern Galilee from the second century C.E. onwards. Zechariah, father of John the Baptist, allegedly belonged to this course (*Luke* 1:5). If, indeed, this identification be accepted, Ḥorvat ha-ʿAmudim would have served as a priestly center during the period under consideration.

[7] See E. Meyers, J.F. Strange, D.E. Groh, "The Meiron Excavation Project: Archeological Survey in Galilee & Golan, 1976," *BASOR*, 230 (1978), 20.

[8] G. Dalman, *Sacred Sites and Ways* (London, 1935), pp. 52, 115–116.

A Synagogue at Beth-Shean

D. Bahat

In 1970, with the increase in shelling in the Beth-Shean area, the government decided to augment the number of bomb-proof shelters; this involved digging broad trenches, during which a mosaic pavement was uncovered adjacent to the "House of Kyrios Leontis." Not far away, the "Imhof" monastery, a "mansion," and other remains had previously come to light, and this area of the ancient city appears to have been a rather wealthy quarter in the Roman-Byzantine period. Following the discovery here, it was decided to initiate a full-scale excavation of the structure to which the mosaic belonged. The building proved to be a synagogue.[1]

The plan of the synagogue. The synagogue lies to the east of one of the gates in the Roman-Byzantine city wall, apparently on a street leading to the gate. This area in the western part of Beth-Shean was apparently the Jewish quarter of the city.

So far we have not been able to establish the exact plan of the synagogue. Most of the area uncovered lies in a large, square courtyard which was paved with mosaics. North, east, and west of the courtyard there were rooms; on the south there were three openings, one leading to the prayer hall. On the northern side several rooms came to light; three of them, uncovered in 1964, comprise the "House of Kyrios Leontis," so called after a person mentioned in an inscription in the floor of the westernmost room.[2] Subsequent-

ly, a series of rooms was built within the courtyard, along with a large silo. These structures destroyed the pavement of the courtyard almost entirely. There may have been various installations in the courtyard, built after the destruction of the complex.

The fact that the walls of the courtyard are not parallel or perpendicular to the rooms of the synagogue should probably be ascribed to changes made in the plan of the entire quarter. Beneath the courtyard there came to light the remains of a structure which contained several ceramic pipes and basins — possibly part of a bath-house of the Roman period. We should note especially several mosaics, some gilded.

The prayer hall of the synagogue complex is square in plan, with two entrances, one on the north and the other on the east, the latter leading to a space whose nature still remains unclear. The mosaic pavement opposite the two openings is quite extensive. Near the northern doorway, two lion-cubs are depicted; near the eastern doorway is a Greek inscription. Around the room, adjacent to the walls, there were benches. A relatively thick wall closed the room on the south; it may have contained a niche. This possibly explains why the inner border of the pavement juts out to the south here. As excavations were expanded toward where we initially thought a large main hall lay, it became evident that this is not a large synagogue, but rather a small prayer hall or chapel. On the east, a small distance from the prayer hall, we found a room with a crude mosaic pavement, in the center of which was a deep pit (about 7 m. have been cleared). Near the shaft are two Greek inscriptions; one relates that the digging of the pit was

[1] The excavations were carried out on behalf of the Department of Antiquities and Museums, and directed by the author. In 1971, the expedition received the support of the Union of American Hebrew Congregations.

[2] N. Zori, "The House of Kyrios Leontis at Beth-Shean," *IEJ*, 16 (1966), 123–134.

completed in the terms of two synagogue superintendents whose names are not clear. The other inscription ends with the Hebrew word *shalom*, and reads: "[Yo]se the great innkeeper and his children made the mosaic of this place." The Greek word for "place" may here refer to the synagogue, as it does at Bar'am and other sites.

The northern entrance to the prayer hall was found blocked, and within the blocking masonry was a coin of the Umayyad period (ca. 650–750 C.E.); the other opening was also found blocked. It appears that in the Umayyad period the courtyard served for some purpose other than as an entrance to the prayer hall, for at that time the floor of the hall was not in use, except for a segment preserved in the west. Many fragments of plaster painted in red were found in the hall, an indication that the walls had been ornamented. Only one vessel was found in the hall, a painted jug of the late Umayyad period. A change in plan is evident within the prayer hall; the inscriptions are also indicative of this, mentioning repairs in the building. It appears that this change in plan stemmed from a replanning of the entire building complex, possibly in connection with the construction of the city wall and the cutting of the street through the quarter toward the city gate.

The mosaic pavement. The pavement comprises a central motif surrounded by wide borders with panels and ornaments outside. In the central panel is a series of medallions formed by a vine sprouting from an amphora, which is located at the middle of the lowest (southern) row. In all, there are nine medallions arranged in three rows. This pattern is known in three other synagogues — at Nirim, Gaza (see pp. 129–132) and Ḥusifa — and in many churches, several in the Beth-Shean region. The *horror vacui* here is most evident; the spaces between the medallions are filled with birds (mainly partridges), grape-leaves, grape clusters, and tendrils. From the preserved remains, we may assume a certain symmetry in the flanking medallions: in the lower pair, there are goats; in the second pair,

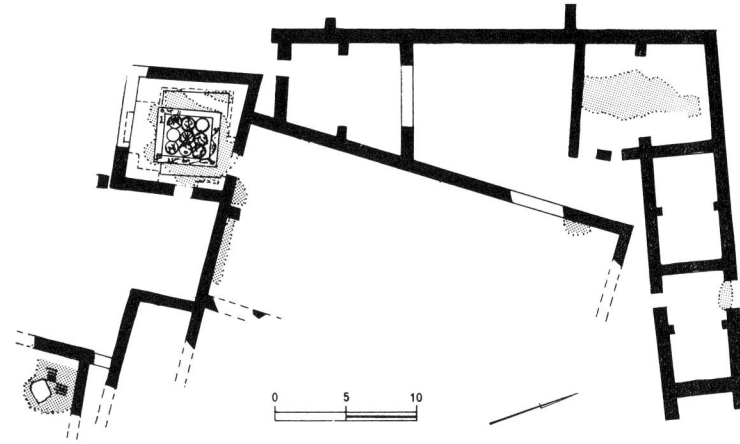

Plan of the synagogue and the "House of Leontis"

pheasants; and in the upper pair, bulls. In the central position of the lower row is, as noted, an amphora with the vine stemming from it. In the central medallion of the upper row is a peacock, and in the center of the panel, a *menorah*. The *menorah* appears within a double border, and is thus not part of the vine pattern proper. The stem and branches of the *menorah* bear well-formed buds, in imitation of the "bud-and-flower" pattern noted in the Bible. The *menorah* stands on a tripod base. The branches terminate above in a horizontal strip; above are cups, in the same color as the branches, within which glass bowls are depicted in green. From the latter sprout red flames with yellow cores. Flanking the stem are several ritual objects: on the left, an *ethrog*, depicted as in mosaics at other sites (e.g. Ma'on); and on the right, a censer hanging from three chains, also found in other mosaics (e.g. at Na'aran); and, further to the right, the upper end of an object, probably a *shofar*.

The depictions within the medallions — as in other synagogues — are entirely independent of one another, and their scale is determined solely by the size of the medallions; no attempt was made to depict scenes here. Surrounding the panel with the medallions, within a similar linear border, various animals appear; in the four corners are amphorae from which vines stem in either direction. The animals preserved include a bear, elephant, fox, hare, dog, deer, and hen,

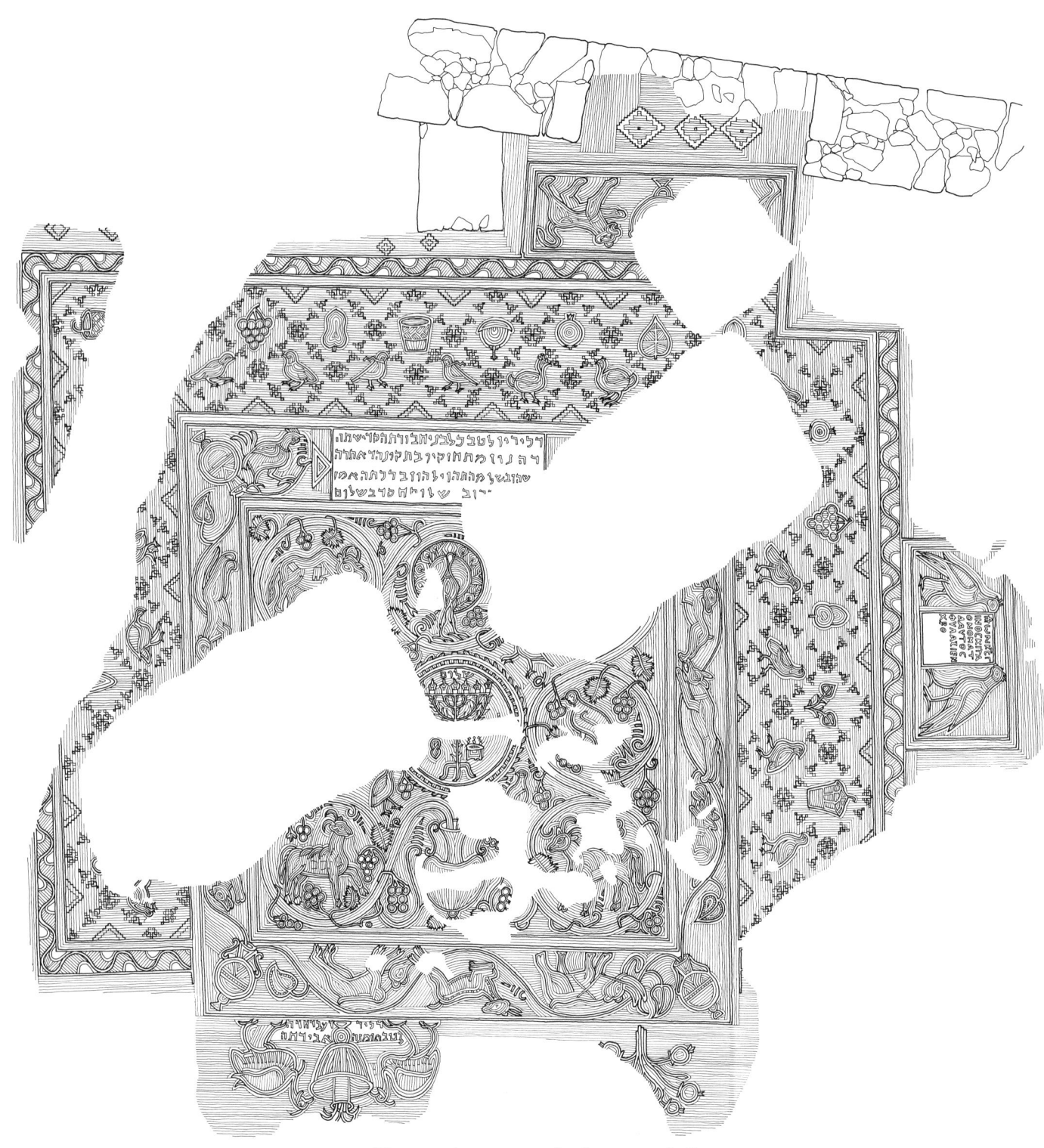

The mosaic pavement in the prayer hall

mostly arranged in simple scenes, such as a dog chasing a deer, a fox chasing a hare, and so forth. In the northern part of this border is a large inscription, in a *tabula ansata*. The outer frame is of a guilloche pattern; between it and the inner frame is a broad border containing an overall floral network, interspersed with small birds (such as guinea-fowl and doves), sprigs, fruit, baskets, and the like. Outside the main frame there are two inscriptions, one on the east and the other on the south. On the north, before the doorway to the courtyard, is a panel containing two lion-cubs flanking a vase or bowl.

The inscriptions. The large inscription, within the inner border, reads in Aramaic:

דכירין לטב כל בני חבורתה קדישתה
דהנון מתחזקין בתקונה דאתרה
[קדי]שה ובשלמה תהוי להון ברכתה אמן
. . . רוב שלום חסד בשלום

Remembered be for good all the members of the Holy Congregation who endeavored to repair the holy place. In peace shall they have their blessing. Amen! . . . Peace! Piety in peace!

A second Aramaic inscription on the south, outside the frame, is also to be read facing north. It is placed within a depiction of two guinea-fowl flanking a vase from which a plant(?) is sprouting. The inscription reads:

דכיר לטב אומנה
דעבד חדה אבידתה

Remembered be for good the artisan
who made this work

The corrupt spellings here, reflecting regional pronunciation, call to mind a passage in the Talmud: "It has been taught . . .: We do not allow men from Haifa, Beth-Shean or Tibeon to lead the congregation in prayers (lit. to pass before the Ark) because they pronounce the letter *he* as *ḥet*, and *'ayin* as *alef*" (B *Megilla*, 24b; J *Berakhot* II, 4d).

The inscription to the east of the outer frame, in Greek, is situated between two pheasants and was apparently inserted some time later, for its frame cut into the beaks and tops of the birds. The lower part of the inscription, containing a date (?), has been removed and replaced by plain, cruder tesserae. The inscription reads: "The gift of those of whom the Lord knows the names, He shall guard them, in times . . ."

On the basis of the ornamentation, the mosaic pavement is to be ascribed to the second half of the sixth century C.E., though the prayer hall itself may be earlier, and the floor, from the time of the major repairs.

The Synagogue at Ma'oz Ḥayim

V. Tzaferis

Early in February 1974, part of a mosaic pavement was exposed during earth-moving operations at Ma'oz Ḥayim in the Beth-Shean Valley; it depicted a *menorah* and a *shofar*, symbols clearly indicating the existence of some ancient Jewish structure on the site. Archeological excavations were subsequently carried out, revealing a synagogue with a rather unusual plan.[1]

[1] The discovery was made by Mr. A. Ya'aqobi, of Kibbutz Ma'oz Ḥayim. Excavations were conducted on behalf of the Department of Antiquities and Museums, and directed by the author.

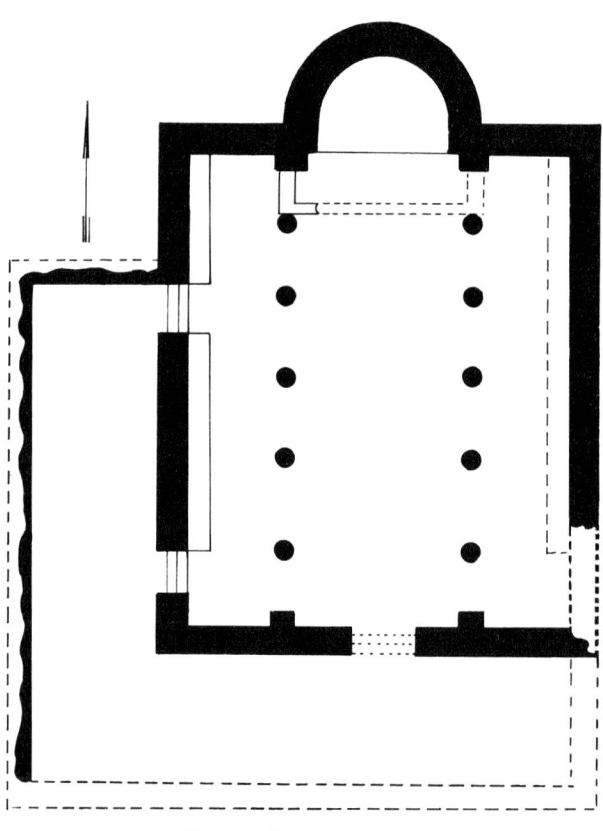

Plan of the synagogue

During the course of excavations, two mosaic pavements were revealed, one overlying the other, attesting to two building phases. The fragment initially discovered, with the *menorah*, was of the lower, earlier phase. The walls of the building had been almost entirely destroyed; however, the remaining fragments, together with the extant mosaic floors, enabled us to reconstruct the synagogue's plan. It was in the form of a simple basilica measuring 14 × 16 m., divided by two rows of columns into a nave and two flanking aisles. Each row had five columns, indicated by bases set into the floors; no actual columns were found. The main axis of the building ran north-south; an apse was located to the south of the nave. In subsequent excavations a third floor was revealed. This floor, paved with flagstones, belonged to a still earlier synagogue structure, which we have ascribed to the fourth century C.E. The plan of this earlier synagogue is uncommon. The prayer hall was almost square, divided into two aisles and a nave by two rows of columns. It had no apse; the apse was clearly added in the later two phases.

The northern part of the later structure — where a courtyard, narthex and main entrances could be expected to lie — was entirely destroyed. The state of preservation of the southern part was better, and the apse and the walls there were preserved to a height of some six courses. The area of the *bema*, including the apse, was raised several centimeters above the floor of the hall. No remains were found to indicate the manner in which the *bema* was enclosed and set off from the nave, but there must have been a chancel-screen with posts and marble slabs, as is the case in many

General view of the mosaic pavement,
looking south

Detail of the lower mosaic floor

The eastern carpet of the lower mosaic floor

The apse, showing the straight wall of the earlier structure

ancient synagogues. Indeed, beneath the floor of the *bema* such a post was found, together with fragments of marble slabs; the latter bore a partial depiction of a *menorah* and several Hebrew letters. These remnants of a chancel-screen were from the earlier phase of the synagogue, of which little is known to date. Behind the *bema*, near the inner wall of the apse, a rectangular installation was found containing several pottery lamps, coins, and fragments of a glass lamp. The installation was paved with two roof-tiles in secondary use, and this cubicle probably served as the *genizah* of the synagogue.

The building, in its later phases, was paved with colorful mosaics. Between the two floor-levels was a layer of fill some 30 cm. thick; this earth was entirely devoid of artifacts and was clearly brought in to raise the floor level. The lower floor, and probably the whole structure, had been destroyed; there were clear traces of a conflagration. In the last phase no changes were made to the basic plan of the structure.

The quality of the earlier mosaic pavement exceeds that of the later one. So far, three panels of the earlier floor have been exposed in the southern part of the building. The two outer panels contain various geometric patterns, with a three-dimensional effect. The central panel is of finer workmanship; the geometric patterns there are richer in effect and color. This central panel is itself divided into three sections, each containing a depiction of a bird, a bunch of grapes, a *menorah*, a running fret pattern, or other motifs. In the upper mosaic pavement, the geometric patterns are simpler in design. This floor was poorly preserved, damaged mainly by the superimposed construction of the Early Arab period.

The excavations yielded relatively few artifacts — several coins of the Roman-Byzantine period, Byzantine pottery lamps, sherds, and glass fragments — all of which can serve in dating the second building phase of the synagogue. An interesting find was a hoard of some fifty coins, which came to light just outside the southern wall of the building. The coins had been wrapped in a cloth and placed within a broken roof-tile. It can be assumed that the hoard was hidden during some emergency, possibly close to the time of the final destruction of the building. The evidence of the pottery and the stratigraphy indicates that the synagogue was destroyed toward the end of the Byzantine period, that is, in the early seventh century C.E. In any case, overlaying its ruins were the remains of private houses of the seventh-eighth centuries C.E. There is no clear-cut evidence for the date of the initial erection of the synagogue or of its earlier destruction.

In the two longer walls of the later building there were doorways, undoubtedly leading to courtyards or auxiliary rooms adjacent to the prayer hall. These latter have yet to be cleared, but they indicate that the synagogue proper was part of a larger complex, situated at the center of an extensive settlement. In a survey conducted by the author in the vicinity of the synagogue, it became clear that this site, today known as Giv'at Hagamadim ("Hill of the Dwarfs"), was occupied by a fairly large settlement in the Roman-Byzantine period. On the basis of the discovery of the synagogue, we may suggest that this was the town of Be'eilah, east of Beth-Shean, mentioned by Cyril of Scythopolis (Beth-Shean). In the Aramaic inscription recently discovered at nearby Reḥob (see pp. 146–152), mention is

General view of the synagogue, showing the earlier flagstone pavement

made of a Jewish settlement of Beth-Shean, with a name apparently similar to that given by Cyril.

The Synagogue at Reḥob

Fanny Vitto

The fields of Kibbutz 'En Hanaẓiv have long aroused the interest of the settlers, because of the numerous ruins, sherds, coins, and architectural fragments found there. Especially rich is the area of Farwana, some 7 km. south of the present town of Beth-Shean and about 800 m. northeast of Tel el-Sarim, the largest of the mounds in the Beth-Shean Valley. F.M. Abel, in the beginning of this century, identified this mound with ancient Reḥob, regional seat of the Beth-Shean Valley at the time of the Egyptian rule in Canaan. Surveys revealed evidence of extensive settlement surrounding the tell in the Roman–Byzantine period. According to Eusebius, in the fourth century C.E., a settlement named *Roób* was located at the fourth mile from Scythopolis

(Beth-Shean). Medieval maps show a town "Riḥib" here. Today, an Arab tomb near the tell is known as Sheikh el-Riḥab. Thus, it can be assumed that a Roman-Byzantine settlement named Reḥob or Roób was in this area.

In 1969, in the course of land-preparation for cultivation, various remains and architectural fragments were destroyed or displaced. Among these were fragments of a marble chancel-screen, carved in relief on one side with a seven-branched *menorah* within a wreath, and on the other side with a rosette. This was the first indication of the existence of a synagogue on the site. Also found was a clay coin box containing 27 Byzantine gold coins, dating to the 7th century C.E., which may have belonged to the hoard of the synagogue. Following these discoveries, plowing was held up, and in the summer of 1973, a limited sounding on the site, carried out by the Department of Antiquities, revealed the presence of a mosaic pavement. One year later, systematic excavations were undertaken, and since then, four seasons have been carried out. The results of the excavations confirm the existence of a synagogue.[1]

The synagogue was a building of basilical plan with an almost square main hall. It is oriented on a north-south axis, with the back wall toward Jerusalem. To the north of the prayer hall is the narthex. The walls, 0.80 m. thick, are built of large fieldstones with a fill of smaller stones. Most of the walls are preserved to a height of one or two courses, and only in the southern wall are four to five courses

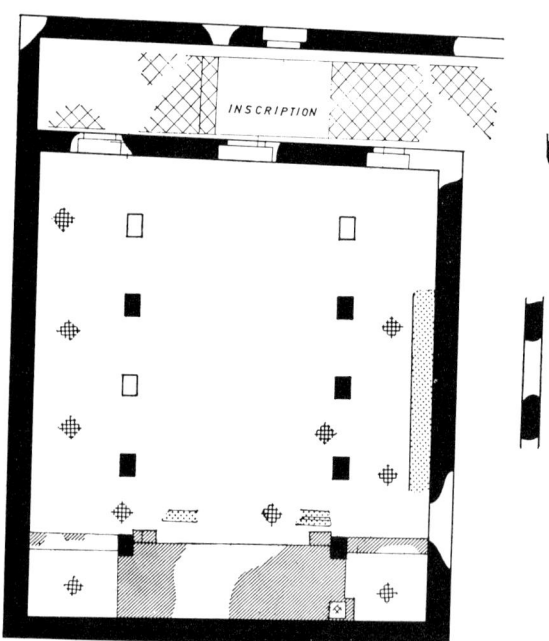

Plan of the synagogue

---

[1] The excavations were carried out on behalf of the Department of Antiquities and Museums, and directed by the author.

90

The mosaic carpet in the room east of the *bema*

preserved. The structure was roofed with pottery tiles, as shown by the abundant tile fragments found among the rubble.

As it appears today, the prayer hall, measuring 17.30 m. × 18.50 m., has two rows of squared pillars dividing it into a central nave and two flanking aisles. These pillars are built of rectangular ashlar blocks, arranged regularly in header and stretcher fashion. The entrance to the narthex from the north is on the central axis. Three doorways, their thresholds found *in situ*, lead from the narthex to the main hall. In the eastern wall, 4 m. from the southeastern corner, the threshold of a fourth doorway to the prayer hall was found. At the southern end of the hall was a *bema*, stretching the full width of the nave. The southernmost pillar of each row juts into the area of the *bema*. On the west, the ashlar-built *bema* was preserved to its original height, ca. 0.80 m. above the floor level, and it seems to have been entirely plastered. In any event, plaster remained on its side panels, and other fragments of plaster were found among the adjacent rubble. Parallel to the *bema* was a low wall; between it and the front face of the *bema* was a fragment of the chancel-screen found prior to the excavations. Flanking the *bema* there were two small chambers, sepa-

rated from the aisles by apparently late walls of rough construction. Low benches, entirely plastered, ran along the walls of the aisles.

The mosaic pavements. The synagogue was paved throughout with mosaics. At least three phases are evident. All that remains of the earliest phase, which shows traces of a fire, is a border of small white tessarae (1 × 1 cm.) laid diagonally and decorated with a single black line. This second phase, richly colored, was also made of small tesserae (1 × 1 cm.), giving rise to geometric motifs of high artistic quality. The borders in the aisles have a triple guilloche enclosing square and rectangular panels, and each panel comprises a different geometric composition executed with great care. This eight-color mosaic was later repaired. The tesserae of the repair are larger (1.5 × 1.5 cm.) and are in only three colors. In the western aisle, the motif was entirely modified by the insertion of a meandering branch with leaves running along a row of large squares. In the eastern aisle, the artist in charge of the repair work attempted to reproduce, very unskillfully, the original motif.

The border in the nave contains meander and chain patterns. The entire central panel, however, is missing, and it appears that the floor here was under repair at the time of the destruction of the synagogue. Piles of as yet unused tesserae, sorted according to color, were found on the foundation bed. Another heap contained waste from the cutting of the tesserae. These materials were obviously intended for the repair of the mosaic.

In the narthex there was only one phase of mosaic. The decorative patterns of the narthex pavement — geometric and simple — are in black 1.5 × 1.5 cm. tesserae on a white background. The floor was divided into several panels, in each of which was a diaper pattern of rhomboids. In the middle panel, however, on the central axis, was a surprising discovery: the panel, preserved almost in its entirety, contained an extensive Hebrew inscription, the largest known in a mosaic floor in Israel (see pp. 146–152).

In addition to the mosaic pavements,

Remains of mosaic floor in eastern aisle of the Reḥob synagogue

evidence of rich wall decoration was found. The interior walls were covered with a smooth, white plaster upon which colorful but simple geometric and floral patterns were painted. In the aisles, numerous fragments of

Fragments of wall frescoes

such plaster were found among the rubble; most of them bore red stripes on a white background. Fragments found in the southern part of the aisles show decorations with triangles and grid patterns with schematic flowers in various colors (red, yellow, black, green). The pillars were also plastered. They were covered with large red-painted inscriptions. Painstaking work in both field and laboratory enabled the restoration of numerous fragments. It seems that each column, on the side facing the nave, was painted with a large wreath, enclosing vine-branches and a *tabula ansata* containing extensive Aramaic inscriptions. These were mainly dedications and benedictions, as well as halakhic laws and other texts related to the worship in the synagogue. After a short period, this plaster with its inscriptions was covered over by a new layer of plaster, and new red and black inscriptions with other dedications and benedictions were then painted.

The synagogue was lit by polycandela in the form of a three-handled glass, suspended by

Remains of inscription found in column. Note layer of plaster which covered it.

three bronze chains from a hook fixed originally in the ceiling. Several of these were found on the floor.

The dating of the synagogue building described above is based upon various factors — coins, pottery, the style of the mosaic pavements — all pointing to a span from the fourth to the seventh centuries C.E. The high standard and fine execution of the poly-chrome pavements in the aisles and the style of its patterns would point to the end of the fourth or fifth century C.E.; the less skillful repair was probably done some time in the sixth–seventh centuries C.E. In addition to these repairs of the mosaic, a number of renovations and structural changes were made directly on the phase-two floor: benches were installed along the walls of the aisles; the *bema* structure was enlarged and the steps to it were moved from the sides to the façade; two small chambers were closed off on each side of the *bema*; a low wall was erected parallel to the façade of the *bema*, perhaps as a base for the

chancel-screen. According to a study of D. Bahat, this chancel-screen stylistically belongs to the 6th century C.E.[2] On the basis of several details in the walls and floor, the narthex was

[2] D. Bahat, "A Synagogue Chancel-Screen from Tel Reḥob," *IEJ*, 23 (1973), 181-183, Pl. 48.

Fragment of marble chancel-screen

93

probably appended to the original structure during this renovation phase. Thus, the mosaic inscription would belong to the last period of the synagogue's existence. The destruction of the building appears to have been sudden, though no traces of fire were found. This, together with indications of a collapse of walls and parallel alignment of the fallen pillars, suggests that the building was destroyed by an earthquake. The synagogue was then completely abandoned, as no material of a later date was found.

Numerous fragments, columns, and composite capitals were found in obvious secondary use in the basilical structure. The period of these fragments is uncertain, but a block of limestone found in the fourth season may give some clue. It is apparently part of a lintel decorated with scrolls formed of acanthus stems. One almost complete scroll and the beginning of a second one are preserved. The former scroll encloses a protome of a lion to the right, with head *en face.* The style of this fragment, typical of late Roman craftmanship, points to a 3rd century C.E. dating. Only further excavations beneath the basilical building will enable us to determine whether these fragments belonged to an earlier building.

Several soundings made around the synagogue indicate that it was set off from the surrounding buildings by a surfaced street. These buildings were apparently dwellings, as shown by the objects of daily domestic use found within them. Since the latest finds there are of the seventh century C.E. or no later than the first half of the eighth century C.E., it appears that neither the synagogue nor the adjacent quarter was resettled.

Despite the large number of inscriptions uncovered, no indication of the identification of the site was found during the excavations. Although the large mosaic inscription emphasizes the Beth-Shean area where the synagogue is located, it does not mention the name of the particular settlement to which the synagogue belonged. Among the dedications listing the benefactors and builders of the synagogue, no indication of their places of residence or business was found. Thus, we are forced to turn back to the literary sources and the local name-place tradition. Since these mention no name of a settlement in the area other than Reḥob, one may suggest that the numerous ruins at the foot and in the vicinity of Tel Reḥob are part of a large settlement, dating to the Roman–Byzantine period, whose name was probably Roób or Reḥob.

Synagogue Remains at Kokhav-Hayarden

M. Ben-Dov

In 1966, with the commencement of excavations in the Crusader fortress at Belvoir (Kokhav-Hayarden; Kawkab el-Hawwa),[1] some carved basalt ashlars were found in secondary use within the walls of the fortress. From the

[1] The excavations were conducted on behalf of the National Parks Authority, and directed by the author. My thanks to Professor N. Avigad for examining the inscription and for reviewing the reading suggested herein. For a fuller discussion, see M. Ben-Dov, "Remains of a Synagogue at Kokhav-Hayarden....," *Eretz Shomron* (Jerusalem, 1973), 86–95 (Hebrew).

motifs depicted on them in relief, it was evident that the stones had originally belonged to a Jewish synagogue of the ancient "Galilean" and Golan type. The relief motifs included, among other patterns, grape-leaves and a double meander, surrounding depictions of flora. Eventually, we found decisive proof that these were indeed remains of a synagogue, for a fragment of a basalt lintel came to light bearing a seven-branched *menorah*, a Torah shrine, an incense shovel, and a *tabula ansata*.

Stone with running fret pattern, in secondary use in the Crusader fortress at Kokhav-Hayarden

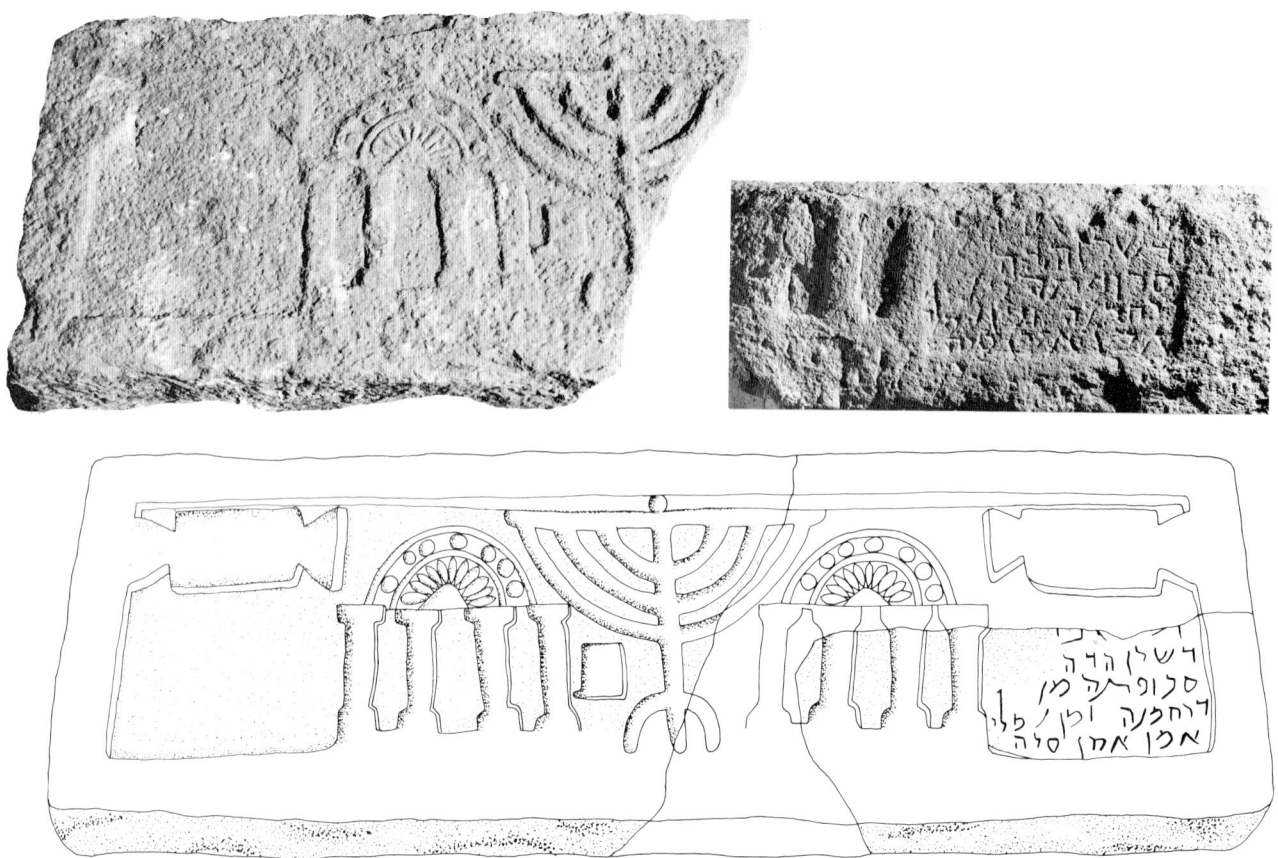

Above: Fragments of a basalt lintel found in secondary use in the Crusader fortress at Kokhav-Hayarden
Below: Restoration of lintel

A year later, another basalt fragment was found, also with traces of reliefs and several lines in Aramaic script. Subsequently we realized that this was an additional fragment of the lintel found the year before, since to the left of the inscription appear columns of a Torah shrine, identical in dimensions and form to those on the other fragment. The dressing and measurements of the stone support this conclusion.

The complete lintel is 1.75 m. long, 0.57 m. high and 0.25 m. thick. In the middle is a *menorah*, with a round dot above the central branch. To the left, below, is an incense shovel; symmetry would call for another such shovel (or possibly some other symbol, such as the *shofar*) to the right. Flanking these on either side is a Torah shrine; only the left-hand one is preserved in its entirety. It is represented by a façade of four columns with bases and capitals, supporting a conch pediment. The extant parts of the right-hand

shrine found subsequently are sufficient to indicate that both were identical in form. At the left side of the lintel, above, is a plain *tabula ansata* — apparently merely decorative. The corresponding part of the lintel on the right is missing, but another stone bearing a blank *tabula ansata* has also been found. The motif of a *menorah* flanked by Torah shrines is unusual in synagogue art. Usually the shrine appears in the center, flanked by *menorot*.

In the lower right-hand corner of the lintel is an Aramaic inscription, of which four full lines remain, with traces of a fifth line above. The inscription reads: ..... /דשרן הדה / סכופתה מן / דרחמנה ומן עמלי / אמן אמן סלה, "... who contributed this lintel from their own and from public funds. Amen. Amen. Selah."

Space would have perhaps allowed for two lines of script above the extant lines; these upper lines, now missing, probably contained the usual formula, mentioning the donors and evoking their blessed remembrance.

Proposed reconstruction of synagogue façade utilizing fragments found at fortress

The location of the synagogue. The large number of stones in secondary use in this Crusader fortress indicates the existence of ruins of a Jewish settlement nearby. In a survey in the vicinity, we have located such a Jewish settlement, as well as its synagogue. At the foot of the fortress, some 700 m. to the southeast, are ruins of buildings. There are still several basalt column drums there, and it could have been the site of the synagogue and other structures from which the stones in the Crusader fortress were taken. The entire site is strewn with pottery of the Roman and Byzantine periods.

The name of the site. The name *Kawkab* (equivalent of Hebrew *Kokhav*, "star") appears in Muslim documents of the Crusader period as the Arabic name for the fortress of Belvoir. This name seems to preserve the name of the early Jewish settlement here: Kokhav (Aramaic Kokhba). In Roman and Byzantine times this name may have been applied to settlements located on heights, but of the examples noted in ancient sources, one can be ascribed to our region with certainty.[2] Whatever the name, the Arabic name bears witness to the fact that the Jewish settlement on this site in the third-fourth centuries C.E. was called Kokhab or Kokhba.

[2] Cf. M. Avi-Yonah, *Gazetteer of Roman Palestine* (*Qedem*, 5) (Jerusalem, 1976), p. 50.

The Art and Architecture of the Synagogues of the Golan

Z. Ma'oz

Synagogues were first discovered in the Golan Heights during surveys conducted in the 18-80's. Lawrence Oliphant, an English "Lover of Zion," explored possibilities in the Golan and Gilead for his dream of resettling the Jews of eastern Europe. Gustav Schumacher surveyed Golan, Batanaea, and Gilead under the auspices of the Ottoman government, to determine the route for a railroad connecting Damascus with the sea-coast. Three synagogue buildings were found at that time — Ḥorvat Dikke, Ḥorvat Kanef and Umm el-Kanatir — as well as remains from synagogues in several villages. Kohl and Watzinger excavated portions of the Dikke and Kanatir synagogues, and sketched their plan and reconstruction. An archeological expedition under E.L. Sukenik, sent by the Hebrew University to complete excavations at Ḥammath-Gader, visited these synagogues in 1932. They photographed and sketched architectural elements of the various synagogues, some of which have since disappeared or have been damaged.

While the study of the Golan synagogues essentially ceased under French and Syrian rule, it was revived after the 1967 war. As a result of the archeological surveys led by S. Gutman and C. Epstein, scores of architectural parts from synagogues were found in various villages and several additional buildings were identified as synagogues. Three of these sites have recently been excavated: Kazrin, Kanef, and 'En Neshut. Buildings identified as synagogues have also been surveyed and measured in the villages of 'Assalieh, Zumimra, Dabiya, and Dir Aziz. A more comprehensive and accurate picture of a definite group of Golan synagogues, homogeneous in type and period, emerges from these new and more extensive data. We shall see that in spite of the superficial resemblance of this group to early "Galilean-type" synagogues noted by previous investigators, it nonetheless possesses its own architectural and artistic style. This chapter attempts to present an overview of extant archeological findings. On the basis of the most recent excavations and surveys, a preliminary evaluation of the style and art of this group and its place in the corpus of the early synagogues of Roman Palestine is offered.

Historical Background: Jewish Settlement in the Golan during the Second Temple Period
The Golan Heights form the western part of the long "desert frontier" in northern Transjordan, extending from northern Israel to the Syrian wilderness and the approaches to Damascus. Archeological surveys exposed many agricultural settlements, mainly in the southern and central Golan, from the second century B.C.E. onward. Urban centers developed around fortresses which were well protected by the natural terrain, e.g., Hippos and Gamla. Such strongholds served as places of refuge for village populations during times of war and also functioned as administrative centers. From the Hellenistic period onward the Golan Heights was divided into three political-administrative units. The southern district included the Hippos-Sussita *polis* and its territory, a densely populated, fertile region with large settlements. The central rural district, "Gaulanitis," had no central *polis* and was itself divided into an "upper" and "lower" region, in the east and west respectively. Because the agricultural potential of the central district fell short of that in the south, only small, sparsely populated villages developed there.

The district of the Paneas *polis* extended across the north; it had an extremely limited agricultural potential and few settlements.

Until Herodian times Jewish settlement was confined solely to the central, "Gaulanitis" district. Alexander Jannaeus, who captured the Golan fortresses of Gamla, Seleucia, and Hippos during a military campaign in 83–81 B.C.E., annexed the region to the Hasmonean kingdom (*Ant.*, 12, 393; *Syncellus* I, 558). This conquest led to increased Jewish settlement in the Golan, a process which culminated at the time of Herod and during the first century C.E.

The central Golan and the districts eastward, Batanaea and particularly Trachonitis, are all regions with rocky terrain, difficult to traverse and thus removed from major transportation routes. For this reason these areas served as a refuge for elements of society opposing the authorities, for example, robbers, fugitives from justice, and political rebels. The area provided the Galilee and the north with what the Judaean Desert offered Jerusalem and central Palestine.

By the middle of the first century B.C.E. young Herod, appointed governor of the Galilee by his father Antipater, had already found it necessary to suppress the "bands of robbers" led by Hezekiah, that periodically invaded the "regions near Syria." This may have been the nascent resistance movement against Rome that subsequently developed into the Sicarii party or "Fourth Philosophy" of Josephus. These bands apparently found refuge in the regions of the Golan and Trachonitis to the east of the Galilee (*Ant.*, 14, 158). The exacerbation of security conditions in northern Transjordan, and the threat to Damascus and the Galilee, forced the Roman emperor Augustus to annex the districts of the Golan, Batanaea, Trachonitis, and Hauran to Herod's administration in 23 B.C.E. The northern part of the Paneas district, until then under Iturean rule, was annexed to the Herodian kingdom in the year 20 B.C.E. (*Ant.*, 15, 360).

To solve the security problem and assert his rule in these regions, Herod initiated an extensive settlement program. He transferred 3000 Idumeans and 500 families of Babylonian soldiers under Zamaris to this newly acquired area. He settled them in new communities organized as paramilitary villages exempt from taxation (*Ant.*, 17, 23). Jewish settlement in northern Transjordan reached its height under Herod. It extended as far as the territory of Damascus, and is reflected in a *baraita* discussing the "boundaries of Eretz Israel" (T *Shevi'it* IV, 10; J *Shevi'it* VI, 33c; *Sifre Deut.* 51; Rehob inscription — see below). Apparently the entire area contained many Jewish agricultural villages; this *baraita* mentions a number by name, located in the districts of Sussita and Naveh.

This settlement policy undoubtedly contributed to the basic security of the region between Damascus and the Herodian kingdom, but failed to subdue completely the Jewish resistance movement against Herod and Rome. Following the death of Herod in 4 B.C.E., Judah, son of Hezekiah, was involved in a rebellion near Sepphoris in the Galilee (*Ant.*, 17, 271), and "Judah the Gaulanite" (the same person?), from a "city called Gamla" led a rebellion against the Romans following the census of 6 C.E. (*Ant.*, 18, 4). With Herod's passing, the districts of Gaulanitis, Batanaea, Trachonitis, and Hauran passed to the tetrarchy of Herod's son Philip, and subsequently to the rule of Agrippa I, 41-44 C.E. (*Ant.*, 18, 237). From the year 50 to circa 100 C.E. the region was ruled by Agrippa II (*Ant.*, 20, 138).

When full-scale war broke out against the Romans in 66 C.E., Josephus was appointed commander of "the two Galilees" (*War*, 2, 568). The list of cities which he fortified includes the names of three sites in Gaulanitis: Gamla, Seleucia in lower Gaulanitis, guarding the two roads from the Galilee, and Sogane in upper Gaulanitis, guarding the eastern approach (*War*, 2, 573; *Life*, 188).

Agrippa II tried to suppress the rebellion in his kingdom with his own resources. He lay siege to the rebel fortresses and, aided by a mobile military force, blocked the road to the Galilee near Julias (*War*, 4, 4; *Life*, 398). With the arrival of the Roman legion in the

Golan, only the city of Gamla continued to resist; the other two fortresses surrendered to Agrippa without a battle (*War*, 4, 4). After a month's siege and two attacks by the legions, the city fell. The inhabitants and defenders were massacred, most committing suicide by throwing themselves into the ravine. The city was destroyed, never again to be inhabited (*War*, 4, 11–83).

Historical developments under the later Roman Empire are unclear due to the paucity of sources. With the exception of the tradition discussed below, neither the Golan nor its settlements are mentioned in the Mishna or Talmud; no names of either settlements or sages from the Golan appear, a surprising phenomenon that requires explanation in view of the wealth of archeological finds and numerous references to settlements in the Galilee. Before attempting to explain this phenomenon, we must examine the important, albeit problematic, text in J *Shevi'it* VI, 36c.

> Rabbi Huna wished to release *Yavlona* (i.e., Gaulanitis, from the agricultural obligations incumbent upon areas regarded as part of Eretz Israel). He came before R. Mani, who said to him: "If you wish, you declare it so," but (R. Mani) would not take it upon himself to make such a decision. The next day R. Ḥiyya b. Madya appeared with him (R. Huna), and said to him (R. Mani): "You were correct in refraining from such a decision, for your father, R. Yona, once said that Antoninius gave Rabbi (Judah I) two thousand parcels of land in tenancy. Therefore, eating (the produce on the sabbatical year) is permissible, but not working the land, as in Syria. (The land is also) exempt from tithing because it is considered gentile land ..."

Two conclusions may be drawn from this source: (1) R. Judah I received a portion of land from a Roman emperor (probably Caracalla); (2) at the time of R. Huna in the mid-fourth century C.E. the region was not densely settled by Jews and at least one sage wished to release it from the commandments applying to Eretz Israel, such as the Seventh Year and tithing

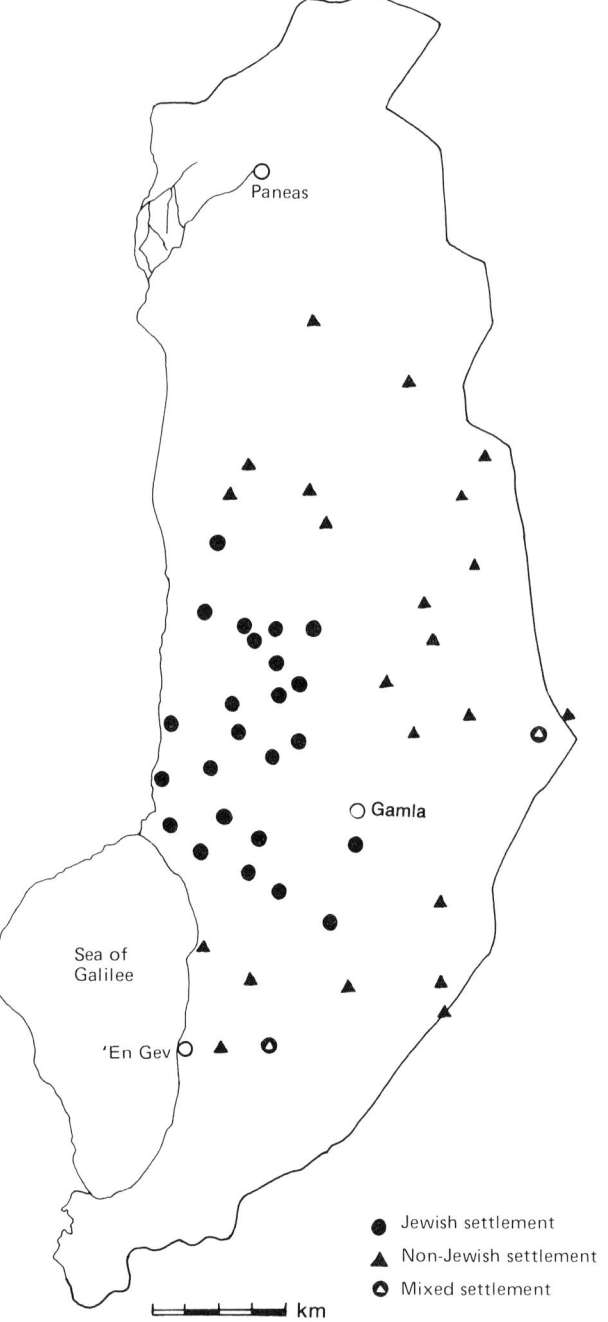

Distribution of the Jewish as well as pagan and Christian communities in the Golan during the Byzantine period

laws. However, the suggestion was not acted upon because of the historical association of the area with Jewish settlement. The first matter suggests Jewish settlement in the Golan at the time of R. Judah I, based on patriarchal holdings, like those in the Jezreel Valley and elsewhere. It also alludes to the autonomous

100

administrative status of Jewish settlement under the Patriarchate, as seen in the Galilee.

The second matter is harder to explain in the light of archeological discoveries in the western part of the central Golan (formerly lower Gaulanitis). Attempts have been made to explain the discrepancy geographically. Jewish settlement in the Byzantine period was concentrated exclusively in this area, which contains no pagan or Christian villages, while the eastern plains of "Upper Golan" are devoid of any sign of Jewish settlement and have yielded only Christian remains. The division is sharp and without exception (see map). On the basis of archeological evidence, it has been suggested that the property leased to R. Judah I was in Upper Golan, which is more suitable topographically for extensive land holding, where Jews resided in the second and third centuries C.E., but that by the time of R. Huna, in the mid-fourth century C.E., significant Jewish communities no longer existed there.

This suggestion is difficult to accept, as we know of no historical catastrophe that would account for so drastic a change in the ethnic character of Upper Golan. In our opinion, Upper Golan was settled by Jews only in the Second Temple period and not at the time of Judah I. The change in population was one consequence of the war with Rome, as in Trachonitis, Batanaea, and the Sussita region. At present, however, we have no alternative solution to suggest for the problem raised by the passage in the Talmud. The answer as to why Jewish settlements are not mentioned in the Mishna and Talmud depends upon the dates of the Golan synagogues, and we shall therefore return to this problem after a short review of the archeological finds. The late history of the Golan settlement and its termination will be resumed after discussing the synagogues themselves.

The Synagogues

Eight synagogue buildings are known to date, all in Lower Golan (see map). Five have been wholly or partially excavated and we are familiar with their plan as well as with architectural elements, allowing for reconstruc-

Umm el-Kanatir: Reconstructed façade of the synagogue (Kohl and Watzinger)

tion of their overall structure. Three others have been surveyed, measured, and photographed, and their general design is also known. One other building, at Dir Aziz, unique in its entrance on the east, has yet to be thoroughly examined, and its identity as a synagogue has yet to be positively established.

Although each building has its own character, all share many common architectural features. The skilled masonry of all the synagogues was executed in the local hard basalt. The outer walls were ashlar and the inner walls, roughly dressed stone. The thickness of all the walls varied between 80 and 100 cm. No mortar was used, but rather dry construction with dirt and small stones as wall fill. All had a monumental façade with a gabled roof and single decorative entrance, with the exception of the synagogue at Horvat Dikke, which had three entrances. Several had a small roofed portico in front of the façade.

The interior plans of the synagogues also display considerable uniformity. As a rule, two rows of stone columns divided the prayer hall into a nave and two aisles, the exception being the Kanatir synagogue with its three rows of columns. The floors are either stone slabs, as at Dikke, Kanatir, and Dabiya, or plaster, as at 'En Neshut and Kazrin. A mosaic pavement appears in one of the levels at Kazrin. Excepting the synagogue at 'En Neshut, where other details are also unique, these buildings do not

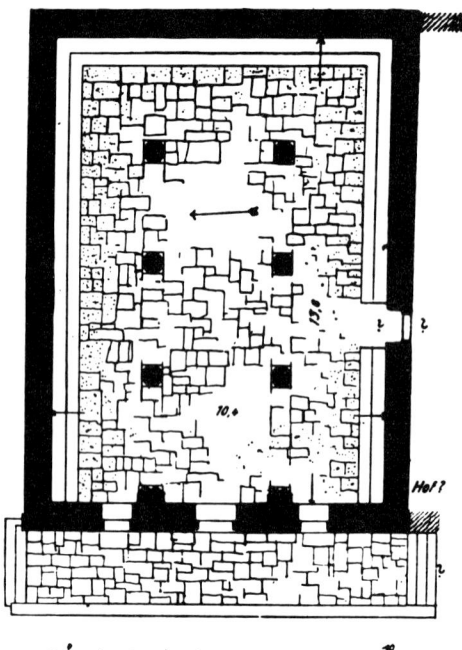

Ḥorvat Dikke: Reconstructed plan of the synagogue (Kohl and Watzinger)

Ḥorvat Dikke: Fragment of the lintel over the central entrance of the synagogue (Note the remains of a wreath and next to it—on left–Victoria, whose head has been defaced)

contain pedestals at the base of columns, so common a feature in the Galilee. The richness of architectural mouldings in these buildings is noteworthy (see below). Around the hall, a pair of benches usually extend from all four sides. To date, Torah shrines have been found in only two buildings, at Kazrin and 'En Neshut, yet these differ so completely from one another

that no common feature is yet distinguishable.

To a great extent this general description also fits the early synagogues in the Galilee, a resemblance that has misled scholars as to their date and plan. After a survey of the buildings and their details, we shall attempt to show that this Golan group, homogeneous within itself, differs in many details from "Galilean" synagogues. The similarity that does exist stems from their common source of influence in southern Syria.

The following description of the buildings does not necessarily progress chronologically, but is organized according to the direction of the façade and its main entrance. First we shall describe three buildings with a westward orientation, then the synagogue at Kazrin which faces northward, and finally, four buildings facing southward. As will be seen, these buildings greatly resemble one another, and reasons for the variation in their orientation will be suggested below.

Ḥorvat Dikke lies 3 km. north of where the Jordan River empties into the Sea of Galilee, east of the river. The westward-oriented façade had three entrances with a narrow porch in front of it. The lintel of the main entrance was decorated with two Victories, one on either side of a circular wreath. Above the main entrance there was a small arch with a vine-scroll ornamentation. The lintels of the side entrances

Ḥorvat Dikke: Reconstructed façade of the synagogue (Kohl and Watzinger)

were decorated with vine-scrolls on convex friezes. At both corners of the façade, flat pilasters were crowned with diagonal Ionic capitals. There was an elaborate window in the second story of the façade. The top of the building formed a Syrian gabled roof, the bottom of which was adorned with a convex frieze of garlands in rotary fashion with a rosette at the center. The 10.4 × 13.8 m. prayer hall was divided by two rows of columns: the first story with Doric capitals, and the second with Corinthian capitals. A pair of benches ran along the walls, and the hall was paved with stone slabs.

Ḥorvat Kanef is located on a high ridge northeast of the Sea of Galilee. Only the outline of the plan has been preserved. The interior of the synagogue was destroyed by the construction of a vaulted building at the end of the nineteenth century. The single main entrance in the western façade was decorated with vine-scrolls on the lintel and doorposts, and a circular relief on either side of the doorposts. One consisted of intertwined squares and a six-pointed star, and the other, of a shell at the center of a meander circle. Above the lintel an Aramaic inscription read: "May Yose b. Halfo b. Ḥanio be remembered for good." A side entrance in the northern wall led to a stone-paved street. The lintel of this side portal bore a relief of birds pecking at grapes. The exterior of the building measured 13.25 × 16 m. Its interior plan has not been preserved, but columns and Doric capitals from both stories have been found.

Zumimra lies north of Naḥal Zevitan and 5 km. south of Kazrin. Surveys have revealed only its exterior outline. The building measured 14.40 × 18.90 m. with a single entrance, 1.58 m. wide, in the western façade. Its doorposts bore an undecorated convex frieze. Parts of an arch that stood over the portal were found, as well as flat pilasters with diagonal Ionic capitals at the corners of the façade, an Attic base, a Doric capital, and a lion relief.

Kazrin, the best preserved synagogue in the Golan, measured 15.00 × 17.20 m. The northern façade had a single entrance, whose lintel was decorated with a circular wreath in the

Ḥorvat Kanef: Remains of an ashlar wall incorporated into a late 19th century building

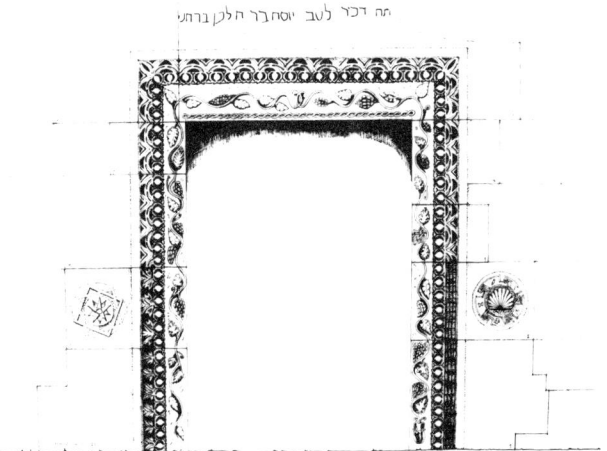

Ḥorvat Kanef: Reconstruction of the main entrance to the synagogue

Ḥorvat Kanef: (Photograph taken in 1932 of the central lintel). Note the inscription above the decoration.

103

Ḥorvat Kanef: Fragment of a lintel from a side entrance, showing birds pecking at grapes

Zumimra: Remains of entrance posts

Kazrin: Drawing of the remains of the entrance

Zumimra: Lion relief, perhaps part of the decoration from the Torah shrine

Kazrin: An Ionic capital typical of synagogues in the Golan

center and pomegranates and amphoras on either side. The doorframes were carved with convex friezes and had Attic bases. A large free-standing arch stood above the portal. Inside there were two rows of columns on Attic bases. The columns of the first story had Ionic capitals of the type peculiar to the Golan ('Assalieh, Rafid, Jehudieh); the second-story columns had Doric capitals. A pair of benches ran along all four walls. There were three stages to the interior plan: (1) a plaster floor decorated with a stone slab pattern and a small stone Torah shrine, of which one double column remains; (2) a colored mosaic pavement; (3) a smooth plaster floor, a large Torah shrine on an elevated stone base, and a dividing wall between columns. An Aramaic inscription was found in the building: "'Uzi made this square (?)." The building was partly destroyed in the seventh century C.E.; in the thirteenth century C.E. its northern section became a mosque.

'Assalieh lies 3 km. west of Kazrin. It is almost identical to the Kazrin building; here the entrance lay in the southern wall and measures 16 × 18 m. The lintel of the main entrance bears a relief of a Torah shrine with a seven-branched *menorah* on either side. The doorposts are identical to those at Kazrin. The interior plan shows two rows of Ionic columns on the first floor and Doric columns on the second floor. Pieces of a large arch from the second-story façade have been found.

Dabiya is located 3 km. east of Kazrin. Only the exterior plan is known; it measures 13.10 × 15.20 m. A single portal, 1.40 m. wide, lay at the center of its southern façade. The doorposts bore an uncarved convex frieze. The inner doorposts of a side entrance in the western wall were decorated with flat pilasters on bases. Part of a lintel was found carved with a "knot of Hercules" and, next to it, a discus with a radial engraving. The hall was paved with stone slabs.

Umm el-Kanatir is located on the northern tributary of Wadi Somek. The façade, oriented southward, had one entrance, in front of which lay a portico with two columns and Justinian basket capitals. The interior of the hall is divided by three rows of columns, which had

Kazrin: A view of the prayer hall before reconstruction; on the right are the stairs leading to the Torah shrine

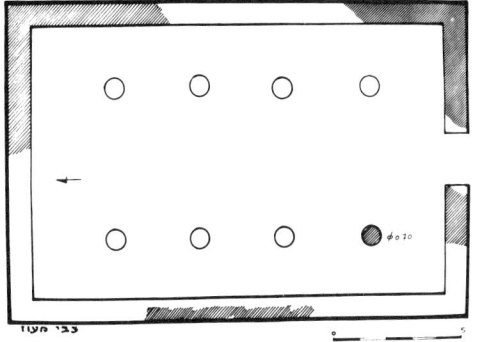

'Assalieh: Reconstructed plan of the synagogue

'Assalieh: A reconstruction of the entranceway to the synagogue

Dabiya: Remains of entrance posts incorporated into a later building

Dabiya: Pilasters next to the side entrance

Umm el-Kanatir: Basket capital from the forward
portico (typical of the 5th and 6th centuries C.E.)

Dabiya: A synagogue fragment showing a pair of incised
menorot

Umm el-Kanatir: An eagle relief on a double columned
capital

Umm el-Kanatir: Remains of the façade

'En Neshut: A fragment of the entranceway lintel showing a lion and a seven-branched *menorah*

'En Neshut: A fragment of a lintel with a rosette inside a wreath

'En Neshut: A general view of the prayer hall, looking west

'En Neshut: A decorated pedestal upon which a column base rests

'En Neshut: A nine-branched *menorah* on a uniquely decorated capital

'En Neshut: A Corinthian capital from the second story

'En Neshut: An inscription on a beam naming one "Abun bar Yose." Above the inscription is a Hercules knot which ends with snake heads

Tuscan capitals on the first floor and Doric on the second. A stone architrave was decorated with vine-scroll and guilloche. Finds also included a pilaster capital, a relief of a lion and one of an eagle, and a corner Ionic capital with a small eagle carved in relief. The hall had a pavement of stone slabs.

'En Neshut, situated on the bank of Naḥal Meshoshim, 2 km. north of Kazrin, measured 11.30 × 12.50 m. Its southern façade had an Ionic-style portal whose lintel was decorated with a rosette at the center of a wreath. A lion relief, one of a pair, with a *menorah* between them, also belonged to the portal. The interior of the hall was divided by two rows of three columns each. The columns were on pedestals decorated with a *menorah* and geometric patterns. The first-story columns had diagonal Ionic capitals, one elaborately ornamented with *menorot*, amphoras, birds, etc.; the second-story columns were crowned with Corinthian capitals. Three-tiered benches ran along the walls of the hall. What remains of the base of a Torah shrine lies to the west of the entrance. The floor of the hall was paved in clear plaster. White plaster with painted red lines covered the walls and columns. One piece of plaster bears the inscription "Amen, Amen, Selah. Shalom." Another inscription was found on a stone architrave: "Abun bar Yose." Reliefs of a lion, lioness, and eagle, as well as floral decorations, were also found among the ruins.

The construction dates of the synagogues have yet to be determined conclusively. The buildings at Kazrin, 'Assalieh, Kanef, and 'En Neshut were probably constructed in the fifth century C.E., Umm el-Kanatir apparently in the sixth century C.E. The other hitherto undated synagogues were most likely built in the sixth century C.E.

Art in the Golan Synagogues

An interesting phenomenon is immediately discernible as one examines the large corpus of relief art found in the Golan, both in the synagogues themselves and in secondary use in modern buildings. Although some similarity to "Galilean" synagogues is apparent, various aspects of Golan art are unique: the choice and predominance of certain subjects, the greater oriental emphasis of the art, and a style of very low relief. This last feature was a result of the utilization of different techniques owing to the Golan basalt stone, a much harder substance than the limestone of the Galilee. The relatively limited range of motifs repeats itself at the various sites and even in a given synagogue, as at 'En Neshut.

The double meander is among the most popular of the formal decorative motifs in the Golan and appears on capitals in the early synagogues at Gamla and Dikke, as well as on an architrave at Kanatir. In many instances patterns of rosettes, shells, and other symbols are incorporated into the meander strip, as we find on the stone doorpost at Dabbura and in the circle encompassing the large shell on the stone doorpost of the Kanef synagogue. (The latter, sketched by L. Oliphant, has since disappeared.) This ornamentation also appears in the synagogue at Bar'am in the Galilee and in the vicinity of Naveh and Nahil in southern Batanaea, where it invariably appears on lintels.

Another popular motif is the winding vine-scroll with leaves and clusters of grapes. This motif appears on the doorposts of the Kanef synagogue, on an architrave at Kanatir, on a frieze at Ahamdieh above the enigmatic inscription "תמוש משמר," and on other architectural pieces at Dikke. The vine motif is also found with birds pecking at the grapes, as on the

Dabbura: Meander design on a doorpost in secondary use

'En Neshut: A stone from the synagogue showing a bird pecking at a cluster of grapes

Dabbura: A lintel bearing a relief of an eagle with outspread wings

Dabbura: A lintel with two eagles, each holding a snake and surrounding a wreath

'En Neshut: A fragment from a relief of a lionness

Dabbura: A fish carved on stone in secondary use

The most striking feature of Golan art is its fauna reliefs. Of particular note is the abundance of eagle and lion reliefs — far more than are found either in the Galilee or in Hauran and southern Syria. The eagles are carved in low relief, as at Dabbura in the northern part of the Golan, or carved three-dimensionally and attached to the tip of gables or to arches. Small eagles ornamenting capitals are also peculiar to the Golan, as, for example, on the corner Ionic capital at Umm el-Kanatir.

Another bird of prey which seems to appear exclusively in Golan art is the short-toed eagle, identifiable by the snake held in its beak. The bird is present on two Dabbura lintels, at either side of a wreath, tied at the bottom by snakes in the form of ropes. One of the wreaths bears an inscription with the name of El'azar Haqappar and a rosette with four leaves is at the center of the other.

Eagles in Golan art are carved in the oriental tradition: wings are spread, the head turned to the side, the stomach round, and the legs sturdy. The depiction of the feathers is schematic and stylized, with no attempt at zoological accuracy. It would be impossible to distinguish between different kinds of eagles, were it not for the fact that the short-toed eagle is the only bird that preys on snakes (hence their name; the Aramaic word for this kind of eagle means snake). To this day large numbers of eagles inhabit the Golan during the summer. In this case the motif of the snake-eating eagle may be derived from local Golan wildlife.

Lion reliefs, which were very prevalent, raise a problem; none of them bears any indication of exactly how they were incorporated in the architecture of the synagogue. Most were carved in relief on rectangular building stones that were inserted in the wall. Some may have been in the façade or perhaps formed part of the Torah shrine ornamentation. The lions are also depicted in oriental style. In most instances the head has not been preserved. The 'En Neshut synagogue contains a large relief of a lioness (recognizable by the teats on its underside) with the mane of a male around her neck, a phenomenon which indicates that in sculpting lions, artisans followed sample pic-

lintel over the side entrance at Kanef and on a stone block at 'En Neshut. These two motifs, meander and vine, are proportionately more popular in the Golan than in the Galilee or in Jewish art generally. Other formal architectural motifs, such as egg-and-dart, astragal, guilloche, and "knot of Hercules" were very prevalent in both the Golan and the Galilee, as well as throughout the Roman–Byzantine Orient.

tures or accepted patterns without actually seeing the animals.[1]

Fish comprise another symbol apparently peculiar to Golan art. They are usually depicted by a mere outline of their profile. The eye is marked by a small depression. Fish appear on two separate blocks from Dabbura: on one, they fill the space beside an eagle under the inscription "who made a gate" and on the other, a smooth building stone, they appear in low relief.[2] What seems to be a fish or dolphin is also found on a window ornamentation at the Dikke synagogue. The fish, a relatively uncommon symbol in the Jewish art of Roman Palestine, is very popular in Christian art. Perhaps here it symbolizes plenty and fertility, as suggested regarding the fish mosaic in the synagogue at Naro in North Africa.

Of the usual Jewish symbols, the most popular in the Golan was the *menorah*, engraved or in relief, depicted simply and schematically,

'En Neshut: A seven-branched *menorah*, and an altar on a diagonal Ionic capital

Pik: A lintel bearing a medallion in which are displayed a seven-branched *menorah*, a *shofar* and an incense shovel, ca. 8th century C.E.

[1] A unique scene appears on a long block found at 'En-Samsam about 1000 m. north of 'En Neshut that also seems to have been removed from the synagogue site. On one of its short sides a large lion's head, entirely covered by a mane, is carved in three dimensions. A low relief within a rectangular frame is carved on the long side of the stone: a human figure holding in one hand a lion raised on its haunches and in the other hand a lioness also rearing with a cub suckling underneath. This is the only composition in Golan art that approaches an actual scene. Its meaning, however, is unclear. It may reflect the motif of Daniel in the lions' den, as suggested by some scholars. However, in the absence of parallels this interpretation is hardly conclusive. The actual carving on the figures is highly schematic, oriental in style, and consists only of the outline without any detail. In two places, Ahamdieh and Kasbieh, highly schematic bulls' heads in frontal pose were found, in both cases on lintels at either side of an eagle.

[2] Fish also appear at either side of the eagle on the Ahamdieh lintel mentioned above, apparently to fill the space, as in the case of other fish carvings.

or in fine, stylistic relief, as in the *menorot* at 'En Neshut and 'Assalieh. At times a *shofar* or incense shovel appears alongside the *menorah*, as on the lintel from Pik bearing a *menorah* in a medallion (very similar in style to the medallions of the eighth-century mosaics from the synagogues at Tiberias and Jericho). The *menorot* vary greatly in the number of branches

'Assalieh: A lintel from the central entranceway of the synagogue showing a Torah shrine surrounded by two *menorot*

— three, five, seven, and nine. Occasionally a horizontal line appears above the branches. Some of the *menorot* probably decorated the lintels of private houses as well as synagogues, as was common in the city of Naveh.

The Torah ark, represented as a shrine, appears only once in the Golan — between the *menorot* on the lintel above the entrance to the 'Assalieh synagogue.

In summing up, we should emphasize the abundance of faunal reliefs and the complete absence of mythological wildlife scenes, so common in the synagogues at Capernaum and Chorazin. The lack of human figures is also noteworthy.[3] In general, both the motifs and execution of detail in Golan art are reminiscent of the funerary art at Beth Shearim, but differ in style from the art in "Galilean" synagogues. Despite the hard basalt rock in which the reliefs were sculpted, the Golan school was very productive and displayed preferences and a style of its own. Apparently representing a local development in style that reflected and continued the stone-carving art of both southern Syria and the Galilee, its oriental-Byzantine character is nevertheless independent and distinct from these possible sources of influence.

Dabbura: A schematic relief of a man

[3] Besides the figure of the man holding the lions on the stone from 'En-Samsam, one other human figure is depicted very schematically on a building at Dabbura. The representation is in very crude outline form. The head is a circle with sunken holes for eyes. In one hand he holds a large, ring-shaped object, and in the other hand, a ball-shaped object. Next to him is something that looks like a keyhole, or maybe a stele with a round head. We have no idea what the relief signifies, nor are we even certain that it belongs to the synagogue. It may have been part of a private house or a tombstone.

A stone found in the village of 'En Samsam, it may have been taken from the 'En Neshut synagogue where it was used for the base of the Torah shrine

The Golan Synagogues and Synagogue Architecture of Roman Palestine

As suggested a few times in our discussion, the Golan synagogues must be examined in the context of their similarity to those of the Galilee. Both groups employed the same building technique and architectural concept of stone construction: stone buildings and columns, monumental façades and architectural sculpture. In these they differ from almost all other synagogues in ancient Palestine. With the exception of the mosaic work in the second stage of the Kazrin synagogue and representation of the *menorah* and Torah shrine, there seems to be little evidence of the influence of those synagogues built in the Byzantine basilica style, executed in concrete, and found west of the Jordan River.

With this in mind, the dating of the Golan synagogues assumes decisive importance. We have already pointed out the evidence supporting a Byzantine date for these synagogues: the coins from 'En Neshut and Kanef, the Justinian basket capitals from Umm el-Kanatir, and the general nature and style of the sculpted art. Although the data are neither final nor complete, they are sufficient, in our opinion, to indicate that these synagogues were constructed and flourished during the fifth and sixth centuries C.E. At the same time, we have shown that differences in structural detail and style of carving existed between the Golan synagogues and those in the Galilee: the preference for a single door in Golan façades as against three in the Galilee, the preference for two aisles in the Golan as opposed to three in the Galilee, the frequent use of pedestals in the Galilee and their absence from every Golan synagogue except 'En Neshut, and the total absence of corner colonnade pillars with heart-shaped cross-sections, found in every synagogue in the Galilee. These are all striking features, without even taking into account the details in architectural moulding, which display marked differences between the two areas.

This architectural analysis, in my opinion, confirms the accepted view that most of the synagogues in the Galilee were built and flourished from the end of the second century C.E. to the beginning of the fourth century C.E. The "Galilean" style originated in southern Syria during the late Roman period and the appearance of synagogues in a similar style in the Golan during the Byzantine period is not surprising, as this style continued to develop in the churches and private houses of southern Syria at least until the seventh century C.E. The architectural technique and general artistic style was derived from the source itself — access for Golan artisans and masons was easy and natural. It continued to develop as part of the local Hauranitic building tradition that was suited to basalt, in the absence of limestone for concrete and tall trees for beams. The tradition began in Hauran during the Hellenistic period and continued in that region through Roman-Byzantine times and, in fact, down to the nineteenth century.

The group of "Galilean" synagogues itself is not entirely homogeneous, neither in stylistic detail nor in date of construction. Two striking examples presented here will hopefully stimulate further study in this direction. The synagogue at Chorazin, both generally and in much of its architectural detail, resembles the Golan synagogues, particularly the one at 'En Neshut described above. It should be emphasized that the Chorazin synagogue is the only one in the Galilee without heart-shaped corner columns or architraves and friezes between its columns in the usual "Galilean" style. The *menorot* carved on its entrance lintel appear nowhere else among the group. It is our opinion, therefore, that the Chorazin synagogue was built about the same time as the Golan synagogues, approximately the fifth century C.E., and perhaps even later.

The synagogue at Nabratein also deviates from the usual "Galilean" style. It had only one entrance whose lintel bore a *menorah* at the center of a wreath carved in relief. In Naveh's opinion, the inscription on the lintel demonstrates clearly — contrary to the views of Avigad and Foerster — that the building was constructed in the sixth century C.E.[4] It is

---

[4] J. Naveh, *On Stone & Mosaic* (Jerusalem, 1978), p. 4 (Hebrew).

noteworthy that a rectangular building stone found at Nabratein bears the profile of a lion, carved in Golan-style, in a form found nowhere else in any "Galilean" synagogue.

We must therefore conclude that the Hauranitic–Galilean building tradition did not fade entirely after the fourth century C.E., even in the Galilee. At least in the two sites noted above, whose physical proximity to the Golan is hardly coincidental, this tradition in synagogue-building continued. This style differed entirely from that prevalent in the other regions of Palestine, from Lower Galilee and Tiberias southward, namely, the ordinary Christian Byzantine basilica style.

The most significant influence of early "Galilean" synagogues on the architectural pattern in the Golan was in the orientation of synagogue façades. Let us return to the question posed at the outset of our discussion: how is the variation in the direction of façades within the Golan group to be explained? In the 1930's Sukenik concluded, on the basis of the synagogues at Dikke, Kanef, and Gerasa (Jerash), that the façades of synagogues in eastern Transjordan faced westward, because in relation to Transjordan, Jerusalem lies to the west. Yet the façades of four buildings that have been dated, 'Assalieh, Dabiya, Umm el-Kanatir, and 'En Neshut, all face southward, which was also the direction of prayer. In our view, this idea was derived from the Galilee, where all synagogues faced southward. The Golan was apparently considered part of the Galilee in laws pertaining to the synagogue. In the Kazrin synagogue, too, one faced south when praying — in the direction of the Torah shrine located in the southern wall, although the entrance was in the opposite wall.

We must now explain why several synagogues face westward. Our suggestion is that the three westward-oriented buildings were the earliest in the group and reflect an older tradition that subsequently changed. Unfortunately, the evidence from Kanef to date does not support this idea, although it is not conclusive. Until we have precise and conclusive data either confirming or disproving the above theory, another possibility might be considered. The three synagogues with western façades are the closest in the group to the Jordan River and the Sea of Galilee; regional differences in prayer traditions may be reflected here.

The synagogues in the Golan and the Galilee shared a common problem — the accommodation of the Torah shrine in the façade wall. We are of the opinion that the synagogues of both the Galilee and the Golan contained two shrines, one on either side of the main entrance. Indications of such a solution have already been found at 'En Neshut in the Golan and Gush Halav in the Galilee. The art work at Beth She'arim and the lintel from Agrippina include a pair of carved shrines, and two shrines were also built at the Sardis synagogue in Asia Minor.

This group of Golan synagogues thus reflects a period of economic prosperity, and architectural and artistic productivity in Golan villages during Byzantine times. The Hauranitic building tradition that influenced the Galilee in the late Roman period survived and flourished in Hauran in Byzantine times as well. Under its influence the synagogues built in the Golan deviated from the building practices known to us in western Palestine, where concrete and mosaics were employed in a basilical plan with apse, nave, and atrium. This reflects an ancient building tradition, and evidences the conservative nature of a rural society that, removed from the influences of the Mediterranean coast and inland valleys, adhered to its native traditions. Yet these factors produced neither stagnation nor degeneration, but rather independent and creative development on the part of the Jewish inhabitants of rural Golan.

Finally, we must consider the historical significance of this archeological evidence. These monumental synagogues indicate a flourishing Jewish community in the Golan, especially in the fifth and sixth centuries C.E., a prosperity based on highly developed agriculture and particularly on the extraction and export of olive oil (two to six olive presses were found in each village of the central Golan). Despite its limited numbers in comparison with the earlier Second Temple period, the population of Lower Golan maintained a crystallized, unique, and unified Jewish ethnicity, even when all neighboring regions to the east, north, and south became Christian (see map). As was the case with Upper Galilee, the terrain and natural features of the Golan affected social, religious, and cultural attitudes of the Jews residing there, contributing to a stable and rather conservative Jewish character in the region. Unlike Upper Galilee, however, Greek inscriptions were also found in Jewish villages, for example, at Dabbura, Dabiya, and Ahamdieh, although they are comparatively rare. Aramaic appears in most inscriptions, though Hebrew is also to be found.

Inscriptions also allude to religious, scholarly activities: rabbis are mentioned in Dabbura and Kazrin, and the former also had a *beth midrash*. The appearance of inscriptions in Hebrew attests to widespread knowledge of the language. In our view, the dating of the heyday of these settlements to the fifth–sixth centuries C.E. provides an answer to the question of why the names of Golan rabbis and communities are not mentioned in rabbinic sources. During the late Roman and Byzantine periods, from the first to fourth centuries C.E., there was no community of such economic and religious strength in the Golan, and the region is therefore not mentioned in these sources, just as other regions populated by Jews in different parts of the land were also omitted. If we had possessed Palestinian Jewish sources relating to the end of the Byzantine period, the picture might have been different. Fortunately, archeology has been able to shed light on aspects of Jewish settlement in Roman Palestine unknown from literary sources, and the picture which emerges is indeed impressive.

The end of Jewish settlement in the Golan is vague. No pottery from the eighth century to medieval times has been found in the excavated villages or in surveys. Evidence from Kazrin attests to alterations and construction of a third stage of the synagogue at the beginning of the seventh century C.E. In the course of the seventh century, after the Arab conquest, security conditions in the region probably changed. The economic basis of the settlements, the export of olive oil, was also undermined by lack of means of transportation and marketing. All these factors contributed to an exodus of both Christians and Jews from the Golan. The Jewish population apparently moved to cities in the vicinity — Naveh, Tiberias, and Paneas — where large Jewish communities continued to exist until medieval times. The Golan reverted to a depopulated wasteland, inhabited only by nomads and Beduins.

Thus ended a period of one thousand years of settlement and creativity among Golan villages in general, and flourishing Jewish communities of the central Golan in particular.

The Synagogue at 'En-Gedi

D. Barag, Y. Porat and E. Netzer

In 1966, during preparation of agricultural land northeast of Tel Goren at the oasis of 'En Gedi, remains of a building and a mosaic pavement were discovered. In the spring of 1970, excavations were commenced on the site,[1] and a second season of excavations was held in the winter of 1971. The results exceeded all expectations, for these proved to be the remains of a synagogue from the Byzantine period, and — thanks to the dry climate and the limited subsequent activity of

man here — the finds were better preserved than in most other locales.

The structure, measuring about 12 × 15 m., was oriented toward Jerusalem (that is, to the north–northwest), as usual in synagogues of the Roman–Byzantine period. To the east, west, and south of the nave were aisles, as in the synagogue at Hammath-Gader. In the southern aisle, step-like benches were preserved. In the western wall there were three openings, leading in from a narthex 4 m. wide and running the length of the western wall of the building. This narthex, paved in white tesserae, has two entrances, one at each end; the northern one leads in from a small

---

[1] The excavations were conducted on behalf of the Institute of Archeology of the Hebrew University, the Israel Exploration Society, the Department of Antiquities and Museums, and the 'En Gedi Field School.

The 'En-Gedi synagogue, looking north

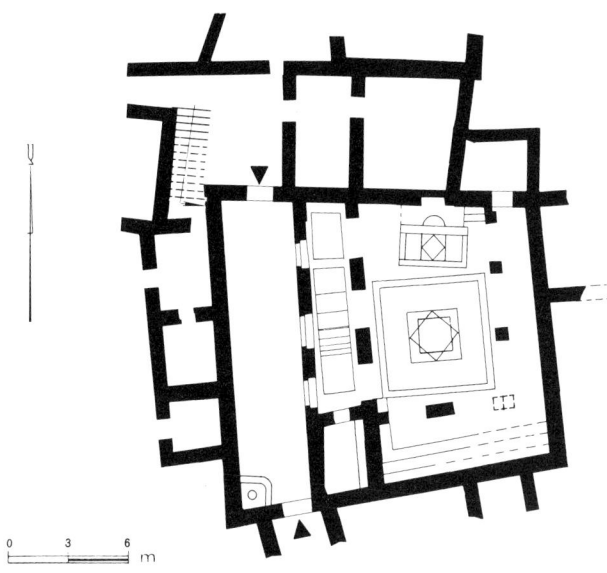

Plan of the synagogue complex

a cast bronze *menorah* of seven branches, some 22 cm. wide. In the niche and to the east, a bronze "goblet" and a hoard of thousands of bronze coins were found. On the rim of the "goblet" there were traces of a hinge, and opposite, a loop — clearly indicating that it had once had a lid. In this area, charred traces of scrolls were observed. In the earth overlying the floor of the niche, a dark lump of matter was found; from its shape and size it is probably a codex or book, burned during the destruction. Pottery lamps, fragments of glass lamps, and traces of posts to support a gable,

courtyard. In the southwestern corner of the narthex, near the southern entrance, was a laver-basin for washing prior to prayer. A stone bowl and a pottery jar were found nearby. This is the first instance of such features actually being found in an ancient synagogue, though they are mentioned in rabbinic sources, and synagogue inscriptions at Na'aran and Hammath-Gader also take note of them.

In the middle of the northern wall, a semi-circular niche was found, undoubtedly serving as part of the Torah shrine. In front of the niche was a rectangular area enclosing a mosaic panel, forming a *bema* measuring 2 × 4 m. At the four corners of the *bema* were small sockets which held the posts of a wooden chancel-screen. East of the niche was a seat, built abutting the wall; this chair, of the type generally identified with the "Seat of Moses," may have been reserved for the head of the congregation or for some other local dignitary. The mosaics in front of the *bema* depict three symmetrically arranged *menorot*.

The synagogue was destroyed in a conflagration, during which first the roof and then the walls collapsed. The building was not significantly looted before its destruction, and thus various objects remained *in situ* — almost all of them behind the niche. In the rubble west of the niche, a unique find came to light,

Laving installation in the narthex (looking south)

The *menorah* found at 'En Gedi, upon discovery

Pottery bowl from the late Byzantine period, found near the niche

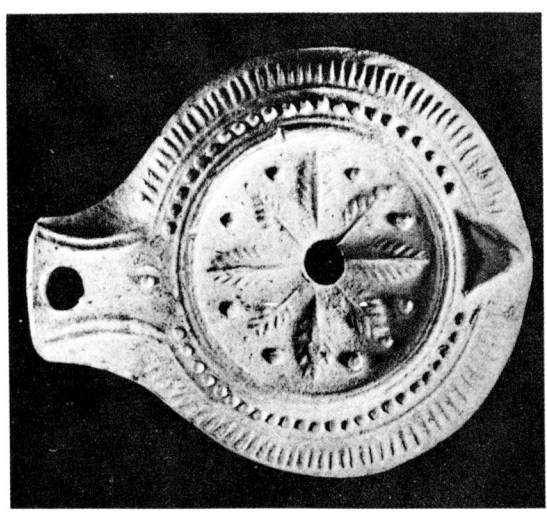

Pottery lamp found in the niche

or possibly a *parokhet* (Ark curtain) were found flanking the semi-circular base of the niche; metal ornaments (possibly from the *parokhet*) were also found.

In the western aisle, another surprise awaited the excavators; the mosaic pavement there included two Hebrew and three Aramaic inscriptions. The first Hebrew inscription lists the ancestors of man according to I Chron. 1:1–4, from Adam to Japheth; a second Hebrew inscription opens with the names of the twelve signs of the zodiac, from Aries (Nisan) to Pisces (Adar), followed by the twelve Hebrew months, from Nisan to Adar,

and then the names of the Patriarchs ("Abraham, Isaac and Jacob. Shalom"). This is followed by the names of Hananiah, Mishael and Azariah, the three companions of Daniel and, finally, by a blessing: "Peace on Israel!"

The third and fourth inscriptions are in Aramaic. The former opens with "May Yose and 'Ezron and Hizziqiyu, sons of Hilfi, be remembered for good"; this is followed by a most interesting oath formula against those causing dissension or revealing the town's secrets. The fourth inscription mentions two of the same donors (see pp. 140–145).

The fifth inscription, also in Aramaic, beginning "May all the villagers be remembered for good," relates that the villagers, including one Jonathan the *hazan*, repaired the synagogue. The reference to "all the villagers" recalls, by contrast, the wording "all the congregation" in mosaic inscriptions in the ancient synagogues at Jericho and Nirim (Ma'on); the 'En Gedi formula was probably applied in places inhabited entirely by Jews, whereas the other phrasing seems to occur in locales with mixed populations. The *hazan* was one of the most honorable positions in a Jewish community; this title also occurs in an inscription in the synagogue at Horvat ha-'Amudim in the Netofa Valley, as well as in one incised on a marble column from the Golan. This inscription, which commemorates the laying of the mosaic, further relates that there had been an earlier synagogue there.

Several parts of the earlier synagogue were uncovered in our second season of excavations. In the eastern aisle we found yet another mosaic pavement, of cruder white tesserae, beneath the later mosaic. Traces of this lower floor were also found beneath the benches in the southern aisle and behind the niche. A wooden ark probably stood upon the earlier floor. The northern wall, facing Jerusalem, appears originally to have had an entrance through it, similar to the doorways of the "Galilean" synagogues of the third–fourth centuries C.E. This opening was blocked up by a thin wall, thereby creating an oblong niche — probably intended to receive a small ark. When the later, more decorative mosaic

Main mosaic floor at 'En Gedi

pavement was laid, and the larger ark and the *bema* were installed, the space of the earlier niche, behind the new semi-circular niche, apparently came to be used for storage or as a *genizah.*

In the small courtyard opening onto the narthex, on the north, the remains of a stairway were found ascending to the south. This may have led up to a story above the narthex and the western aisle, possibly including a women's gallery. The thickness of the piers of the western aisle tends to support this assumption.

Adjoining and surrounding the synagogue there are various rooms and houses, all bearing evidence of the conflagration which destroyed Jewish 'En Gedi. A hoard of coins found there dates from the reigns of the Byzantine emperors Anastasius I, Justin I, and from the beginning of the reign of Justinian (early sixth century C.E.) — demon-strating that the destruction probably took place early in the days of Justinian (ca. 530 C.E.). The small segments of the earlier mosaic floor seem to indicate that a synagogue was founded here before the Byzantine period, probably early in the third century C.E.

In the excavations conducted in recent years by B. Mazar at the oasis of 'En Gedi, few remains have come to light from the period between the Bar-Kokhba Revolt (ca. 135 C.E.) and the end of the Byzantine period. It should be noted, however, that the church fathers, Eusebius (early fourth century C.E.) and Jerome (late fourth–early fifth centuries C.E.), mention 'En Gedi as "a very large village of Jews." These new discoveries help to fill the void for this period, representing a further link in the historical chain from the period of the later Judaean monarchy down to the late Byzantine period.

The Synagogue of Eshtemoa

Z. Yeivin

The synagogue at Eshtemoa was discovered in 1934 by L.A. Mayer and A. Reifenberg. In 1936 these two scholars began excavating the site but were forced to abandon their work because of civil disturbances. At the time, the synagogue structure served as a dwelling site, with houses in and around it. The excavators were thus able to restore the plan of the building only on the basis of the architectural fragments then visible. Despite this handicap, they presented a surprisingly accurate plan of the synagogue, which needs little correction or emendation today.

In 1969 a project of excavation and restoration was begun. This synagogue is a rectangular structure (interior: ca. 20×10 m.), with an east–west orientation.[1] All three

[1] The excavations were conducted on behalf of the Military Command, Judea and Samaria, and directed by the author.

entrances to the building pierce the narrow, eastern wall. Before these entrances lies a narthex, beyond which is a courtyard, paved with large slabs of stone. The courtyard is preserved almost in its entirety. It should be noted that the steps of the synagogue do not run parallel to the rows of flagstones in the court, possibly indicating that the synagogue was erected *after* the laying of the court pavement.

Three steps led up from the court to the narthex, as is shown by the remains on the south. On the façade of the narthex there were four columns, between which one entered the building. The central doorway was broader than the side openings, and all three openings had a raised, ornamental moulding. On either side of the entrance, north and south, were pilasters. Inside the southern wall

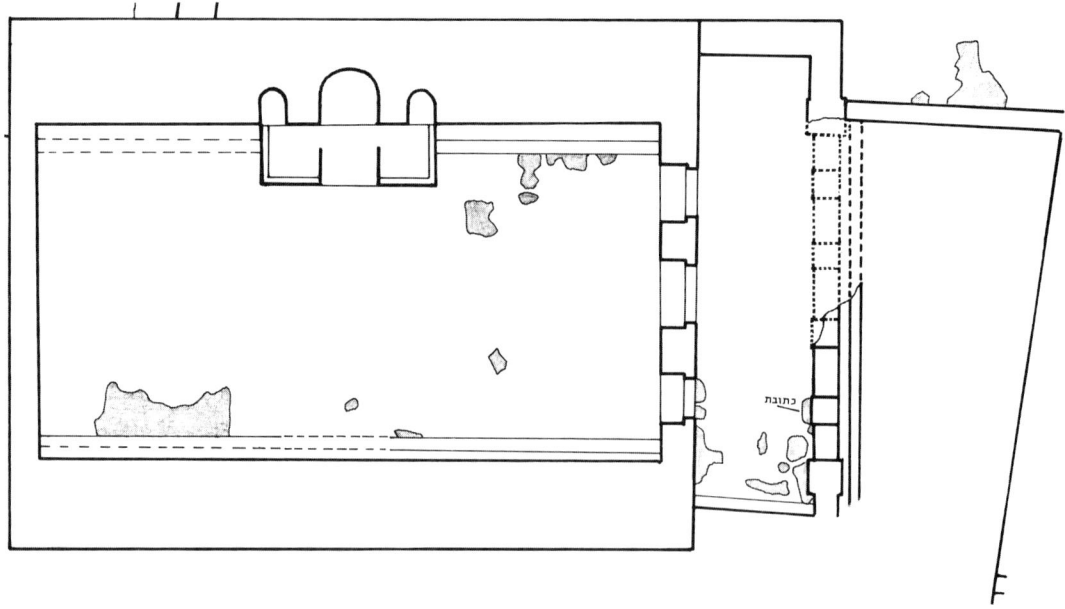

Plan of the synagogue

of the narthex were found remains of a stone bench. The façade, the stones of which are well joined, is preserved to ca. 2 m.

The interior of the synagogue is one continuous, free space. The long walls are 3–3.5 m. thick, while the shorter side walls are only 1.2–1.5 m. in thickness. The central elements of this synagogue are the niche for the Torah shrine and the *bema* before it. It seems that these two elements were joined by a flight of steps, which reached the middle of the *bema*. Flanking the shrine were two smaller niches, in which *menorot* may have stood.

Along the northern wall, in the space between the *bema* and the eastern wall, two broad stone benches were preserved, one higher than the other. In the section between the *bema* and the western wall, no traces of benches were found.

Along the southern wall, too, benches were built; these were later cut into by a *miḥrab* (Muslim prayer niche), when the building was converted into a mosque. According to a tradition among the local population, the mosque and the *miḥrab* were inaugurated in the days of Saladin.

In the open expanse of the synagogue, no trace of columns was found. It appears that the structure was covered over by a gabled tile roof of broad span, supported by a stout wooden frame. This frame would have rested upon the northern and southern walls, dismissing the need for columns within the hall.

Attached to the northwestern corner were the remains of a chamber, one of a series of buildings surrounding the synagogue and apparently contemporary with it. East of the synagogue stands the village mosque. Continuing the line of the mosque wall southward are traces of an ancient wall, containing an opening. This wall also continues the line of the wall of the synagogue court. On the southeast, outside the synagogue, remains of later walls were uncovered running out perpendicularly from the southern wall of the synagogue; they are founded upon the bedrock. A cave hewn into the bedrock was not cleared.

The floor of the synagogue was paved in

Narthex and façade of the synagogue

The *bema*, showing the niches in the wall behind

The benches along the northern wall, with the eastern edge of the *bema* on the left

mosaics. On the west, only the bed of the flooring remained, comprised of pebbles mixed with cement. Of the mosaic itself, only a few scattered fragments survive. The extant

Lintel-stone bearing a *menorah* relief

Relief of *menorah*

parts include floral and geometric patterns; in one small fragment in the narthex, near the southern doorway, there is a depiction of a tree, executed in fine colors. The original mosaic was made of small tesserae (1 × 1 cm.), but later repairs were made in larger stones (1.5–2 cm. sq.), all in white.

Of special interest is another fragment of mosaic paving found in the narthex, adjacent to the second pilaster on the south. It includes an Aramaic inscription, executed in black and white tesserae in the manner of the original mosaics. The inscription is of the same width as the adjacent pilaster. It reads:

דכיר לטב לעזר כהנ[א]
ובוני דיהב חד טר
[   ] [מ]יסין מן פעל[ו]

Remembered for good be [E]l'azar [the] priest and sons
(?) . . . who donated one tri[m]isis from his wages [   ].

The first line is preserved almost in its entirety except for the last letter, of which only one black tessera survives, in the upper right corner. It would seem preferable to restore an *alef* here, rather than *he*. This line mentions the name L'azar, a short form of El'azar; this form is not unusual in the Hebrew and Aramaic of Roman Palestine,[2] and is also

found in manuscript versions of the Mishna,[3] as well as in several Aramaic and Greek inscriptions. This form is also found incised on a chancel-screen pillar at Ḥorvat Susiya (see pp. 123–128).[4]

The first word in the second line appears to be corrupt: בוני instead of בנוי ("sons"). Further on appears the verb "donate," in the singular, though several donors seem to have been mentioned. Of the final word in this line, only the first two letters survive — the first, a clear *ṭet* and the other, which is broken, probably a *resh*; the word can be restored to read "tri[m]isis,"[5] a coin worth a third of a Roman gold denarius. This coin is mentioned twice in the synagogue inscriptions from Ḥammath-Gader, once in the same wording — "one trimisis." Of the third line, only the middle is preserved. The first word is damaged and is beyond restoration. The last word, also broken, can possibly be restored [ה]פעל, "his wages" or "his property," similar to the usage of this word on the "Seat of Moses" from Chorazin; in this case it should be related to the clear word preceding it, "from."

[2] Y. Kutscher, "The Language of the Sages," *Sefer Yellin* (Jerusalem, 1963), pp. 255–256 (Hebrew).

[3] J.N. Epstein, *Introduction to the Text of the Mishna* (Jerusalem, 1948), pp. 1266–1267 (Hebrew).

[4] Cf. Z. Yeivin, *IEJ*, 24 (1974), 203.

[5] Cf. now J. Naveh, *Leshonenu*, 38 (1974), 297, n. 12 (Hebrew).

Excavations in the Synagogue at Ḥorvat Susiya

S. Gutman, Z. Yeivin and E. Netzer

A century ago, Ḥorvat Susiya was first described by the British *Survey of Western Palestine*. A. Reifenberg and L. A. Mayer, who excavated the synagogue at nearby Eshtemoa (see pp. 120–122), noted the existence of a synagogue at this site, but gave no details. During the extensive archeological survey conducted in the late sixties, the site of the synagogue was covered. Ḥorvat Susiya was re-examined in a more thorough manner in 1969 by S. Gutman, and in a trial excavation, the narthex of the synagogue was uncovered. This led to the decision to expand the project and excavate the entire structure in 1971–1972.[1]

[1] The excavations were sponsored by the Military Command, Judea and Samaria, the Ministry of Education and Culture, the

The synagogue is situated on the southeastern slope of a hill to the west of Ḥorvat Susiya itself. An enclosed entrance courtyard east of the main hall was paved with large rectangular flagstones. Doorways led into the court from the north and east, and porticos bounded the courtyard on three sides. The southern portico contained a mosaic pavement with a dedicatory inscription at one end. The porticos were roofed over by arches supported on square pillars. In the two eastern corners of the courtyard there were small chambers, apparently store-rooms.

Department of Antiquities and Museums, the Hebrew University Institute of Archeology, and the Israel Exploration Society. The excavations were directed jointly by S. Gutman, Z. Yeivin, and E. Netzer.

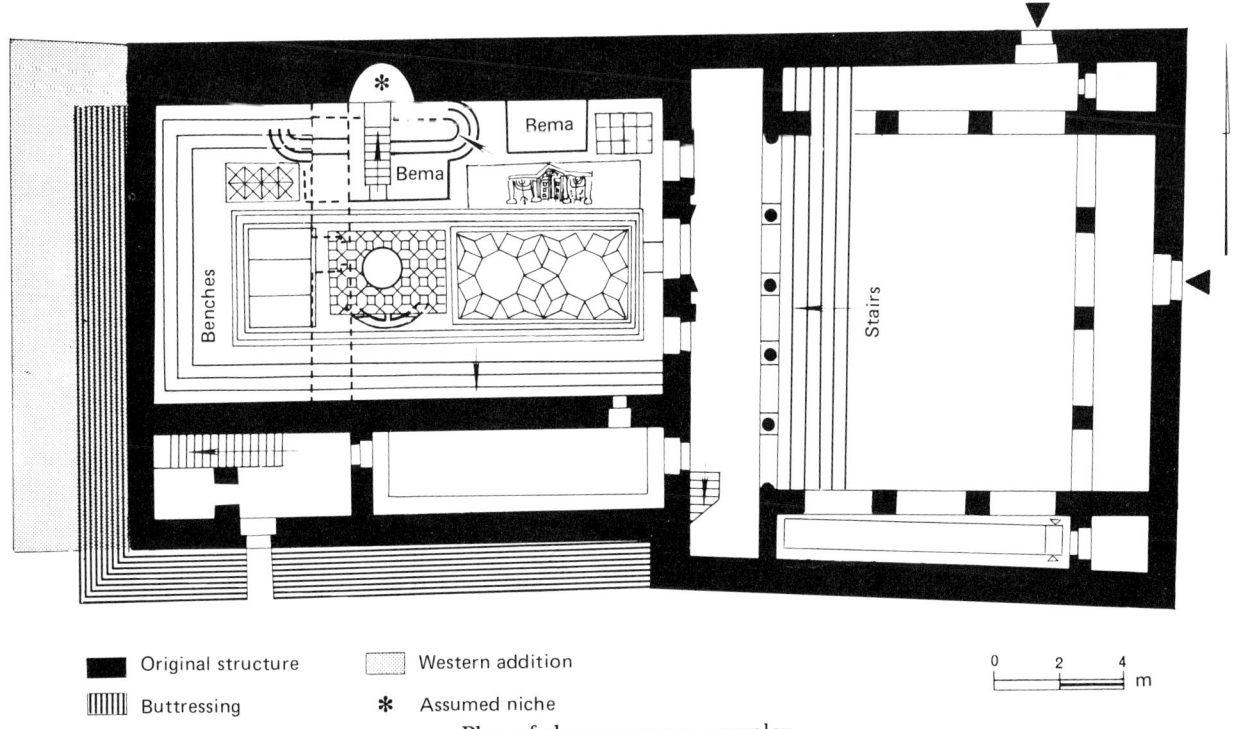

Original structure
Buttressing
Western addition
* Assumed niche

Plan of the synagogue complex

Reconstruction of the façade and courtyard, looking west

The floor of this courtyard was 1.50 m. lower than that of the synagogue, following the local topography. Within the courtyard, on its western flank, five broad steps led up to the narthex through a colonnade. In the floor of the courtyard two pits were discovered, one a cistern for gathering rain-water and the other the opening to a series of caves, which may originally have been a quarry, but at the time of the synagogue were used for storage.

The building itself was divided into three parts: the prayer hall (interior: 9 × 15 m.), the narthex on the east, and a long, narrow wing on the south. At the southern end of the narthex, steps led up to a second story which lay above the southern wing. The hall itself most probably rose the full two-story height of 8–9 m.

In southern auxiliary room, looking east; note the window into the prayer hall, in the wall on the left

The façade also apparently rose the full height of the gabled building. The columns of the narthex, *in antis*, had Corinthian capitals of a late type. Two of the columns and three of the bases were found *in situ*. The missing base, the remaining columns, two capitals, and parts of the architrave were found in secondary use in the mosque, which was built within the courtyard at a later date. This mosque included a plastered *miḥrab*, installed in the southern wall of the courtyard, with another *miḥrab* built between two columns of the southern portico. Crude stone benches were built on the north.

The floor of the narthex was paved in mosaics, in geometric patterns, and contained several inscriptions. This floor underwent many changes and only small fragments of it have survived.

The southern wing of the main building was divided into two chambers. Entrance to the eastern, larger chamber was through the narthex; the western room was entered from the exterior on the south. A wall dividing the two rooms was pierced by a doorway. The eastern room was paved with flagstones, similar to the paving in the courtyard. Along three of its walls (western, southern, and eastern) there were stone benches. A small window pierced the northern wall, opening out into the prayer hall. At a later stage, a flight of steps was constructed within the western chamber, over a small vaulted store-room. At this stage, the courtyard was repaved with a crude mosaic floor.

From the narthex, three doorways led into the prayer hall. The middle doorway was larger than the flanking ones. Two *bemas* abutted the northern wall of the hall, which was of double thickness. No niche was found in the northern wall here, probably because of the considerable destruction, but its existence can be surmised from various remains.

The synagogue at Ḥorvat Susiya, like that at Eshtemoa, was clearly a "longhouse" type on an east–west axis, yet it was oriented northward, toward Jerusalem — an unusual arrangement making the hall into a "broadhouse" in effect. At Eshtemoa only one

The mosaic panel and the secondary *bema*

bema was discovered, located exactly at the center of the northern wall; two *bemas*, however, were found at Horvat Susiya. The main *bema* stands slightly west of the center of the northern wall; the secondary *bema*, to the east, was one of the peculiarities of this synagogue.

The main *bema* was built in the form of stepped benches, while the secondary *bema* more closely resembles a cube. The main *bema* underwent numerous changes: initially it was formed by several benches, plastered over in white (like the benches around the hall), with a flight of steps in the middle leading up to the niche behind. Eventually a socle was installed in front of the *bema* and benches were added; at the same time, the posts and the chancel-screen around the *bema* were erected. Finally, at the synagogue's height, the entire *bema* was

faced in grey marble and flanked with semi-circular flights of steps. Most of the posts of the chancel-screen have been preserved (some in secondary use), and many parts of the screen itself, ornamented with such motifs as a *menorah*, a tree-of-life surrounded by lions, and a palm-tree surrounded by eagles, have also survived. Several of the marble posts, as well as the chancel-screen itself, bore dedicatory inscriptions.[2]

Changes also took place in the secondary *bema*; for example, it was extended at the time when the white pavement was replaced by the polychrome mosaic (see below). In one of its corners a carved stone column was preserved, perhaps pointing to the existence of a canopy above the *bema*.

[2] Z. Yeivin, "Inscribed Marble Reliefs from the Khirbet Susiya Synagogue," *IEJ*, 24 (1974), 201–209, Pls. 42–44.

125

Along the southern and western walls of the hall, as well as the northern wall up to the main *bema*, were three rows of stone benches. The walls were built mostly of ashlars on the exterior and field-stones within; only the western wall of the hall was built entirely of ashlars. The roof was tiled, as indicated by the many pottery tile fragments within the debris in the prayer hall.

The remains of mosaic pavement found near the main *bema* clearly show that originally the floor of the prayer hall was paved mainly in white tesserae. But already at a relatively early phase this floor was replaced by a polychrome mosaic, divided into three panels over the length of the hall. In the western part three scenes were depicted: a hunt; Daniel in the lions' den (?); and a damaged section, the nature of which is unclear. In the middle panel was a large circle divided into segments, probably for the signs of the zodiac. This was enclosed by a border containing a meander pattern alternating with metopes depicting birds or floral motifs. In the eastern panel was a geometric carpet containing a pair of octagons, with birds interspersed. Within the octagons there were scenes which cannot be discerned.

An additional panel was placed next to the eastern one, before the secondary *bema*; in its center is a Torah ark flanked by two *menorot*, all within a four-columned, gabled façade; flanking this are two stags. The position of this panel emphasizes the importance of the secondary *bema*, which apparently served for the reading of the Torah. In the northwestern corner of the prayer hall there are two small panels containing geometric designs.

Eventually, the zodiac circle was replaced by a geometric pattern with a rosette at its center, and only a small part of the round border of the circle survives. This mosaic floor was repaired many times, following accidental or intentional damage. These repairs were executed mainly in coarse white tesserae, though in several places colored tesserae from ruined sections were re-utilized.

At the center of the floor of the narthex is an especially noteworthy panel of small colored tesserae, forming a geometric pattern in the center of which is an inscription. This is the earliest part of the pavement in the narthex and seems to have been laid at the same time as the white floor in the prayer hall.

Later, several motifs and inscriptions were inserted into the pavement of the narthex — for example, the inscription on the north. Repairs were also carried out here, using white tesserae. The rather popular representation of the Torah ark in the northern part of the narthex may also be attributed to these repairs.

There were four inscriptions in the mosaic pavement: two inscriptions were in the narthex, one at the center and one near the northern wall. A third inscription was discovered in the main hall of the synagogue, immediately within the central doorway; and a fourth in the southern corridor of the courtyard.

Inscription 1. The inscription in the middle of the narthex was enclosed within a geometric pattern. The inscription and the pavement around it were comprised of small, polychrome tesserae (measuring 1×1 cm.). This part of the floor is apparently the oldest in the synagogue, belonging to the first stage. Only three lines of script are extant.

Remembered [be for good]	דכיר
Yoshu'a Yudan	יושיע יודן
[ ]who gave	דיהב[ ]
[ ]	[ ]
[ ]	[ ]

Within the original pattern, alongside the guilloche, part of another word was later inserted: חומה . . . This word is from another locus and is related to the inscription near the northern wall of the narthex (No. 2). It is probably to be restored מנ[חומה].

Inscription 2. The second inscription in the narthex was in one line, set between two stripes. One letter is missing at the beginning, and the end is also lacking (see No. 1, above).

[Re]membered be for good	כירין לטב[ד]
Menaḥemah Yeshu'a the witness	מנחמה ישוע שהדה
and Menaḥemah Sh[ ]	[ש]ומנחמה

The name *Menaḥemah* is rare, but is found in

the sources. *Yeshuʻa* is very common, in both the inscriptions and the sources. The word for "witness" is generally spelled with a *samekh* (סהדה). In Syriac, this word has the connotation of a martyr.

Inscription 3. The most important inscription, of six lines in Hebrew, was near the central doorway of the prayer hall. The left half is damaged and was repaired in antiquity with white tesserae.

Remembered be for good and for	זכורין לטובה
bles[sing]	ולב[רכה]
who endeavored and made [ ]	שהחזיקו ועשו [ ]
the se[co]nd of the week	הש[ני]ה שלשבוע
[year]	שנת]
four thousa[nd]	ארבעת אלפי[ם]
when the world was creat[ed]	שנברה העול[ם]
[ ].. in it.	[ ] לי בו]
Let there be pea[ce	יהי של[ום]

Inscription No. 3

Several persons were apparently mentioned at the end of the first line. An expression similar to the first word in the second line, also in context with the root "to make," appears in Aramaic inscriptions such as that in the synagogue at Naʻaran. The actual deed performed is lacking. The word "year" is probably missing here, as well as at the very end of the line.

The third line begins with a word damaged in its middle, but which should probably be restored to mean "second." The use here of the term "week" in this context is interesting, recalling the method of dating in the apocryphal Book of Jubilees, where jubilees (49-year cycles), "weeks" of years (seven-year cycles) and single years are used in recording dates; a similar mode is found in the Mishna and in medieval Jewish contracts.[3] The fourth line includes a more concise method of dating, based on the era of the Creation of the Universe, as is seen in the fifth line. Regrettably, the notations for the century and year are missing (in the latter part of line 4). The Hebrew phrase for "when ... was created" in line 5 appears to be spelled wrong. The fifth

line is badly damaged, at beginning and end, but seems to have included a common closing formula.

Inscriptions written in Hebrew rather than in Aramaic are rare in synagogues of this period. No less important is the fact that there are two systems of dating here, one according to the Seventh Year and the other — for the first time in so early an inscription — according to the era calculated from the "Creation of the Universe."

Inscription 4. A fourth inscription — the clearest and most complete — was located in the southern portico of the courtyard. The entire six-line Hebrew text is preserved, within a *tabula ansata*.

Inscription No. 4

---

[3] We wish to thank Professor Y. Yadin for bringing the use of this method of dating to our attention.

Remembered be for good the sanc-	זכור לטובה קדושת מרי
tity of my master and rabbi	רבי
Isai the priest, the honorable, the	איסי הכהן המכובד
"venerable," who made	בירבי שעשה
this mosaic and plastered	הפסיפוס הזה וטח את
its walls with lime,	כותליו בסיד מה
which he donated at a feast	שמתנדב במשתה
Rabbi Yoḥanan the priest, the	רבי יוחנן הכהן הסופר
venerable scribe,	בירבי
his son. Peace on Israel!	בנו שלום על ישראל
Amen!	אמן

The style of this text differs from that of the other inscriptions found in the synagogue, as well as from the usual style of synagogue inscriptions from the later Roman–Byzantine periods. The abundance of honorific titles here is unusual in such inscriptions. The use of "the sanctity of" as part of an appellation is likewise uncommon in inscriptions and literary sources of antiquity, though it is found in the salutations of letters from the period of the Geonim (ninth–tenth centuries C.E.) on.[4] The honorific "master and rabbi," in its several variant forms, was also quite common in the salutations of the Byzantine and Gaonic periods. The title "the honorable" is also rather uncommon in the sources and inscriptions of the earlier period. The term בירבי appears not in its usual meaning of "son of Rabbi X," or "of the house of Rabbi X," but as a special honorific added after the function of the person so honored. A similar use of this word is also found in talmudic sources (B *Ḥullin* 28a): "Rabbi El'azar Haqappar the *venerable* says: ..."; which the medieval Jewish commentator Rashi interpreted as: "בירבי — a person great in his own generation."[5]

The spelling of the Hebrew word for "mosaic" reveals a local pronunciation close to the Greek, from which it was borrowed. The word for "which he collected," in this particular grammatical form, is common in mishnaic Hebrew; and the phrase "feast of ... his son" commonly serves in the Mishna and Talmud to denote wedding festivities.

Within the courtyard, near the northern wall, a series of caves was revealed, sealed either prior to or at the time of the construction of the mosque there. These caves contained no remains from a time later than the ninth century C.E., and thus we can assume that they subsequently remained closed. The mosque and the area of the synagogue, in contrast, were strewn with remains from the tenth–fifteenth centuries C.E. Thus, the mosque was probably built in the tenth century C.E., at the earliest, after the synagogue had fallen into ruin.

Beneath the benches in the southern part of the prayer hall, cut through by the foundation trench of the later partition wall, a coin of Justinian (sixth century C.E.) was discovered. Various remains found in trial-trenches indicate that the site was occupied prior to this, in the third–fourth centuries C.E. Beneath the mosaic pavement of the narthex, a coin was found — apparently of the Byzantine emperor Honorius (ca. 400 C.E.); since this mosaic floor is of the first phase of the flooring, it must have been laid after that date.

The synagogue, therefore, seems to have been founded toward the end of the fourth or in the fifth century C.E., and to have flourished at least until the eighth or ninth century C.E. During this span the building was renovated several times, a fact in turn testifying to its continuous use. It would thus seem that the building was not destroyed suddenly, but that it was abandoned and slowly deteriorated until its final collapse. It was upon these ruins that the mosque was erected.

[4] S. Assaf and L.A. Mayer, in: *Sefer Hayishuv*, II (Jerusalem, 1945), p. 52, No. 10 (Hebrew).

[5] This inscription has been treated extensively by S. Safrai, "The Synagogues in the Southern Judean Hills," *Immanuel*, 3 (1973–74), 44 ff. (Hebrew).

PLATE I

A–C: Two inscriptions and a *menorah* in the mosaic pavement of the synagogue at Beth-Shean

D–F: From the mosaic pavement in the synagogue at 'En Gedi: representations of a *menorah* near the *bema* (D), a bird from the southern aisle (E), and two birds from the nave (F)

PLATE II

Monumental inscription from the courtyard of the synagogue at Ḥorvat Susiya

Mosaic pavement in the outer southern aisle of the synagogue at Gaza. David playing the harp before the animals

PLATE IV

The blinded Samson being led to the pagan temple, from the mosaic pavement of the synagogue at Mopsuestia in Cilicia

The Synagogue at Gaza

A. Ovadiah

In 1965, a colorful mosaic pavement was discovered on the sea-shore at Gaza, about 300 m. south of the modern port. The Egyptian Department of Antiquities cleared the pavement, and a brief note was published on the results.[1] According to the publication, the mosaic pavement belonged to a fifth-century C.E. church and contained depictions of various animals and of "a figure of a female saint playing on a lyre." There were also two inscriptions, in Greek and in Hebrew. On the basis of the photographs, and especially the inscriptions, the late M. Avi-Yonah concluded that the building was a synagogue, and that the figure represented King David.[2] After the Six Day War, archeological excavations were carried out on the site, in order to preserve the remains.[3]

Of the synagogue only the mosaic pavement is extant, and even this only in part. These and other remains point to a large building with a southeast–northwest orientation, measuring about 26 × 30 m. It consisted of a wide nave and two aisles on either side, making five halls in all (thus differing in plan from most contemporary synagogues in Israel). These were apparently set off from one another by rows of columns, whose location could be reconstructed from various traces. There seem to have been three doorways on the northwest, the central one opening onto the nave and those on either side leading into the inner northern and southern aisles. In the

[1] See *Orientalia*, NS 35 (1966), 135. A fuller version of the present article appears in *IEJ*, 19 (1969), 193–198.

[2] *BIES*, 30 (1966), 221–223 (Hebrew).

[3] The excavations were conducted under the direction of the author, on behalf of the Department of Antiquities and Museums, in cooperation with the Gaza Military Government.

southwestern wall was an additional entrance. At the southwestern end of the building there was presumably an apse, some 3 m. in diameter, intended for the Torah shrine.

The nave was originally paved with mosaics, though later it was mostly repaved with large slabs of marble, almost all of which have disappeared. The extant western section of

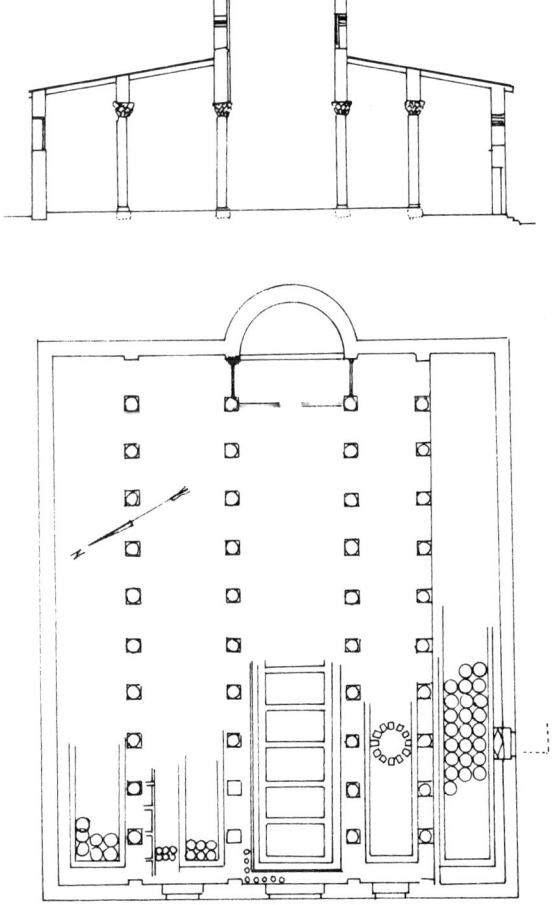

Restored plan and section of the synagogue

The "David" mosaic, as initially discovered

the central panel depicts King David as Orpheus, dressed as a Byzantine emperor and playing a lyre. Above the musical instrument is the Hebrew inscription דויד, "David." Around the king are a lion-cub, a giraffe and a snake, all listening to his music. The whole is surrounded by a border of geometric patterns.

In the southernmost aisle is a better preserved mosaic, with a floral motif forming medallions which enclose various animals, including a bear, an antelope, peacocks, a lioness suckling her cub, a donkey, a leopard, flamingoes, giraffes, a zebra, partridges, a bird in a cage, a goat, foxes, and others. Again, a geometric border surrounds the whole. This mosaic floor is very similar to those in the Nirim (Ma'on) synagogue[4] and the Shellal and Ḥazor (south) churches,[5] which are of the same period. We may assume that the floors of these three sites, all in the Gaza region, were made by the same workshop.

Within one of the medallions is a Greek inscription commemorating the names of the Jewish donors: "Menaḥem and Yeshua the sons of the late Isses [Jesse], wood merchants, as a sign of respect for a most holy place, have donated this mosaic in the month of Loos, 569" (of the era of Gaza = 508/509 C.E.).[6]

The aisles north of the nave were also paved with mosaics, depicting geometric patterns and floral and faunal motifs.

An interesting find in the eastern part of the synagogue was hundreds of fragments of four marble chancel-screens. The carving is in the drilled technique and the motifs include bunches of grapes, pomegranates, stylized rosettes, birds, a ram, etc. On two screens the motifs are contained in medallions similar to those in the mosaics in the southernmost aisle. The borders of the screens were still partly covered with the red paint which served as the base for a gold-leaf overlay, and some fragments were incised with Greek inscriptions. Together with the screens was a marble window-grille bearing a pattern of an intricate double meander with stylized rosettes; this window is reminiscent in technique and decoration of those found in the Umayyad palace at Khirbet el-Mefjer near Jericho (though the latter are made of stucco). Alongside the screen fragments were many pieces of ornamented bone plaques, bearing floral and geometric designs, which probably decorated a wooden box. Two large marble basins were also found here, they had apparently stood on pedestals at the center of a nearby courtyard. One bore a Greek inscription on its edge: "For the salvation of Roubelos [Reuben] and Isses [Jesse] and Benjamin."

The chancel-screens are additional support for the assumption that this large building with its colorful mosaic pavement was indeed a synagogue. Other indications are the typically Jewish names, and the phrase "a most holy place," in the Greek inscriptions, the figure of King David and his name written in the square Hebrew script, and the east–west orientation

[4] See M. Avi-Yonah, *Rabinowitz Bulletin for the Exploration of Ancient Synagogues*, 3 (1960), 25 ff.

[5] Cf. A.D. Trendall, *The Shellal Mosaic* (Canberra, 1957) and A. Ovadiah, *Revue Biblique*, 82 (1975), 552–557.

[6] The reading is that of M. Avi-Yonah.

130

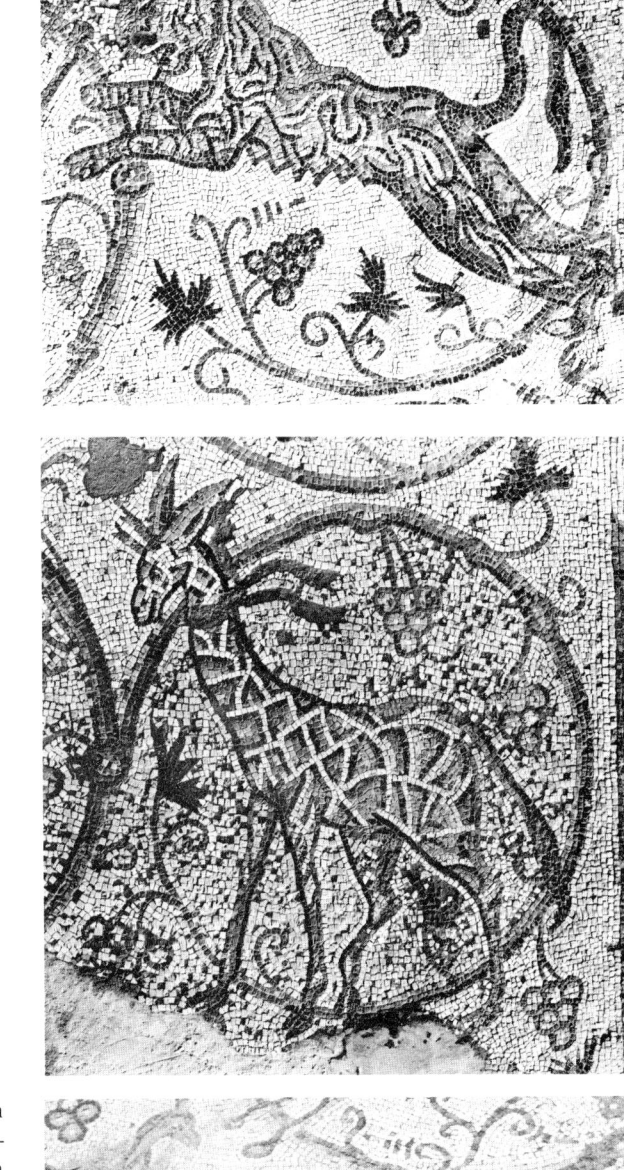

Medallions in the southern aisle: upper — lioness with suckling cub; upper right — leaping tigress; lower left — prancing zebra; lower right — giraffe, with ribbon around neck

Greek dedicatory inscription in southern aisle, as initially discovered

Fragmentary marble chancel-screen

of the building. The depiction of King David here is most significant, for after 427 C.E. such figures were forbidden in Christian churches. Further, a column and a chancel-screen bearing Greek and Hebrew inscriptions, as well as a fragment of a chancel-screen bearing a *menorah* motif with *shofar* and *lulab* — all indicative of a synagogue — were found many years ago in Gaza.[7] Our synagogue seems to have belonged to maritime Gaza — Maiumas Neapolis — named Constantia from the fourth century C.E. on.

As for the date of the synagogue, pottery lamps of "Sassanian" type were found dating

[7] See M. Avi-Yonah (ed.), *Encyclopedia of Archaeological Excavations in the Holy Land*, II (Jerusalem, 1976), p. 414, lower right.

Chancel-screen showing *menorah, shofar* and *lulab*

from the end of the Byzantine period (late sixth–seventh centuries C.E.); such types continued just into the early Arab period. Thus, the synagogue was most probably destroyed during the Persian occupation (614–627 C.E.) or shortly after the Arab conquest.

Ancient Synagogue Inscriptions

J. Naveh

The corpus of North-West Semitic epigraphic material has grown substantially during the last decades. We have now arrived at a stage when collecting and editing these inscriptions should be a primary aim.

Such collections will afford scholars and students who are not specialists in epigraphy easy access to the inscriptions, which are at present scattered in many publications. The epigraphist will also profit from having all the material at hand; he will be able to discern points which have previously been overlooked, revise incorrect readings, and suggest better reconstructions for fragmentary inscriptions. He may also be able to offer a more precise interpretation of words and idioms occurring in these texts.

In 1925 Samuel Klein collected the Hebrew, Aramaic, and Greek synagogue inscriptions from Palestine known at that time; they numbered only thirty, of which ten were discovered at Na'aran in 1920. Two of these inscriptions have not been seen in modern times; they are known only from the letter of Rabbi Shmuel bar Shimshon, who described his journey to Palestine in 1210. The inscriptions discovered up to the late thirties were collected, with other material, in *Sefer ha-Yishuv*, Vol. I (edited by S. Klein) and in J.B.

Frey's *Corpus Inscriptionum Iudaicarum*, Vol. II, published in 1952. The Greek synagogue inscriptions were collected and published in 1967 by B. Lifshitz in *Donateurs et fondateurs des synagogues juives*. This corpus contains about a hundred inscriptions, mainly from the western Diaspora (Egypt, Cyrene, Spain, Sicily, Greece, Asia Minor, and Cyprus) and from ancient Jewish communities in Syria. However, about twenty-five are from Palestine, mostly from Greek-speaking cities such as Ascalon, Caesarea, Gaza, Scythopolis, and Tiberias. [To these should be added sixteen Greek inscriptions from the Beth She'arim synagogue and some ten from excavations conducted since 1967. Thus, at present we know of over 50 Greek synagogue inscriptions from Palestine. The dedicatory inscriptions were generally in the languages spoken by the community. All the Greek inscriptions are dedicatory texts and stem from areas where Greek was undoubtedly a widely used, if not universal, language. — Ed.]

Most of the Palestinian synagogue inscriptions, however, are in Aramaic; Hebrew is less common. The number of Aramaic and Hebrew synagogue inscriptions known today is about one hundred and ten. Most were found at sites from Upper Galilee and the Golan

Ascalon chancel-screen with Greek inscription

כתב יהודה
זכור לטוב
אמן שלום
אמן

Hebrew inscription from south Yemen

Heights in the north to Beer-sheba in the south. Single inscriptions were found at Gerasa, today in Jordan, and at Naveh in Syria. About fifteen Aramaic inscriptions of various lengths were discovered in the mid-third century C.E. synagogue of Dura Europos. Two Hebrew synagogue inscriptions have recently been found in Yemen, at Beit el-Ashwal and Beit el-Khader. That of Beit el-Ashwal is bilingual; beside a longer Sabaean text, there is a short Hebrew note כתב יהודה זכור לטוב אמן שלום אמן — "The inscription of Judah, may he be remembered for good, Amen Peace Amen." The Beit el-Khader inscription contains a large fragment from the list of the 24 priestly courses.

Many of the synagogue inscriptions were carved on stone, often on such architectural members as lintels and columns, marble slabs, and chancel-screens. At Chorazin there is an Aramaic inscription on a basalt seat. Numerous inscriptions are found in mosaic pave-

Inscription from "Seat of Moses" — Chorazin synagogue

Inscription from Yemen listing some of the 24 priestly courses

Zodiac cycle and other inscriptions in mosaic pavement,
Na'aran synagogue

Aramaic inscription from Na'aran synagogue

As to their content, the synagogue inscriptions can be divided into two main groups: (a) dedicatory inscriptions, and (b) so-called "literary" texts. Although the dedicatory inscriptions follow specific formulae, their texts were composed by the members of the congregation. The texts of the second group, however, were copied from literary sources.

To the second group belongs, of course, the halakhic inscription found at Reḥob in the Beth-Shean Valley; this text is known from talmudic sources (J *Demai*, II, 22c–d; J *Shevi'it*, VI, 36c [see also pp. 146–152]). Fragments from the list of the 24 priestly courses, known from *piyyutim*, were found in Caesarea, Ascalon, and in the fields of Kissufim, a kibbutz near the Gaza Strip. The longest fragment of this kind was discovered in 1970 at Beit el-Khader in Yemen. The inscription on the 'En Gedi mosaic pavement begins with the list of the pre-diluvian patriarchs from Adam to Noah, the three sons of Noah, Hebrew names of the signs of the zodiac and the names of the months; then the three Patriarchs — Abraham, Isaac, and Jacob — and the three companions of Daniel — Ḥananiah, Mishael, and Azariah — are listed (see also pp. 140–145). The twelve signs of the

ments. They are also painted onto plastered surfaces and, at Dura Europos, on the tiles which had formed the ceilings.

Inscribed lintel, 'Alma synagogue

zodiac and the four seasons, written in Hebrew, occur in zodiacs depicted on mosaic pavements found at Ḥammath-Tiberias, Beth Alpha, and Na'aran. Among the "literary" texts one should also consider the short inscriptions which accompany the biblical figures or scenes on mosaic pavements, such as "Daniel" at Na'aran (and perhaps also at Ḥorvat Susiya) and "David" at Gaza. The biblical scene of the "Binding of Isaac" on the Beth Alpha mosaic pavement contains four short inscriptions: (a) Isaac, (b) Abraham, (c) אל תשלח, "do not stretch forth your hand," (d) והנה איל, "and behold a ram." These short texts are from the biblical narrative in Gen. 22.

The vast majority of the synagogue inscriptions are dedications, most of which are in Aramaic. The number of Hebrew dedicatory or building inscriptions is very scanty. At Dabbura in the Golan Heights an inscribed lintel reads as follows: זה בית מדרשו שהלרבי אליעזר הקפר ("This is the academy of R. Eli'ezer ha-Qappar" — see pp. 153–155). Eli'ezer ha-Qappar lived in the late second century C.E., and thus it seems likely that the inscription should be dated to this period or slightly later. A precise date appears in the Hebrew inscription from Kefar Neburaya: למספר ארבע מאות ותישעים וארבע שנה לחרבן, הבית ניבנה ... (the synagogue was built 494 years after the destruction of the Temple), i.e. in 564 C.E. (Most of the dates mentioned in Palestinian synagogue inscriptions are from

the sixth century C.E.) In the lintel inscription from the small synagogue of Kefar Bar'am discovered in 1861 (of which only half is preserved in the Louvre), we read:

יהי שלום במקום הזה ובכל מקומות ישראל, יוסה
הלוי בן לוי עשה השקוף הזה. הבא ברכה במע[ש]יו
של[ום]

"May there be peace on this place and in all the places of Israel, Yose the Levite, son of Levi made this lintel. May his activities (or: property) be blessed. Shalom."

On the lintel from 'Alma, not far from Kefar Bar'am, the same donor is mentioned in a very similar way:

יהי שלום על המקום הזה ועל כל מקומות עמו ישראל
אמן סלה

"May there be peace on this place and on all the places of His people Israel Amen Selah,"

but the continuation of the text is in Aramaic:

אנה יוסה בר לוי הלוי אומנה דעבדת [הדן שקופה...]

"I, Yose, son of Levi the Levite, an artisan, who made [this lintel...]"

In addition to the above-mentioned Hebrew inscriptions, three Hebrew dedicatory inscriptions were found at Ḥorvat Susiya in the south: two of them are on mosaic pavements and the third on a marble slab (see pp. 123–128). Thus, there are altogether six non-literary inscriptions.

The dedications generally begin with the phrase דכיר לטב — "may X be remembered for good." The name of the donor and the

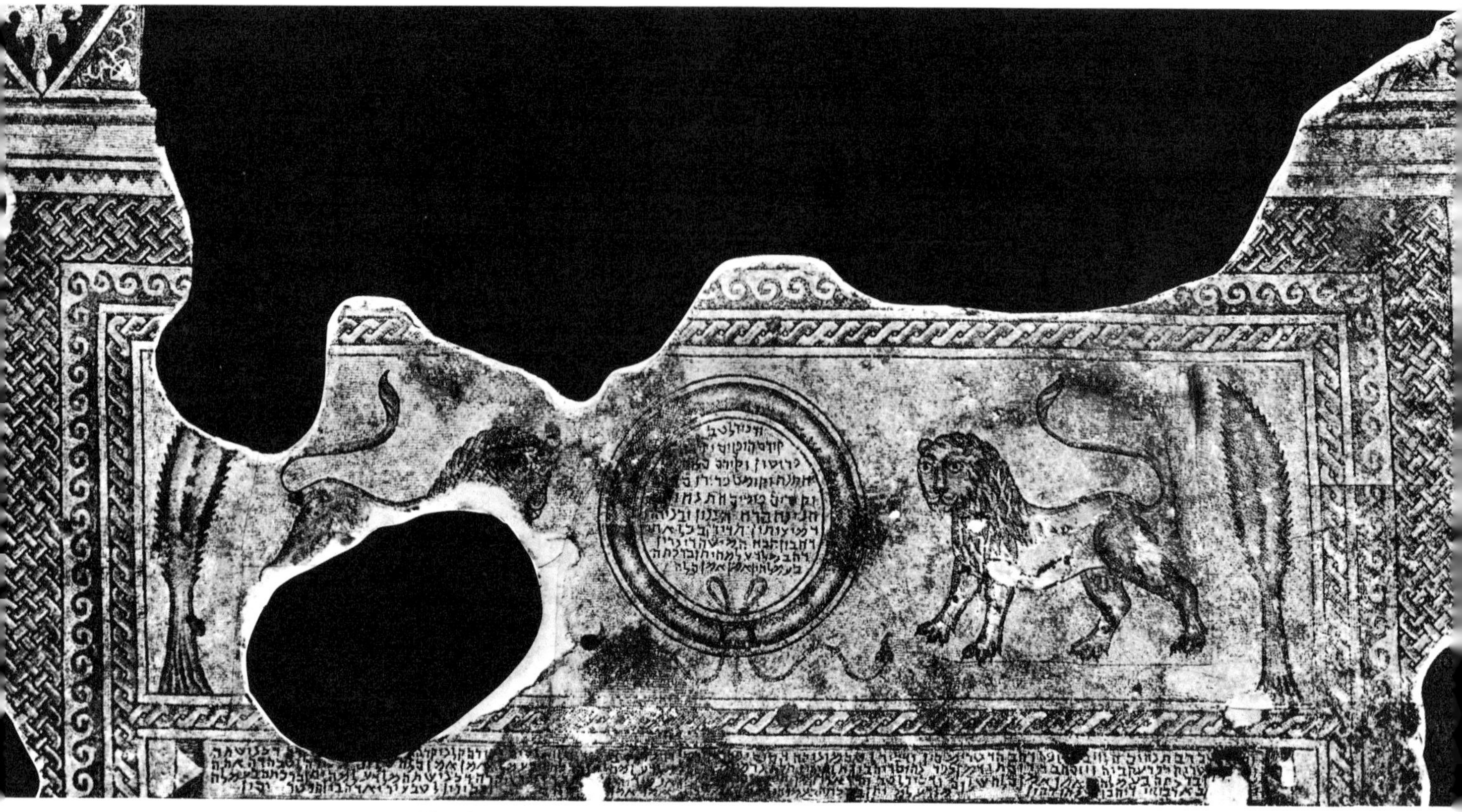

Mosaic pavement with inscriptions, Ḥammath-Gader synagogue

description of the donation then follow, and the texts end with blessing formulae.

The donation was generally made in money and the amount is sometimes mentioned. The highest sum known to date was given by a whole family, which donated five golden denarii for the synagogue of Ḥammath-Gader. It was more usual to contribute one denarius, a half, a third (*ḥd ṭrymysyn*), or even

Inscribed panel in mosaic pavement, Jericho synagogue

less (e.g., a *gramma*, which is thought to be a quarter of a denarius). Whenever the contribution is mentioned in money, the verb *yhb*, "to give," is used. In the Na'aran inscription we read of one "who gave the price (or the value) of the mosaic." However, when the donation is an object, for instance, a column, or a mosaic pavement, the verb is Aramaic *'bd* or Hebrew *'sh*, "to make, to do." These verbs do not indicate that the object was made or built by the donor himself, but rather that the objects were made at the donor's expense. In the inscription on a column found at Beth Guvrin (Eleutheropolis), we read: "May ... Shimáy ... be remembered for good, for he bought this column for the honor of the synagogue. Shalom." Thus we should translate *'bd* and *'sh* as "contributed." On the seat at Chorazin (see pp. 161–162) we read "contributed this colonnade and its stairs from his property." A similar text occurs in the mosaic at Eshtemoa (see pp. 120–122): "who gave a third denarius from his property" (the noun *po'al* in the meaning of "property" is attested also in *Genesis Rabba*, LXVIII, ed. Theodor, Albeck, p. 784). The parallel Greek expression is *ek ton idion* and the Palmyrene one is *mn kysh*, "from his pocket" or "purse," i.e. "at his own expense."

The contribution at times was given by the whole community. In this case we find the expressions "the holy congregation," "all the members of the holy society," or "all the members of the village." There are other general descriptions of the donors which do not mention their names, as at Hammath-Tiberias (see pp. 63–69): "May peace be upon all those who gave charity in this Holy Place and who will give charity."

The deity is never mentioned by name in the synagogue texts. Beside "the King of the Universe," we find here the epithets "the Merciful" or "the Lord of Heaven." Sometimes there are longer epithets; for example, at Jericho we read: "May He who knows their names and (the names) of their children and (the names) of their households, write them in the Book of Life together with all the Just." Another blessing for future life occurs at Chorazin: "May he have a share with the Just." The most common blessing formula is "May he have the blessing" or "May the King of the Universe bless his property." On the other hand, the mosaic floor of the 'En Gedi synagogue has preserved a remarkable text which warns the members of the congregation "not to commit certain sins," and concludes with a solemn curse on all who transgress (see pp. 140–145). This section of the 'En Gedi text concludes with the sentence "and may all the people say Amen, and Amen Selah," also a biblical phrase (1 Chron. 16:36).

The words Amen and Selah are usual at the ends of dedicatory inscriptions. Very frequently the short blessing "Peace," in its Hebrew form, closes the dedications, even when they are written in Aramaic or in Greek. Another Hebrew blessing formula is "Peace upon Israel." It occurs as short independent inscriptions at Jericho and Husifa on Mt. Carmel, as the concluding sentence at 'En Gedi and Horvat Susiya, and at the beginning of an inscription from Gerasa. An enlarged version of this blessing occurs at Kefar Bar'am and 'Alma (see above).

Aramaic inscriptions which, as noted, are the most numerous, were found principally in the north, from Kefar Bar'am in Upper Galilee and Dabbura in the Golan Heights as far as Husifa on Mt. Carmel and various sites in the Beth-Shean Valley. However, the number of the inscriptions discovered in the south is also quite large. They were found in the eastern part of Judaea, at Na'aran, Jericho, and 'En Gedi; at Beth-Guvrin, Eshtemoa, Horvat Susiya and Beer-sheba in southern Judaea; and at Ascalon and Ma'on, southwest of Judaea. Thus, the Palestinian Aramaic inscriptions can be divided into a northern and a southern group. However, from the stylistic, linguistic, grammatical, and orthographic points of view there is no reason to distinguish between northern and southern inscriptions. Only ten years ago it was generally assumed that the Upper Galilean synagogues are earlier than those found in Lower Galilee and in the south. However, there is no linguistic justification for drawing any distinction between the northern and southern inscriptions. Thus, we would conclude that the majority of Aramaic and Hebrew synagogue inscriptions, both northern and southern, should be dated to the late fourth–seventh centuries C.E.

I have attempted here to summarize briefly some of the salient features of the Aramaic and Hebrew synagogue inscriptions. However, there remain several aspects which could not be treated on this occasion. The interested reader will be able to find a detailed discussion of each text in the recently published corpus of Hebrew and Aramaic inscriptions.[1] It is to be hoped that this corpus will encourage further investigations into the epigraphic material and Jewish history and literature of the Byzantine period, and that it will throw further light on the languages used by the Jews at that time.

[1] J. Naveh, *On Stone and Mosaic: The Aramaic and Hebrew Inscriptions from Ancient Synagogues* (Jerusalem, 1978) (Hebrew).

The Inscription in the 'En Gedi Synagogue

Lee I. Levine

The inscription preserved in the mosaic floor of the narthex to the west of the 'En Gedi synagogue sanctuary contains 18 lines and 118 words. Until the recent discovery at Reḥob, this was the longest synagogue inscription known from Roman Palestine. The inscription reads as follows:

1. Adam, Seth, Enosh, Kenan, Mahalalel, Jared,
2. Enoch, Methuselah, Lamech, Noaḥ, Shem, Ḥam and Japheth.
3. Aries, Taurus, Gemini, Cancer, Leo, Virgo,
4. Libra, Scorpio, Sagittarius, Capricorn, and Aquarius, Pisces.
5. Nisan, Iyar, Sivan, Tammuz, Av, Elul,
6. Tishrei, Marḥeshvan, Kislev, Tevet, Shevat
7. and Adar Abraham Isaac Jacob. Peace.
8. Ḥananiah, Mishael, and 'Azariah. Peace unto Israel.
9. May they be remembered for good: Yose and 'Ezron and Ḥizziqiyu the sons of Ḥilfi.
10. Anyone causing a controversy between a man and his friend, or whoever
11. slanders his friend before the Gentiles, or whoever steals
12. the property of his friend, or whoever reveals the secret of the town
13. to the Gentiles — He whose eyes range through the whole earth
14. and Who sees hidden things, He will set his face on that
15. man and on his seed and will uproot him from under the heavens.
16. And all the people said: Amen and Amen Selah.

אדם שת אנוש קינן מהללאל ירד
חנוך מתושלח למך נוח שם חם ויפת
- - - - - - - -
טלה שור תאומים סרטן ארי בתולה
4 מאוזניים עקרב קישת גדי ודלי דגים
ניסן אייר סיון תמוז אב אילול
תשרי מרחשון כסליו טבית שבט
ואדר אברהם יצחק ויעקב שלום
8 חנניה מישאיל ועזריה שלום על ישראל
- - - - - - - -
דכירין לטב יוסה ועזרון וחזיקיו בנוה דחלפי
כל מן דיהיב פלגו בן גבר לחבריה הי אמר
לשן ביש על חבריה לעממיה הי גניב
12 צבותיה דחבריה הי מן דגלי רזה דקרתה
לעממיה דין דעינוה משוטטן בכל ארעה
וחמי סתירתה הוא יתן אפוה בגברה
ההו ובזרעיה ויעקור יתיה מן תחות שומיה
16 וימרון כל עמה אמן ואמן סלה
- - - - - - - -
רבי יוסה בר חלפי חזקיו בר חלפי דכירין לטב
דסגי סגי הנון עבדו לשמה דרחמנה שלום

17. Rabbi Yose the son of Ḥilfi, Ḥiziqiyu the son of Ḥilfi, may they be remembered for good,
18. for they did a great deal[1] in the name of the Merciful, Peace.

Lines 1–2 name the thirteen ancestors of the world and are taken from I Chron. 1:1–4. Lines 3–4 list the twelve zodiac signs; these signs appear in design as well as in name in the synagogues of Ḥusifa, Tiberias, Beth Alpha, Na'aran, and perhaps Yafia and Ḥorvat Susiya as well. It would seem that the absence of the zodiac figures was deliberate;

[1] Alternatively, following Naveh: "They made a large staircase (or upper stair)"; J. Naveh, *On Stone and Mosaic* (Jerusalem, 1978), 31–32 (Hebrew).

Inscription on mosaic floor at 'En Gedi

141

'En Gedi is the only example among ancient synagogues where only the names appear. This may be indicative of a more conservative cultural–religious orientation of the members of the community. Such a posture is likewise reflected in the main mosaic pattern within the synagogue, where only representations of birds appear.[2] Furthermore, the exclusive use of Hebrew and Aramaic reflects a cultural setting somewhat removed from the main currents of the day (fifth–seventh centuries C.E.). Such influences clearly affected the synagogues along the coast and in the north. In these locales, Greek plays a far greater role in synagogue inscriptions.

Lines 5–7a follow with a list of the twelve months of the year, again an unusual feature in ancient synagogues. However, in ancient synagogue poetry (piyyutim) dating from this period, the listing of zodiac signs and the corresponding months is common. It would thus appear that the 'En Gedi inscription was inspired by one such pattern.[3] A further association with the practice of contemporary piyyutim would also seem to be indicated in the unusual appearance of the conjunctive vav with the word Aquarius, instead of with the last word of the list, Pisces, which one would normally expect. Mirsky has suggested that this change is intentional and, as elsewhere, it alludes to the existence of two competing traditions, each listing Aquarius and Pisces in a different order. Both these traditions find expression in later Byzantine piyyutim. As the

issue had not been settled when the mosaic floor of 'En Gedi was laid, the inscription was made to reflect this unresolved question through the unusual location of the conjunctive vav. At Hammath-Tiberias and Beth Alpha, somewhat different methods were invoked to allude to this issue.[4]

Lines 7b–8a name two sets of biblical personalities: Abraham, Isaac, and Jacob on the one hand, Hananiah, Mishael, and 'Azariah on the other. Both series conclude with special endings, "Peace" or "Peace unto Israel." Such phrases frequently mark the end of a paragraph or of an entire inscription, as is the case with the inscriptions of Rehob (cf. below), Husifa, Jericho and Horvat Susiya.

Lines 1–8 comprise the first half of the inscription and form an independent entity. Hebrew is used throughout, and each subdivision is clear and self-explanatory in and of itself. What is not so obvious, at first glance, are the reasons for inclusion of certain material and the relationships between the various paragraphs. For example, why are the forefathers of the world mentioned and what is the connection between them and the remainder of the inscription? Why indeed mention both the zodiac signs and months of the year? While this may have been the accepted practice in piyyutim, it is unprecedented in a synagogue inscription. Perhaps the key to understanding this section lies in the concluding lines, which list two sets of biblical heroes. We are better informed regarding the significance of these names, owing to the following rabbinical tradition preserved in Midrash Tehilim I, 15:

> And this is what people say: upon whom does the world rest? Upon three pillars. Some say (that they are) Abraham, Isaac, and Jacob; others say Hananiah, Mishael, and 'Azariah, and still others say the three sons of Korah.

It would seem, therefore, that the first

[2] Birds appear to have been a neutral symbol/decoration even for Jews who scrupulously avoided any imagery. Hellenistic and early Roman Jerusalem (the late Second Temple period) can certainly be characterized by its avoidance of any sort of imagery. Of the hundreds of artistic remains (mosaics, wall-paintings, stone-carvings, etc.) from this period, only representations of birds have been discovered to date, and these in but one location. See M. Broshi, "Excavations in the House of Caiaphas, Mount Zion," Jerusalem Revealed, ed. Y. Yadin (Jerusalem, 1976), pp. 57–60.

[3] See Y. Yahalom, "Traces of Greek Culture in the Ancient Hebrew Piyyut," Proceedings of the 6th World Congress of Jewish Studies, 3 (Jerusalem, 1977), pp. 203–213 (Hebrew), who suggests that the zodiac inscriptions and representations may have been intended to accompany and give visual expression to these synagogue piyyutim.

[4] See A. Mirsky, "Aquarius and Capricornus in the 'En Gedi Inscription," Tarbiz, 40 (1971), 376–384 (Hebrew); Y. Yahalom, Review of J. Naveh, On Stone and Mosaic, Kiryat Sefer, 53 (1978), 349–355 (Hebrew).

section of our inscription attempts to fix the basic order of the universe. Commencing with the founders of the world, it names the heavenly divisions of time, zodiac symbols, followed by the months of the year. The section concludes with names associated with pillars upon which the world is sustained. If the thirteen ancestors are considered the pillars of the world generally, the two sets of heroes at the end represent the same view, but from a Jewish perspective. Similarly, the universally accepted zodiac signs are matched by a list of Hebrew months. We thus discover a very clear chiastic pattern (ABBA) to this section: thirteen world ancestors, zodiac signs, Hebrew months, two sets of Jewish pillars. The movement here is not only chronological, but also ties the general to the particular, the universal to the Jewish.

Interestingly, we see here, once again, that the authors of this inscription adopted a compromising stance in the face of competing traditions. As with the variant Aquarius–Pisces traditions noted above, so too with the differing versions of biblical heroes who sustain the world; the 'En Gedi community included both (in the latter case) or clearly indicated the existence of a rival tradition (in the former case). Why the sons of Korah, who, according to tradition, repented and were given the gift of song and prophecy are not mentioned, is unclear.

We thus conclude that the first eight lines constitute a distinct unit. This is indicated by the following considerations: (1) the lines are accompanied by a well-attested ending; (2) they contain an all-Hebrew section; what follows is entirely in Aramaic and deals with very different matters; (3) these eight lines comprise about one-half of the inscription, and are followed on the mosaic by a black line dividing the inscription into two sections.

There yet remains the intriguing question as to the meaning, if any, of the section as a whole. Is it merely a conglomeration of lists of names with no identifiable purpose? Does it relate in some way to the second half of the inscription? It has been suggested that the names of these biblical heroes are to be associated with what follows. In *Canticles Rabba* VII, 5 these two sets of figures are mentioned as the pillars of the world in whose names people were wont to take oaths. Perhaps all those named — the ancestors of the world, the zodiac signs, months, and biblical figures — serve the purpose of bearing witness to the community oath and adjuring members to stand fast in their vows. True, the second section itself invokes a curse (lines 13–14), and this preliminary formula might seem redundant. However, given the obvious importance of this oath to the community at large, invoking any and all figures and forces respected and feared by the people might not be unlikely.

The second section of our inscription is radically different from its predecessor, in terms of both language and content. Nevertheless, an attempt has been made to relate the two parts, at least with regard to their outward form. Most obvious is the division into sub-paragraphs. Just as the first section is divided after two lines by a double line, so the latter section is divided by a double line just before the concluding two lines. Moreover, as the opening lines list the ancestors of the world, the last lines constitute a paean to the leaders of the community. In fact, the whole second section bears a form quite similar to the first. The first begins and concludes with a list of the great of antiquity; the second part commences and ends with a list of prominent local personalities. Thus, despite the radically different topics of the two sections, an attempt has been made to bestow a unifying form on the various parts.

The dedicatory inscriptions at the beginning and end of the second section are clearly related. The same salutation — "May they be remembered for good" — appears, as well as the same personages; Yose, 'Ezron, and Hizziqiyu the sons of Hilfi are mentioned in line 9, and R. Yose the son of Hilfi, and Hizikiyu the son of Hilfi in line 17. Clearly, we are dealing with the same people, despite the slight variation in the name of the latter. The two most notable changes are the absence of 'Ezron the second time around, and the title

143

"Rabbi" bestowed on Yose. It has been suggested that the last lines were added at a later date, after 'Ezron had died and Yose had acquired the title "Rabbi." However, in light of the uniform format of this inscription noted above, it would appear that the entire mosaic was conceived and executed at more or less the same time. The differences between the two lists may merely reflect two different kinds of dedication. Three brothers were first honored for their donation (the mosaic floor?), the egalitarian nature of the donation being reflected in the form of the dedication: "Yose, 'Ezron, Ḥizziqiyu, sons of Ḥilfi." It would seem, however, that in addition to this donation, Yose and Ḥizikiyu were active in communal life in many other ways (line 18), and they are subsequently singled out for special mention, with the appropriate title added for Yose.[5]

However, it is the core of the second section which contains the most surprises and has intrigued scholars for the past decade. Lines 10–16 commence with a list of four cardinal offenses for which members of the town would be held responsible: (1) sowing seeds of controversy; (2) slander; (3) stealing; and (4) revealing the secrets of the town. Then follows a dire warning to those who ignore this admonition. Almost three full lines are devoted to the curse; He who sees and knows all will remove from the face of the earth both the offender and his offspring. Dothan has pointed out the extent to which this particular section draws upon biblical terminology:[6]

Line 13 — He whose eyes range through the whole earth	Zech. 4:10 — the eyes of the Lord which range through the whole earth

Lines 14–15 — He will set His face on that man … and will uproot him	Lev. 20:3 — I myself will set My face against that man, and will cut him off
Lines 14–15 — He will set His face on that man and on his seed	Lev. 20:5 — Then I will set My face against that man and against his family
Line 15 — from under the heavens	Jer. 10:11 — from under the heavens
Line 16 — and all the people said Amen and Amen	I Chron. 16:36 — And all the people said Amen

The four offenses named vary greatly. Three of the four deal with speaking (1, 2, 4), the other with stealing (3). Two involve the Gentiles (2, 4), and two seem to be confined to the community itself (1, 3). Three offenses originate in interpersonal relations between a man and his friend (1, 2, 3). The first three transgressions are not uncommon; causing dissension, slander, and stealing are oft-mentioned offenses in Jewish tradition. References to them are legion in both biblical and rabbinic literature. The last-named sin, "revealing the secret of the town to the Gentiles," is, however, most unusual. Because of its uniqueness, this phrase has drawn the attention of almost all commentators, and explanations range far and wide. The central issue, of course, is the nature of the secret which the town is sworn to keep.

Urbach suggests that the secret of the community be seen in the context of oaths imposed on religious societies, guilds, and citizens of a Greek *polis* in antiquity.[7] The oath taken by the citizens of Chersonesus (Crimea) in the third century B.C.E. is a case in point, as is the oath of the Essenes, which included a clause prohibiting the revealing of secrets (Josephus, *War* II, 139–141). The oath in our inscription would thus constitute a further example of a civic oath imposed on members of a town. Urbach further suggests that it was this Essene oath which may, in some way, have

[5] The different script used for the last two lines — which can be interpreted as indicating a somewhat later date of composition — may merely reflect the work of a different artisan. This would not be the first case known of a single inscription being the product of more than one hand; cf. the inscription in the Nabratein synagogue, Naveh (note 1), pp. 31–33.

[6] "The 'Secret' in the Synagogue Inscription of 'En Gedi," *Leshonenu*, 35 (1971), 211–217 (Hebrew).

[7] "The Secret of the 'En Gedi Inscription and its Formula," *Tarbiz*, 40 (1971), 27–30 (Hebrew).

inspired that of 'En Gedi, since Pliny notes that Essenes lived there as well. The major weakness of Urbach's proposal is that the 'En Gedi oath is removed by hundred of years from the parallels cited. The *polis* oaths stem from the Hellenistic and early Roman eras and, as is the case with the Essenes, they belong to a different historical setting.

Mazar interprets the town's secret as relating to various political alliances.[8] Dating the inscription to the early seventh century C.E., just prior to the synagogue's destruction,[9] he suggests that the Persian–Byzantine conflict of 614 and after gave rise to political controversy. Some members of the community tended to support the Persian cause, others maintained their allegiance to the Byzantine authorities. These conflicting loyalties gave rise to tensions within the community, including slander and the revealing of the town's secret, which is a reference to the town's divided loyalties. According to Mazar, it was this political controversy which led to a schism, contributing, in the end, to the destruction of the community. The validity of this interpretation is based on the claims regarding the date of the inscription, the existence of conflicting political loyalties, and the interpretation of the term "secret" to refer to this particular controversy. These suggestions, however, are all conjectural, and thus the proposal remains no more than a possibility.

In contrast to Mazar's political interpretation, Dothan has suggested that the events behind this inscription are religious in nature and related to the restrictions imposed by Justinian (sixth century) on the reading of the Scriptures and the study of the Oral Law (*Deuterosis*).[10] Basing himself on the report of the ninth-century Babylonian, Pirqoi ben Baboi, who referred to the burning of Torah scrolls in late Byzantine Palestine, Dothan suggests that Jewish communities accordingly hid their scrolls, and this is the "secret" referred to in our inscription. Furthermore,

he proposes reading "the secret of the Scriptures" (רזה דקרייה) instead of "the secret of the town" (רזה דקרתה). Aside from the fact that a questionable emendation is required (cf. the comments of Barag[11]), the resort to a later Babylonian tradition, which has no bearing on the inscription as it stands (and very little even after the emendation!), renders this approach problematic in the extreme.

Finally, Lieberman has offered an entirely different approach, relating the inscription to the secrets of the balsam industry centered in 'En Gedi.[12] Given the fame of this product, the secrets of its cultivation and preparation might well have been regarded as a trade secret not to be divulged to outsiders. The strength of Lieberman's suggestion derives from the fact that he is able to relate the four prohibitions of the inscription to the delicate relations between trade guilds, governmental authorities, and Gentile competition. This he accomplishes on the basis of rabbinic traditions which speak of (1) the prohibition of revealing secrets of one's trade to the Gentiles; (2) slander and dissensions between members of a guild over issues of taxation owed the authorities; and (3) a partner in a business enterprise unlawfully using (i.e., stealing) shared property. Lieberman's suggestion is most intriguing. Whether the rabbinic material from the Galilee of the third and fourth centuries C.E. is relevant for sixth-century Judaea, however, remains an open question. Moreover, the nature of this particular secret is not entirely clear. Greek and Roman writers were well informed regarding balsam and described this industry in detail. What, then, might the community wish to hide?

Thus, despite the valiant efforts made to elucidate this paragraph, none has succeeded in providing a totally satisfactory answer. Some explanations are more plausible than others, but questions remain, even in the best of circumstances. For the present, at least, "the secret of the town" remains just that.

[8] "The Inscription on the Floor of the Synagogue in 'En Gedi," *Tarbiz*, 40 (1971), 18–23 (Hebrew).

[9] For a different dating, see above, p. 119.

[10] Cf. above, n. 6.

[11] "'Qarta' in the Inscriptions from the Synagogue of 'En Gedi," *Tarbiz*, 41 (1972), 433 (Hebrew).

[12] "A Preliminary Remark to the Inscription of 'En Gedi," *Tarbiz*, 40 (1971), 24–26 (Hebrew).

The Inscription in the Synagogue at Reḥob

J. Sussmann

The inscription found in the mosaic floor of the synagogue at Reḥob (see pp. 90–94) is one of the outstanding recent archeological discoveries from the Roman–Byzantine period in Israel. The inscription is unique in both content and size, and its importance is not only archeological, but historical, geographical, literary, halakhic, and linguistic as well. It is surprisingly well preserved and will undoubtedly occupy the attention of scholars in various spheres for many years to come. Here we will treat only one or two aspects of this text, focussing upon its philological and halakhic context.[1]

The twenty-nine line inscription contains 365 words and is by far the longest mosaic inscription ever found in Israel. For instance, it is over three times as long as the extensive mosaic inscription in the synagogue at ʿEn Gedi (see pp. 140–145), which was previously the longest such inscription known.

Our inscription is further remarkable in its contents. As a rule, the brief lines of synagogue inscriptions relate to construction work within, and thus are generally dedicatory, or list the months of the year, the signs of the zodiac or the like (see pp. 126–128, 133–145). Only at ʿEn Gedi does an inscription touch upon the community as such, rather than upon the building (see pp. 140–145). However, at Reḥob the entire text is devoted to matters of halakha, with successive, specific, and detailed halakhic passages.

The text deals with agricultural precepts concerning the Holy Land, that is, tithes and seventh-year produce in the various districts of the country (see Glossary). The inscription can be divided into eight paragraphs, each of which is devoted to a particular region. Most of the text is known to us from talmudic sources; it is to be found in the Palestinian Talmud, tractates *Demai* II and *Shevi'it* VI, and also in several tannaitic sources (T *Shevi'it* IV and *Sifre-Deuteronomy* 51). The only new material is the final paragraph and part of the first: in the former hitherto unknown cities of Samaria are listed, and in the latter a precise topographical description of the gates of the city of Beth-Shean and its vicinity is given. Although the inscription thus offers little new material and, in this respect, is something of a disappointment, it is of major significance in its philological and textual ramifications. Foremost, this is the earliest surviving talmudic exemplar known. It is the first instance of a talmudic text which is close in time and place to the centers of talmudic creativity in Israel — an inscription made apparently not long after the completion of the Palestinian Talmud, and at a site not far from Tiberias, the rabbinical center in the talmudic period. The text is entirely independent of and free from the textual manuscript traditions, through which we have received the Palestinian Talmud, and it has not been corrupted by innumerable copyists and readers. In this lies its importance for talmudic textual criticism. Of particular note is the decidedly Palestinian spelling and the original renderings of the many toponyms — a realm particularly vulnerable to the whims of later copyists and readers. Moreover, the text is apparently derived from the Palestinian Talmud, but not directly copied from it, and thus it represents a significant contribution to our

[1] See also the author's articles in *Tarbiz*, 43 (1974), 88–158 (Hebrew); 45 (1976), 213–257 (Hebrew).

Overall view of the mosaic inscription

knowledge of Palestinian literature in the period following the completion of the Talmud, a period about which we know very little.

The inscription is in the main a detailed list of fruits and vegetables forbidden or permitted during the Seventh Year in particular regions (lines 1–9, 18–26; see pp. 151–152) and of "towns" and other localities where they were forbidden or permitted (lines 9-18, 26–29). Altogether, some ninety cities and "towns" (that is, rural agricultural settlements) and about thirty kinds of fruit and vegetables are named. The regions involved include the areas around Jewish Galilee; that is, Beth-Shean, Sussita (Hippos), Naveh, Tyre, Paneas, Caesarea and Sebaste (Samaria). The inscription opens with Beth-Shean, the area of the synagogue, and then lists the other regions in order from south to east to north to west and then again to the east. All the "regions" specified were strictly pagan, and thus presented a problem in matters of tithes and seventh-year produce.

The agricultural precepts concerning the Holy Land played an important role in halakha during the days of the Second Temple and later. This fact, so evident in the sources, is confirmed by archeological discoveries. Throughout the existence of Jewish settlement in Israel — down to the end of the Byzantine period and the beginning of the early Arab period, at the very least — the Jewish community observed the precepts concerning tithes and seventh-year produce, despite an increasingly difficult economic situation. The observance of these precepts, relating specifically to those living in the Holy

147

Land, demanded considerable devotion and we can well understand why the biblical phrase "You mighty ones who fulfil his word" (*Psalms* 103:20) was applied by the Sages to the "upholders of the Seventh Year," who left their fields and vineyards fallow one year in seven despite the heavy burden of taxation — "Be there a more mighty one than this?!" (*Leviticus Rabba* I).

The sages sought ways of alleviating this burden; one solution was to reduce the territory within which these laws applied. Already in talmudic times, the principle came to be acknowledged that the full severity of the precepts concerning the Holy Land was binding only within the reduced boundaries of the land held by those "who came up from Babylonia"; that is, the fields which reverted to the Jews in the days of the return from Babylonian exile. It was in this respect that the *baraita* concerning the boundaries of Eretz-Israel established by the Babylonian returnees (lines 13-18) defined the general limits of the area within which these agricultural precepts were applicable. Moreover, the "forbidden towns" within the exempt areas, that is, the Jewish "towns" in particularly pagan areas (lines 9-13), were also denoted, as well as the exempt "towns" within the "forbidden" areas — those localities in central Israel in which, apparently, no Jews were settled (lines 27-29). The pagan towns of Palestine were exempt; "Rabbi released Beth-Shean; Rabbi released Caesarea; Rabbi released Beth-Guvrin; Rabbi released Kefar Zemah" (J *Demai* II, 22 c). But even in the exempt locales, fruits known to have been brought from areas liable to the precepts concerning the Holy Land, or produce considered as grown in definitely Jewish areas, were forbidden. This led to lists of "forbidden fruits" (lines 1-9, 19-24), that is, fruits considered as brought from those areas of the Holy Land liable to the Seventh Year and tithes. Such lists of "towns" and fruits appear in the Talmud, and it is these lists which appear in the Reḥob inscription. Let us now examine the contents of the inscription, section by section.

A. Beth-Shean (lines 1–9). After opening with the word "Shalom," the first paragraph treats the halakhot concerning Beth-Shean. This paragraph is found also in the Talmud: "Rabbi Yose of Kefar-Dan, in the name of Rabbi [?] b. Ma'adiya: The species which are forbidden in Beth-Shean ..." (J *Demai* II, 22 c). The first part of this section — the list of fruits — appears almost word-for-word in the Talmud, but here it is given anonymously, in keeping with an inscription addressed to the public. The minor differences (such as the order of fruits) are important for an understanding of the nature of the connection between the text before us and the talmudic version. The second part of this paragraph — "the Beth-Shean region" — appears in very brief form in the Talmud; however, in our inscription, which is addressed to the inhabitants of this very region, it is presented in full detail according to the four cardinal directions, with Beth-Shean at the hub — from a given gate, פילי (= Greek πύλη), toward a specific locality.

Beth-Shean, which was a clearly pagan city, is included among the four places which were released by Rabbi Judah the Prince. But certain fruits, considered as imported from the areas liable to the Seventh Year and tithes, were forbidden here too; that is, they were forbidden during the Seventh Year, and during the other six years of the cycle they were liable to the tithe. The later rabbis were divided as to whether application of the tithe to the fruits was "certain" (*vadai*) or "dubious" (*demai*). The author of our inscription ruled *demai*, in accord with the talmudic sage Rabbi Jonah. Bread, however, was liable to the "dough-offering" (*hallah*) "eternally," i.e., throughout the seven-year cycle, for this offering was not a matter specific to this region.

The detailed inscription of the gates of Beth-Shean and its vicinity is especially interesting. In the literary sources there is no topographical description of this city (also known as Scythopolis) in the Byzantine period, despite its size and importance; only a small part of the remains of its walls and gates has been uncovered by archeologists. This is the first instance of such a detailed description of the limits of the city and, on this basis, together with the few extant remains, it may be possible to propose a topographical reconstruction, at least in outline.

B–D. Sussita (Hippos), Naveh and Tyre (lines 9–13). These three sections, stemming from T *Shevi'it* IV, are also found in J *Demai*. They list the "forbidden towns" which were located on the periphery of the Jewish community of Palestine, in areas considered principally pagan. The areas themselves were exempt from the agricultural injunctions and only the "towns," considered as Jewish agricultural settlements, were forbidden. The names of the "towns," which are generally quite corrupt in the various recensions of the Talmud, appear here in their authentic spellings, and this in itself is of the greatest importance for topographical identifications.

The note "and all [land] purchased by the Jews is forbidden," at the end of this list, is not found in the Tosefta, but it would appear that this reflects the teaching of Rabbi Manna in J: "That was so at first, but now there are [other towns held by Jews which are forbidden]" (the bracketed phrase is lacking in the printed versions, but appears in manuscripts). In other words, the second-century rabbis who first compiled this list named "towns" in which Jews owned property, but from their day until Rabbi Manna's (fourth century C.E.), further places where Jews resided were added, and these too were "forbidden."

E. The Boundaries of Eretz-Israel (lines 13–18). This is the famous *baraita* concerning the "boundaries of Eretz-Israel," one of the most important texts in talmudic literature concerning the historical geography of Palestine. This brief passage is found in several sources, with minor variations: T *Shevi'it* IV (directly continuing our sections C–D); *Sifre-Deuteronomy* 10; J *Shevi'it* VI, 36c. This short text has often been treated by modern scholars, and a large body of literature has grown up around it. The main problem facing scholars was textual, for most of the names in this list have been corrupted by copyists, and the attempt to reconstruct a more accurate

text has involved much effort. The present inscription now provides an authentic version of this *baraita*, quite close to that appearing in *Sifre*, and thus provides a solid basis for determining the correct names.

As noted, the *baraita* was intended to denote the boundaries of the territory possessed by the returnees from Babylonian exile; that is, those regions which were obliged to observe the agricultural precepts concerning the Holy Land. This is the only text in all our ancient literature which specifies in detail the borders of the country. The *baraita* commences on the western coast, moving northward from Ascalon to 'Akko, northeast to Caesarea Philippi, south-eastward to Bostra, southward to Rekem de Gaia (Petra), and finally westward, back to Ascalon.

Whereas most of the borders are stated only in very general terms, the northwestern border, from 'Akko to Caesarea Philippi, is given in much detail. This would indicate that the intention of the *baraita* was primarily to delineate this short border segment on the edge of the dense Jewish settlement in the Galilee, and to define precisely the limits of the land as denoted in M *Shevi'it* VI ("which the returnees from Babylonia took possession of in Eretz-Israel all the way to Chezib"). Hence, what we have here is plainly a halakhic *baraita* expanding upon the Mishna, rather than an early historical–geographical document, as assumed by the majority of scholars.

F. Paneas (lines 18–22). This paragraph, like that on Beth-Shean, deals with the forbidden fruits in an exempt region; it is found also in J *Demai* II, in the name of an Amora: "Rabbi Jonah, in the name of Rabbi Shim'on b. Zachariah, the listing of the forbidden things at Paneas; ..." The Paneas region, on the northern border, was also considered pagan; nevertheless, the fruits brought there from Jewish settlements were liable to agricultural injunctions. This prohibition also applied to those parts of the Paneas region which lay beyond the boundaries of Jewish Palestine; that is, "even from Upper Tarnegola and beyond" — previously noted (in line 16 of the inscription) as being on the

Detail of the lower left corner of the mosaic inscription

border. This final phrase is also found in the name of Rabbi Jonah (J *Demai* II), though the version there is slightly different.

G. Caesarea (lines 22–26). This is the third list dealing with the fruits of a region which was exempt, like the Beth-Shean region: "Rabbi released Caesarea" (J *Demai* II, 22c). Like the Beth-Shean list (paragraph A), here too the exempted area is delineated: "and until where is the territory of Caesarea ..."; that is, the territory in which the fruits listed were forbidden. At the end of this list, we again find the note on any "place purchased by a Jew," as in paragraph D, lines 12–13.

The word "Shalom" at the end of this paragraph was apparently intended to denote the transition from the preceding sections (A–G) — (all of which are also found in the literary sources) — to the final one (H).

H. Sebaste (lines 26–29). This section contains entirely new material; it is close to home, and its author clearly emphasized this point by setting it off from the above by the word "Shalom." Here we find a list of the exempted "towns" in the Sebaste region, an area about which our knowledge in the Roman–Byzantine period is sketchy, at best. Here, in the heart of Israel, the exempt "towns" are given, in contrast to the forbidden "towns" listed on the pagan periphery of the country. The list itself is unknown from any other source, but it may well be alluded to in J: "Towns of the Cutheans [Samaritans] in which permission was given" (*Shevi'it* VI, 36c). The "towns" listed here are known in part from the Bible (Dothan, Jibleam), the Samaria Ostraca (Yazit, [Kefar] Yehudit [?]) and other sources; most have yet to be identified.

We have seen that most of the sections of the Reḥob inscription are to be found in the Palestinian Talmud, but our text is no mere copy of the talmudic passages in question; rather, it represents a paraphrasing of the talmudic material. Names of the sages have been omitted and the formulation is straightforward and unambiguous, as befitting a text intended for the instruction of practical law. It can be assumed that such versions, in the form of halakhic judgments, were quite common in those days. It may even be that the text before us is related to the literature of practical law, remnants of which have come to light among the literary material from the Cairo Genizah, that is, fragments of *Sefer Hama'asim* ("The Book of Decisions"), which also contains decisions based on J, in a practical and simple formulation.

In any event, the Reḥob inscription presumes a text later than the original of the Palestinian Talmud, and the inscription should thus be ascribed to the fifth century C.E. at the earliest. The few archeological finds discovered in the synagogue at Reḥob appear to indicate that the inscription is even later than this, and it should possibly be placed as late as the seventh century C.E., a little before the Arab conquest (though possibly even after it). It is hoped that further excavations on the site will uncover evidence for a more precise dating.

The existence of such a monumental inscription in the mosaic floor of a synagogue, while unique, is nevertheless understandable. In those days the synagogue was the focal point of Jewish public life, especially in smaller settlements; "a 'small town' — this is a synagogue" (*Lamentations Rabba* 3). The populace would gather there daily to discuss current community affairs and, in the words of El'azar Haqappar (whose academy has also been found in recent years; see pp. 153–155), "Love the synagogue that thou mayest take thy reward every day" (*Derech Eretz Zuta* 9). It is hardly surprising that the building was so sumptuously decorated, and that the pavement was utilized to bring to the notice of the community important matters concerning adherence to daily precepts, especially those of such importance to the Beth-Shean region.

In this manner, the inscription achieved several purposes: ornamentation, instruction in the Law, and expression of regional "patriotism."

As noted, for the present this inscription is unique, but it was probably not an isolated phenomenon. Until a relatively short time ago, very few synagogue mosaic floors and inscriptions were known. Only a few generations ago, scholars held that a lack of mosaics and inscriptions was a typical feature of ancient synagogues; today these two elements are considered distinctive, almost essential, elements of ancient Jewish houses of prayer. We can only hope that this is the first of a series of such discoveries which will come to light in future archeological excavations.

The Reḥob Inscription: A Translation

1. Shalom! These fruits are forbidden at Beth-Shean in the Seventh Year, and in the other sabbatical cycle years they are tithed (as) *demai*: the marrows,

2. and the melons, and the cucumbers, and the parsnips, and the mint which is bound by itself, and Egyptian beans which are bound

3. in shavings, and leeks from the holiday (of Succot) until Ḥanukkah, and seeds, and dried figs, and sesame, and mustard, and rice, and cummin, and dry lupine,

4. and large peas which are sold by measure, and garlic, and village onions sold by measure, and onions,

5. and pressed dates, and wine, and oil; in the Seventh Year (they are considered) Seventh Year (produce), the other years of the sabbatical cycle (they are tithed as) *demai*, and the bread for *ḥallah* (dough-offering) is eternally (due). These are the places

6. which are permitted around Beth-Shean: on the south which is the "campus" gate till the "white field"; on the west

7. which is the gate of the (oil-) press till the end of the pavement (?); on the north which is the gate of the watchtower (or "of Sekuta") till Kefar Qarnos, and Kefar Qarnos

8. is as Beth-Shean; and on the east which is the "dung" gate till the tomb of *pnwtyyh*, and the gate of Kefar Zimrin and the gate of the uncleared field (or "*'gmh*").

9. Before the gate it is allowed and beyond it is forbidden. The forbidden towns in the territory of Sussita: Ayyanosh, and *'ynḥrh*, and *dmbr*,

10. Iyyon, and Yaarut, and Kefar Yaḥrib, and Nob, and Hasfiya (= Caspein), and Kefar Zemaḥ, and Rabbi permitted Kefar Zemaḥ. The towns which are doubtful within the territory of Naveh:

11. Ṣir, and Ṣayyer, and Gasimea, and Zeizun, and Raneb, and Ḥarbata, and *'ygr ḥwṭm*, and Charax of bar *ḥrg*. The forbidden towns in the territory of Tyre: *šṣt*,

12. Bezeth, and Pi Masoba, and Upper Hanotha and Lower Hanotha, and *bybrh*, and *r'š myyh*, and *'mwn*, and *mzh*, which is Castella, and all (the lands) which Jews have purchased,

13. is forbidden. The territory of Eretz-Israel: the place which they that returned from Babylon [held], the Ascalon junction, and the wall of Strato's Tower, Dor, and the wall of Acco,

14. and the head of the waters of Gaaton, and Gaaton proper, and Kabr[atha, and B]eth-Zenitha, and the *castrum* of Galila, and *qwb'yyh* ("peaks"?) of Aita, and *mmṣyyh* of Jorcatha,

15. and the fort of Kuryaim, and the neighborhood (or "enclosure") of Jatti[r and the brook] of *bs'l*, and Beth-Aita, and Barshata, and greater Houle, and the channel (?)

16. of Iyyon, and *mṣb spnḥh*, and Karka of Bar Sangora, and Upper Tarnegola of Caesarea (Paneas), and Beth-Sabal, and Canatha,

17. and Rekem (of) Trachonitis, Zimra of the limits of Bostra, Jabbok, and Heshbon, and the brook Zered, Igar Sahaduta, Nimrin,

18. the fort of Raziza, Rekem of Gaia, and

the garden of Ascalon, and the great road leading to the desert. These fruits

19. are forbidden in Paneas in the Seventh Year and in the other years of the sabbatical cycle they are tithed as full (?) *demai*:

20. the rice, and the nuts, and the sesame, and Egyptian beans. Some say even choice plums,

21. for these in the Seventh Year are (considered) Seventh Year (produce) and in the other years of the sabbatical cycle they are tithed as *demai*, and even

22. from Upper Tarnegola and beyond. These fruits are tithed (as) *demai* at Caesarea (Maritima): the wheat and the bread

23. for *hallah* (which is) eternally (due), and the wine, and the oil, and the dates, and the rice, and the cummin, for these are permitted in the Seventh Year at Caesarea

24. and in the other years of the sabbatical cycle they are due (as) *demai* and there are some who forbid white onions from

25. the King's Mountain. And until where is the region of Caesarea? Till Ṣoran, and the inn of Tibetah, and the column,

26. and Dor, and Kefar Saba, and if there is a place which was purchased by Jews our rabbis are suspicious of it. Shalom! The towns

27. permitted within the territory of Sebaste: *'yqbyn*, and Kefar Kasdayah and Ṣir, and *'zylyn*, and Safirin, and *'nnyn*, and Upper Jibleam, and Mezḥaru,

28. and Dothan, and Kefar *myyh*, and Silta, and Pentakomias Livias and Pardisalya, and Yazit, and *'rbnwryn*, and Kefar

29. Yehudit, and *mwnryt*, and half of Shalaf.

Jewish Inscriptions from the Village of Dabbura in the Golan

D. Urman

Following the Six-Day War, in 1967, an extensive survey was carried out in the Golan. Hitherto unknown remains from the Roman–Byzantine period, including architectural fragments bearing inscriptions, were found in the village of Dabbura. A subsequent survey revealed additional inscriptions, giving a total of one Hebrew and five Aramaic inscriptions — all of them Jewish in nature.[1]

Inscription 1. A fragment of an Aramaic inscription, carved on a basalt lintel. The fragment measures 0.36 m. long and 0.28 m. high; the letters are 8 cm. high:

... son of Yudah   [ב]ר יודה

This appears to be part of a memorial inscription, mentioning a person whose name is lost; only his father's (or grandfather's) name is preserved.

Inscription 2. A fragment of a two-line Aramaic inscription, carved on a basalt lintel. The fragment measures 0.30 m. long and 0.34 m. high; the letters are about 8 cm. high:

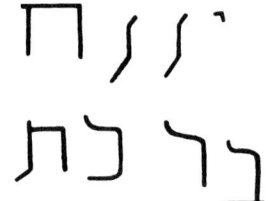

Facsimile of inscription No. 2

... Ḥinana   ח]ינה [ ]
... [may he (or "they")] be blessed. ברכת[ה]

[1] The initial survey was carried out by the Society for the Archeological Survey of Israel, and headed by S. Gutman and A. Druks. The subsequent survey was conducted on behalf of the Department of Antiquities and Museums and the Military Command of the Golan, under the direction of the author.

This commemorates the name of a person whose name has not been preserved, only that of his father (or grandfather) remaining. The name Ḥinana, though spelled with *alef* at the end instead of *he*, is known as a Galilean name. The preserved word in the second line is the ending of a common blessing in synagogue inscriptions, such as at Capernaum, Gush Ḥalav (Gischala), and other sites.

Inscription 3. A fragment of a three-line Aramaic inscription, carved on a basalt lintel. The fragment measures 0.26 m. long and 0.28 m. high; the letters are 3 cm. high:

Inscription No. 3

They made the house (synagogue?) עבדו בית [כנישתא?]
May [they?] be blessed. תהי לה[ון?] ברכתה

At the center of the lintel there had been a wreath, a trace of which remains on the right of the fragment, and the full inscription probably flanked it on either side. The missing part of the lintel certainly bore the first part of the inscription, including the names of those who "made the house." The blessing at the end, as noted for Inscription 2, is quite common in memorial inscriptions in ancient synagogues (an example, in the plural, is found among the inscriptions ascribed to the synagogue of Kefar Kana).

Inscription 4. A fragment of an Aramaic inscription, carved on a narrow strip at the top of a basalt lintel. The fragment measures 1.08 m. long and 0.60 m. high; the letters are 1.5–2 cm. high:

עבד תרעה ... made the gate.

This appears to be part of the lintel of an elaborate door or gate, bearing in relief an eagle with outstretched wings and holding a wreath in its beak; near the wingtips are two fish, with an additional fish below each wing. It may be assumed that the name of the person who "made the gate" was carved above the now-missing wing. The second Aramaic word also appears in an inscription ascribed to the synagogue at 'Abellin.

Inscription 5. Three fragments of a basalt architrave bear a carved Aramaic and Greek inscription in two lines. The total length of the fragments is 1.10 m. and the letters are about 6 cm. high:

(In Aramaic:) El'azar the son of [Ra]bbah made   אלעזר בר[ר]בה עבד
the columns above the arches   עמודיה דעל מן כפתה
and beams...   ופצ[ימיה]...
"Rusticus built (it)."   [PO]YCTIKOC EKT(ICEN)

It can be assumed that the architrave is from a synagogue. The inscription mentions the person who erected the upper columns. It would appear that this refers to the columns of a second story, thus that the gallery was supported by arches and beams. This is the first instance of such architectural terms appearing in an Aramaic inscription, and it warrants further study; the matter may be of considerable significance in understanding ancient synagogal architecture.

The Greek addition following the Aramaic inscription seems to record the name of the actual artisan who made the columns. Such Greek inscriptions alongside Aramaic donors' inscriptions are known at other sites, such as in the mosaic pavement of the synagogue at Beth Alpha.

Inscription 6. A Hebrew inscription, carved on a basalt lintel measuring 1.70 m. long and 0.42 m. high. Near either end of the lintel is an eagle in relief, each holding a snake in its beak. The two snakes curve and meet at the center of the lintel, forming a "wreath" tied with a "Hercules' knot." Within this wreath, and flanking it, appears the inscription:

This is the academy   זה בית מדרשו
of the Rabbi   שהלרבי
Eli'ezer ha-Qappar   אליעזר הקפר

It appears that the lintel was part of the main entrance to the School of Eli'ezer ha-Qappar. The lintel, its workmanship, and the incised script are reminiscent of the third century C.E. "Galilean" synagogues at Capernaum, Chorazin, and other sites. The motif of an intertwined wreath and eagles is common in synagogues, such as on the lintel of the synagogue discovered at Safed, on that at

Lintel fragment bearing inscription No. 4; above, facsimile of script

Inscription No. 5 on lintel fragments

Japhia, and on the keystone from Capernaum.

R. Eli'ezer ha-Qappar was a famous tannaitic sage who flourished toward the end of the second century and the early third century C.E. Talmudic sources often mention "Bar Qappara," also called "R. Eli'ezer the son of R. Eli'ezer ha-Qappar" (T *Beza*, I, 7; J *Beza*, I, 3, etc.). Scholars of the Talmud are divided as to whether the two figures are one and the same person, or one was the son of the other; the generally accepted opinion holds that Bar Qappara was R. Eli'ezer ha-Qappar's son. It would seem that the lintel should be ascribed to one of them.

The title "Qappar" (Hebrew) or "Qappara" (Aramaic) can be interpreted in two different ways: either that R. Eli'ezer was from Qefira, an ancient village some 4 km. northeast of Dabbura, where remains dating from the Roman–Byzantine period have been found; or that R. Eli'ezer dealt in some manner with medicaments or spices made from the caper plant (*capparis*). This plant is often mentioned in early Jewish medical literature.

The spelling of the last word within the wreath (שלהרבי) is also noteworthy. In the inscriptions of the period under discussion, especially those from the cemeteries at Jaffa and Beth-She'arim, the form שלרבי, in one word, is quite common. In our instance, it is not clear whether one or two words was intended; but in the light of the other sources, the former seems more likely.

This group of inscriptions is indicative of the existence of a large Jewish settlement at Dabbura in the Golan, including the School of R. Eli'ezer ha-Qappar and possibly also one or more synagogues (see pp. 98–115). This settlement flourished in the second-third centuries C.E., and possibly even till the mid-fourth century C.E. This raises the problem of the name of the settlement in this period. A hint might be found in *Targum Jonathan*, Deut. 4:33, mentioning Dabara as a city of the Golan.[2]

[2] I am grateful to Prof. E.E. Urbach and J. Naveh, who assisted me in reading the inscriptions. See also D. Urman, *IEJ*, 22 (1972), 16–23.

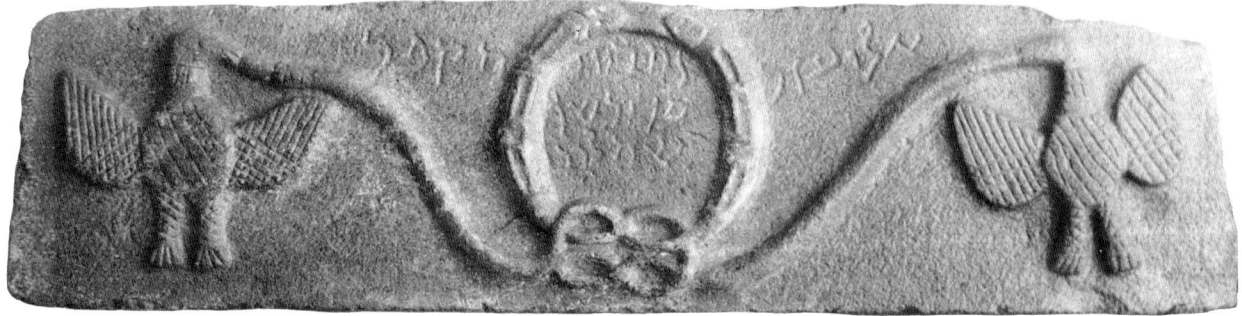

Lintel from academy of R. Eli'ezer ha-Qappar, bearing inscription No. 6

156

Fragmentary Inscriptions from an Ancient Synagogue at Tiberias

M. Ben-Dov

At the fourth convention of the Jewish Palestine Exploration Society, held in Tiberias in 1947, the late Moshe Schwabe presented several Aramaic and Greek inscriptions, including three fragmentary Aramaic inscriptions.[1] Schwabe thought that two of them were the beginning and the end of a single inscription; that is, that the three fragments represented two inscriptions. He ascribed one to a sarcophagus, the other, to a tomb-plaque. Re-examination of these fragments shows them to be three inscriptions from an ancient synagogue, entirely unrelated to any funerary purpose.

The first inscription is quite clear: שלום, "Peace." The word is followed by a single ivy leaf. The letters on the second fragment are also quite clear: הדן מש ... Schwabe restored this to read: הדן מש[כבא דפב׳׳פ, "This is the gr[ave of X son of Y]," and placed the word "Peace" of the first fragment at the end, as is

[1] M. Schwabe, "Tiberias Revealed through Inscriptions," *Kol Eretz Naphtali* (Jerusalem, 1976), pp. 180-191, Pl. 10: 1-4. The drawings in the present article were prepared by Martha Ritmayer.

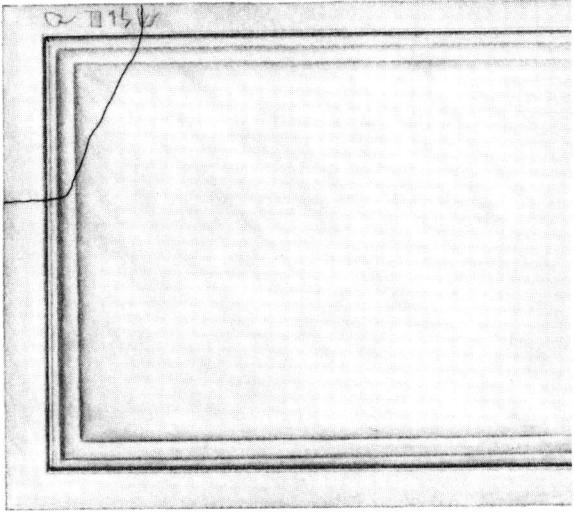

Photo (left) of marble fragment bearing first inscription, with restoration of original position in a chancel-screen

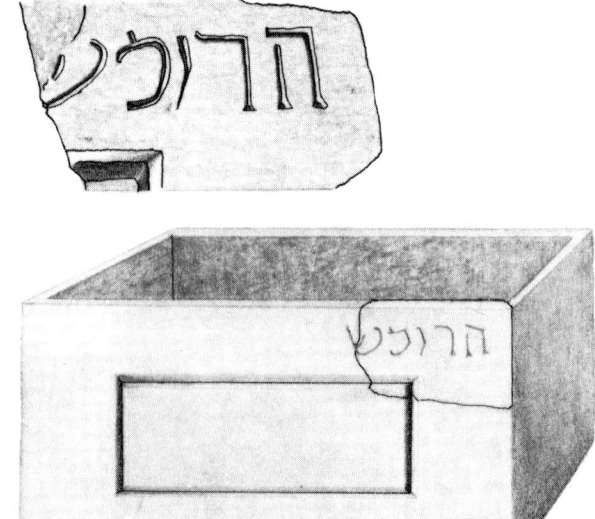

Photo (left) of stone fragment bearing second inscription, with restoration of original position in a laver basin

usual in burial inscriptions. He based this on the features supposedly held in common by the two fragments: the form and size of the letters, the working of the stone and, primarily, the fact that the back of the second stone was smoothed, as on the third. Examining the illustrations published by Schwabe, we can clearly see the differences between these two fragments, in both the profile and in the technique of dressing — not to speak of the script. Clearly, these are two independent inscriptions. One stone was finely smoothed prior to the incising of the inscription whereas on the other traces of a toothed chisel are still discernible.

The inscription of the word "Peace" is actually part of a typical chancel-screen, which explains the finish on both sides. Such chancel-screens are well known from several ancient synagogues in Israel. On one such screen at least, the word "Peace" appears at the end of the dedicatory inscription.

The second fragment can be restored to read [כילתא]הדן מש[קולית or הדן מש[כילתא], "This is the basin ...." This refers to an ornamented stone basin which stood near the entrance of the synagogue. A remnant of such a basin has been discovered in the ruins of the synagogue at Gush Ḥalav (Gischala). It can be assumed that, among the objects or architectural

elements donated to the synagogue, there were also laver basins, which were placed in a prominent position near the main entrance and which had an important function in the ritual. Thus, we seem to have here an inscription attesting the donation of a basin. The inscription may well be restored to read הדן מש[כילתא עבד פב'/פ], "This is the ba[sin which X, son of Y, made]." A Greek inscription, found at the beginning of this century at Philadelphia (Ala-Shehr) in Lydia, mentions the donation of a laver basin to a synagogue.[2] The entire inscription reads:

> To the most holy synagogue of the Hebrews, I, Eustathios the God-fearing, in memory of my brother, Hermophilos, dedicated the laver basin, together with my wife, Athnasia.

The third fragment is clearly a synagogue inscription. Our reading differs from that of Schwabe (להאי סימן בן ען[בדיה], admittedly difficult). He interpreted the word סימן as denoting a tomb, but we have no doubt that the reading here is האי סכופתה, "This is the

[2] B. Lifshitz, *Donateurs et fondateurs dans les synagogues juives* (Paris, 1967), p. 31. I am most grateful to L. Roth-Gerson, whose article in *IEJ* drew my attention to the existence of this inscription.

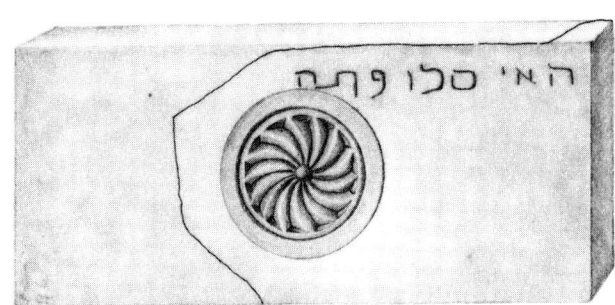

Photo (left) of stone fragment bearing third inscription, with restoration of original position in a synagogue lintel

lintel ...."[3] The stone fragment is of basalt, and at its center is a decorative motif common in ancient synagogues. Both the shape of the stone and the inscription indicate that this was a lintel which was donated to the synagogue. This unusual form of the word for "lintel" also appears in a dedicatory inscription on a basalt lintel from the synagogue at Kokhav Hayarden (see pp. 95–97). So similar is the incising that it might be suggested that the two lintels were made in the same workshop.[4]

In any event, these are fragments of inscriptions from an ancient synagogue in Tiberias. Most interesting in this context is a comment by G. Landau, former Municipal Engineer of Tiberias, made during a lecture at the same convention in 1947; within the modern city-limits, near the southern wall built by Dahr el-Amr, winter torrents would occasionally uncover "marble columns of synagogues and various other objects." If the above inscriptions were from this region, these would constitute remains of a further synagogue — the first within the town proper.

[3] I am grateful to M. Magen who drew my attention to this inscription.

[4] J. Naveh has proposed reading the two inscriptions as [הד]ה איסכופתה, with the same meaning as our reading; however, since the letters are lacking on the stone, we prefer our original reading.

A Lintel with Menorah Relief from Ḥorvat Kishor

A. Kloner

In 1958 a limestone lintel bearing a *menorah* motif in relief was discovered at Ḥorvat Kishor.[1] The site (Khirbet Umm-Kashram) is located some 9 km. north of Kibbutz Lahav and about 5 km. west of Tell Beit Mirsim (map ref. 1364 0970), in the heart of the southern Shephelah, in the hilly mass separating the coastal plain from the Hebron hills. The lintel was found in secondary use as a building stone, in the northeastern part of the ruin.

The extant length of the stone is 1.25 m. and it is 0.43 m. high. The left end is broken off, but it is clear that to the left of the *menorah* there was originally an ornamental strip identical to that on the right. The original length of the lintel thus would have been 1.42 m. The block of stone is not an exact rectangle and it is evident that it had to be cut in order to fit it into its secondary position. The *menorah* itself and the other motifs were

carved in shallow relief (3–5 mm.); only the surfaces immediately around them were sunken. The lintel and its ornamentation had been damaged by natural wear.

The *menorah* is 0.53 m. wide. The branches are perfectly semi-circular with a horizontal bar above which, in continuation of the branches, are flames or oil-lamps. The base is tripodal, with a short stem above. This precise design is well known from lintels, chancel-screens, tomb doors, capitals, mosaic pavements, and the like.

From each end of the horizontal bar of the *menorah* hangs a flower-like object. Such objects are often depicted flanking the stem of the *menorah*, but upright rather than dependent. They may be intended here to represent schematic bunches of grapes like those depicted on tomb-façade friezes, sarcophagi, synagogues, oil-lamps, and other objects of ancient Jewish art. This motif is quite common in both oriental and classical art. It could, however, also represent pendant lamps, like those depicted in the Na'aran synagogue

[1] I wish to thank D. Alon for having brought this lintel to my attention; it is now preserved at Kibbutz Mishmar Hanegev. See also A. Kloner, *IEJ*, 24 (1974), 197–200.

Lintel bearing a *menorah* relief

pavement and on the chancel-screen from the Susiya synagogue (see pp. 123–128).

Flanking the *menorah*, 18 cm. from it, are vertical strips containing a meandering vine pattern with leaves and flowers. A similar motif is found in many mosaic pavements in this region, such as at el-Maqerqesh at Beth-Guvrin and the Orpheus floor in the Musrara quarter of Jerusalem. The present relief lacks the plasticity of the mosaic depictions achieved by shading.

The strips and the *menorah* lead us to ascribe this lintel to the fifth or perhaps late fourth century C.E. The dimensions of the stone indicate that it originally came from a public building, such as a synagogue or academy.

The discovery of such a lintel is in keeping with the finds from the Jewish cemeteries north and east of Ḥorvat Kishor, and, indeed, with numerous discoveries attesting the Jewish settlement of the southern Shephelah in the days after the Bar-Kokhba Revolt (ca. 135 C.E.). The settlement at Ḥorvat Kishor, the ancient name of which is not known, was one of a chain of Jewish villages and towns extending from the Beth-Guvrin area to Ḥorvat Tillah and Ḥorvat Rimon near the modern Kibbutz Lahav.

Two Lintels with Menorah Reliefs from Chorazin

Z. Yeivin

During examination of various architectural fragments found in excavations at Chorazin in 1961–1964, our attention was drawn to four basalt fragments, for they bore traces of reliefs. A closer look showed the motif in relief to be the seven-branched *menorah*.[1]

On fragment A, parts of two branches of a *menorah* and half of a wreath are visible; on fragment B, parts of two branches, a small segment of a wreath and part of a base-line; on fragment C, the central branch and stubs

of six other branches; on fragment D, parts of two branches and a trefoil pattern, with a definite corner preserved, apparently the lower left.

The depiction on fragments A and B differs from that on fragments C and D: on the two former, the *menorah* branches are rather thick, while on the latter two they are much thinner. Thus, it would seem that we have here fragments of two separate reliefs — two lintels of entrances to a synagogue (possibly the side doors, as suggested to me by G. Foerster).

The height of the two lintels is indicated by fragments B and C; the restored length can be

[1] The excavations were conducted on behalf of the Department of Antiquities and Museums, under the direction of the author.

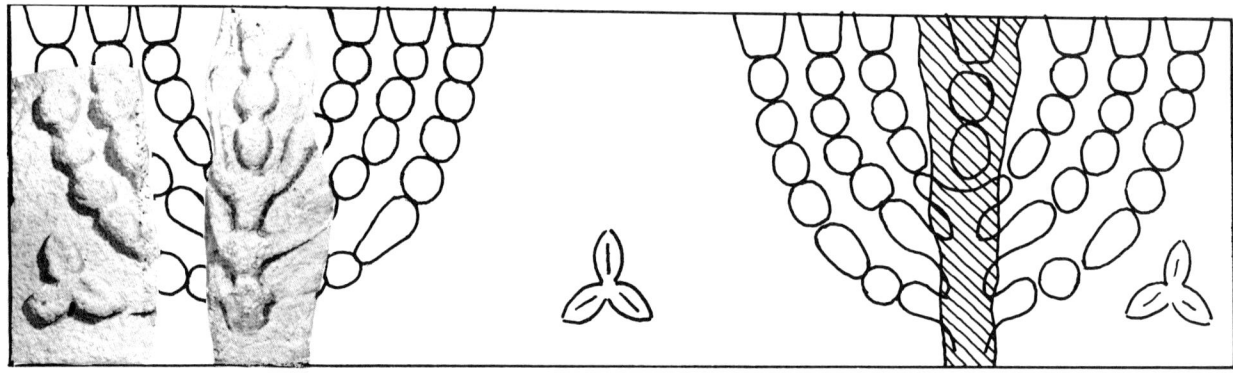

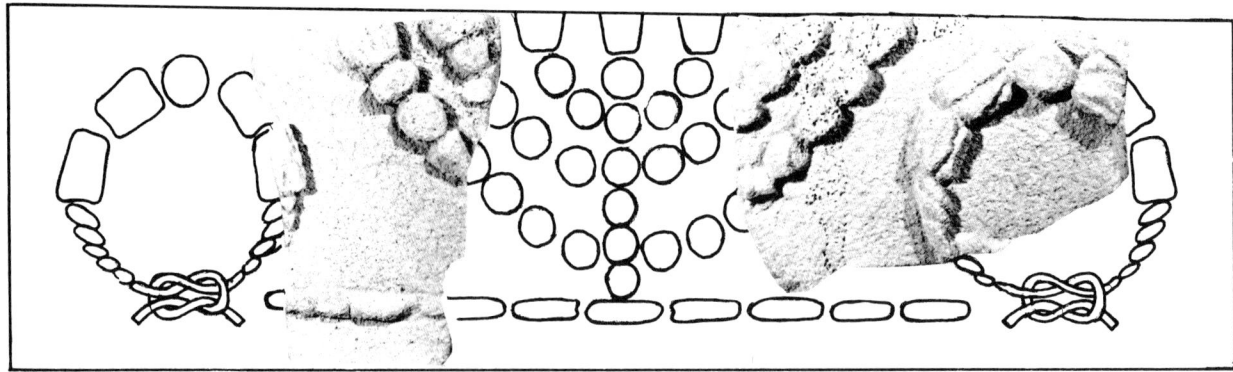

Above: restored view of lintel A-B; below: restored view of lintel C-D, with fragment E in position

based on the reconstruction of the original motifs. In this light, the two lintels were probably of identical dimensions: 0.40 × 1.40 m. If the lintels are from the synagogue already discovered at Chorazin, however, then the dimensions of the side doorways there would be decisive in determining the size.

On lintel A–B, there seems to have been a large *menorah*, without any base, at the middle. The branches are composed of crude beads. The form and workmanship of the branches recall the painted *menorah* in the Dura Europos synagogue and several *menorot* at Beth-She'arim. Flanking the *menorah* are two wreaths; these may well have terminated below in "Hercules' knots." There seem to be traces of subsidiary motifs between the *menorah* and the wreaths, and a sort of chain pattern forms a base-line parallel to the bottom of the lintel.

Of the other lintel, C–D, a third fragment appears to have been published sixty years ago[2] (see fragment E in the lower figure). At first glance, it resembles our fragment C, but a more thorough examination reveals (despite the lack of clarity in the published photograph) that the two are not strictly identical. Fragment E depicts the central branch of a *menorah*, but its lower part is defaced. Thus, it may well be part of a second *menorah* carved on lintel C–D. In contrast to the central *menorah* of lintel A–B, therefore, lintel C–D seems to have had two *menorot*. The closest parallel to this second lintel is that at Naveh, which also bears two flanking *menorot*, depicted without bases.

The trefoil in the corner of fragment D would probably have been repeated in the opposite corner as well; in this, our lintel further resembles the Naveh lintel. There may have been a third trefoil, or some other motif, between the two flanking motifs.

Thus, we may now add two more examples to the list of synagogue lintels bearing the *menorah* motif in Israel.[3]

[2] See H. Kohl and C. Watzinger, *Antike Synagogen in Galilaea* (Leipzig, 1916), p. 50.

[3] For the history of this motif, see A. Negev, *Eretz-Israel*, 8, pp. 194–210 (Hebrew, with English summary).

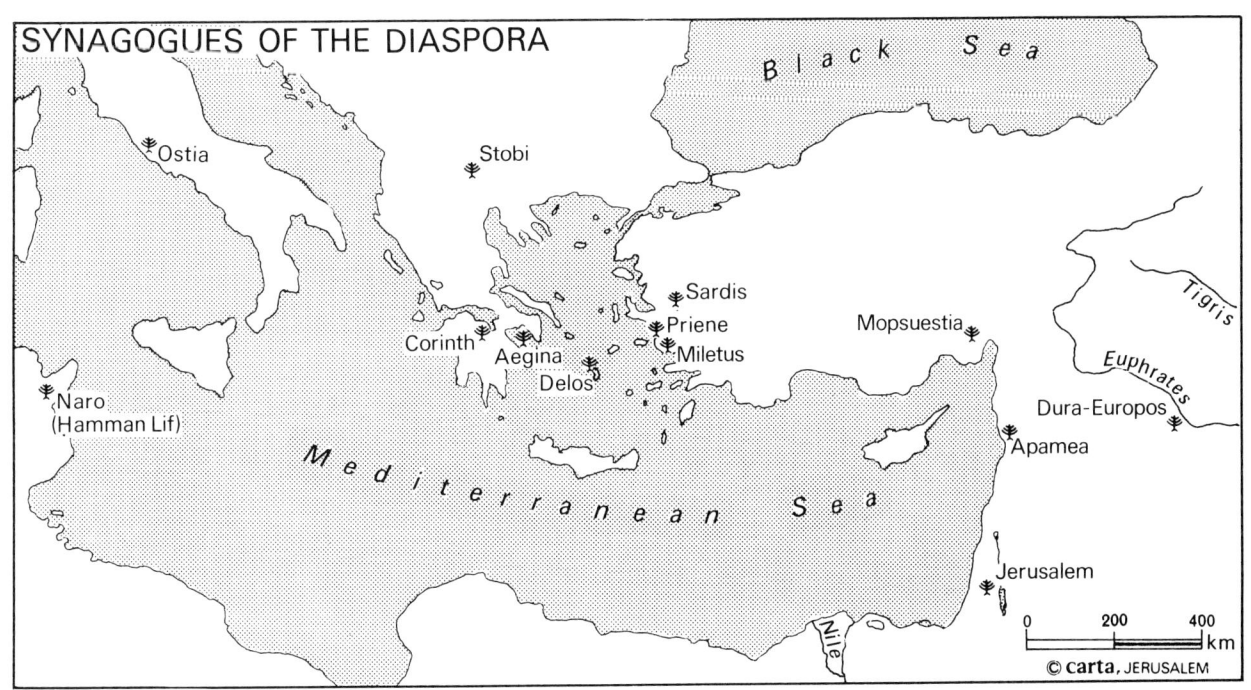

163

A Survey of Ancient Diaspora Synagogues

G. Foerster

The synagogue remains discovered to date in the Diaspora are much fewer than those found in Roman Palestine, and it is hardly possible to speak of any typological homogeneity amongst them, let alone of any clear-cut resemblance to those in Israel. This can probably be explained by their wide distribution: at Dura-Europos in Syria; Miletus, Priene and Sardis in Asia Minor;

Mosaic floor from Apamea

Corinth, Delos and Aegina in Greece; Stobi in Macedonia; Ostia in Italy; Elche in Spain; and Naro (Ḥammam Lif) in Tunisia. If several synagogues were discovered within a more limited geographical area, it would probably be found that they possess common features in plan and ornament, as is the case with the ancient synagogues of Israel. The Diaspora synagogues were part of their own artistic and architectural environments, and any attempt to compare them must take regional factors into account. Such differences, and the individual tendencies of their congregations, led to considerable variation in plan and ornamentation. All the Diaspora synagogues do, however, conform in certain broad essentials —general orientation toward Jerusalem and the use of Jewish motifs such as the *menorah*, *shofar*, incense shovel, *ethrog* and *lulab*, in mosaics and other decorations. It must be added that numerous isolated remains and objects (mainly inscriptions) from ancient synagogues have been found scattered throughout the Diaspora, but these are generally insufficient to provide a picture of a complete synagogue.

Below we shall review the remains of ancient synagogues found at some of the sites mentioned above. Separate chapters are devoted to the synagogues at Dura-Europos (pp. 171–176) and Sardis (pp. 177–183).

Apamea.[1] At Apamea on the Orontes in Syria, remains of a synagogue were found beneath those of a church by a Belgian expedition in 1934. Splendid mosaics and

[1] V. Verhoogen, *Apamée de Syrie aux Musées royaux d'Art et d'Histoire* (Bruxelles, 1964); E.L. Sukenik, "The Mosaic Inscriptions in the Synagogue at Apamea on the Orontes," *Hebrew Union College Annual*, 23 (1950–1951), 541–551.

many interesting inscriptions in Greek were found, mentioning *inter alia* the head of the Council of Elders at Antioch and his family; it is known that these very persons were buried at Beth-She'arim, for they are mentioned in inscriptions discovered in catacomb No. 12. One of the inscriptions dates the mosaic pavement at Apamea to the late fourth century C.E. The plan of the synagogue at Apamea has never been published.

Miletus.[2] At Miletus, also in Asia Minor, a modest structure came to light in the excavations of a German expedition; it was apparently built in the third or fourth century C.E. on a basilical plan. The hall measures 11.6×18.5 m., and has a peristyle forecourt with benches to the east. It has been identified as a synagogue on the basis of analogy with synagogues of Roman Palestine. It should be noted, however, that it is incompletely excavated, and no direct evidence has been found in or around the building for any specifically Jewish use.

Priene.[3] At this Hellenistic city, again in Asia Minor, extensive excavations by a German expedition at the end of the nineteenth century revealed the remains of a small synagogue which the excavators regarded as similar to a "house church." The planners of the building converted a private dwelling on the street of the west gate, sometime in the fourth or fifth century C.E. The small hall, measuring 10×14 m., had a niche in the eastern wall, toward Jerusalem, measuring 1.5×1.5 m., and apparently used for the Torah shrine. There are benches on the north wall, and there is a small forecourt to the west. The identification of this modest building is quite clear; three reliefs bearing definitely Jewish symbols were found. On all three there is a *menorah*; one bears, in addition, rolled Torah scrolls, an *ethrog* and a *lulab*; on another, the central motif is flanked by peacocks. Within the hall there is a large laver

[2] A.V. Gerkan, "Eine Synagoge in Milet," *Zeitschrift für die neutestamentliche Wissenschaft*, 20 (1921), 177–181.

[3] T. Wiegand and M. Schrader, *Priene, Ergebnisse der Ausgrabungen* (Berlin, 1904), p. 480; E.R. Goodenough, *Jewish Symbols in the Greco-Roman Period*, II (New York, 1953), p. 77.

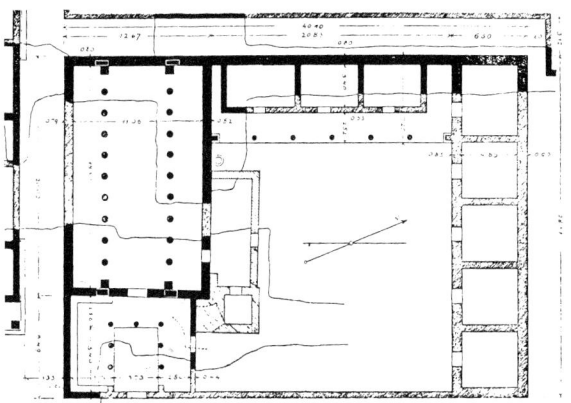

Plan of synagogue from Miletus

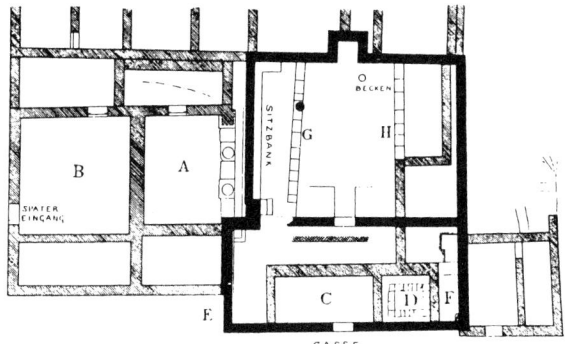

Plan of synagogue from Priene

Menorah relief from Priene

Menorah relief from Priene

basin, but its use within the hall is obscure. This building indicates the existence of a Jewish community here in the late Roman period, but there is no proof for its existence in the Hellenistic period, when the city was at its zenith.

Delos.[4] On this Aegean island, whose Jewish community is mentioned by Josephus and in inscriptions, a structure discovered at the beginning of this century has been identified as a synagogue built in the first century B.C.E. and continuing through the first and second centuries C.E. The identification, at first somewhat controversial, is now accepted by a majority of scholars.

This structure, like that at Dura-Europos and others, is part of a residential quarter, in the northeastern corner of the island, very close to the sea-shore. The main hall measures 14.4 × 16.9 m. The entrances are on the east, and on the northern part of the western wall are well-formed marble benches, at the center of which is a splendid marble "throne," recalling the "Seat of Moses" as found at Chorazin and Hammath-Tiberias (see pp. 63–69). South of the hall is a row of smaller rooms; beneath one of them is a cistern in which a group of lamps bearing particularly pagan motifs was found. In front of the entrance on the east is a covered portico. Within the hall, no focal point for the Torah shrine was found. Though the plan of the structure indicates that it was used for assembly, there is no positive evidence that it was actually a synagogue, except for several *ex voto* inscriptions, the contents and significance of which are debatable. The inscriptions contain dedications to *Theos Hypsistos*, a form of the Divine Name which is used in the Septuagint version of the Bible, but which occasionally appears in pagan contexts as well. Inscriptions of certain Jewish origin employing this term have been found on an adjacent island. In other inscriptions in this structure, there appears the Greek term *proseuche*, generally referring to a synagogue or prayer-

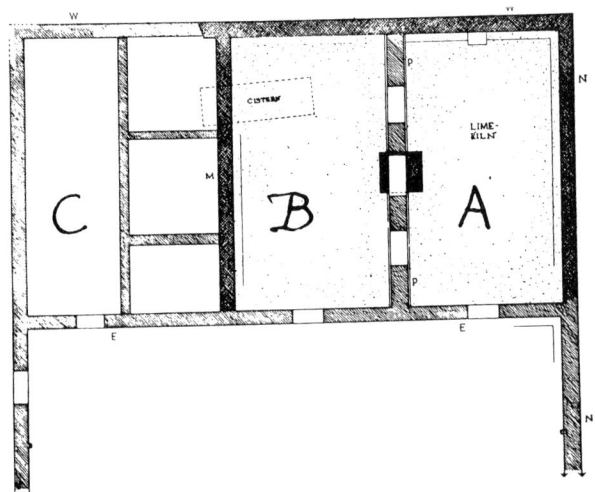

Plan of synagogue at Delos

Reconstruction of "Seat of Moses" from Delos

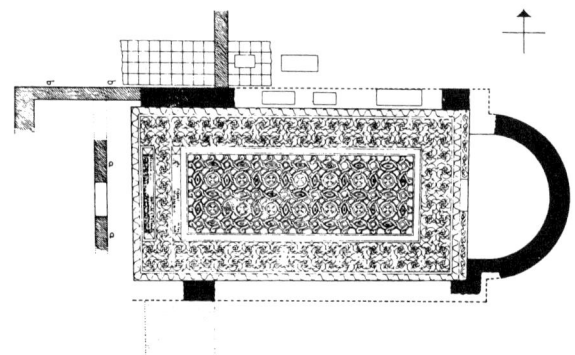

Plan of synagogue at Aegina

house in the Hellenistic period. Thus, despite the problems, this structure would appear to be the earliest synagogue yet discovered, dating from the first century B.C.E.

Aegina. The ruins of a synagogue on the island of Aegina were first noted by a German scholar in 1829; the building was studied again in 1901 and 1904, and in 1928 by E.L.

[4] P. Bruneau, *Recherches sur les cultes de Délos à l'époque hellénistique et à l'époque impériale* (Paris, 1970), pp. 480–493.

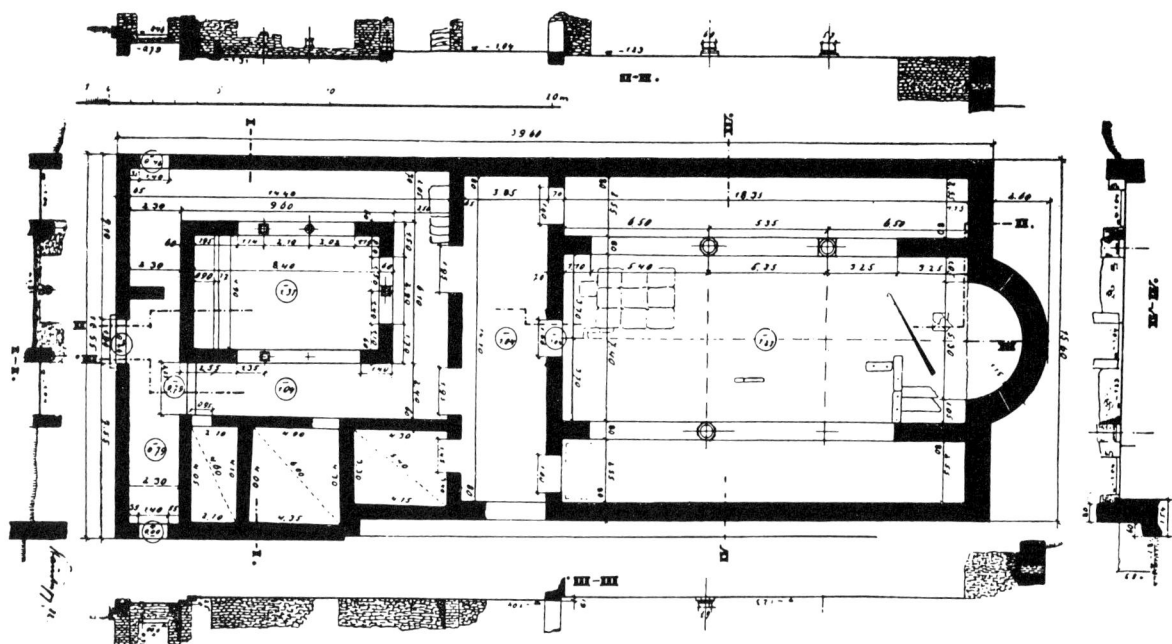

Plan of synagogue at Stobi

Sukenik. It was thoroughly excavated by a German expedition in 1932, and the Greek Department of Antiquities has recently completed the work. The hall of the building, located not far from the harbor, measures 7.6 × 13 m., with an apse (?) on the eastern wall. There was apparently a portico before the hall. The mosaic pavement of the hall is in blue, grey, red, and black, and includes two inscriptions, within *tabulae ansatae*, both referring to donors. Remains of an earlier structure were noted beneath the building, which seems to have been in use till the seventh century C.E.

Stobi.[5] At Stobi in Macedonia (Yugoslavia), a long inscription in Greek was found some forty years ago. This inscription, ascribed to the third century C.E., is dedicated to a donor, Claudius Tiberius Polycharmos, who is described as "the Father of the Synagogue at Stobi," and who donated a considerable sum of money for the repair and expansion of the building. He may have donated his own house for use as the synagogue structure. In

excavations on the site in recent years, inscribed fragments of stucco were found, also mentioning Polycharmos and his donation. The large inscription, of 32 lines, is incised on a column in the forecourt of a basilical structure of the fifth century C.E., discovered in 1931. This building was therefore identified as the synagogue, but the identification, accepted in the scientific literature, has been demonstrated as incorrect in the light of more recent work on the site. It appears that the column is in secondary use in the basilica, which was actually a church built over two earlier buildings, probably synagogues. The church is of the late fourth–fifth centuries C.E., while the earlier synagogue, of Polycharmos, is of the third century C.E. and the later one, of the fourth century C.E. The plan of the earlier structures is still not clear and thus it is impossible to identify those parts which are mentioned in the inscription (such as the *hagios topos*, *triklinion*, and *tetrastoön*). The later synagogue, directly beneath the entrance to the basilica, has a mosaic pavement of geometric patterns; the main hall measures 7.9 × 13.3 m. and is oriented to the east; a small platform, possibly a base for a Torah shrine, was found abutting the wall closest to

[5] J. Wiseman and D. Mano-Zissi, "Excavations at Stobi," *American Journal of Archeology*, 75 (1971), 395–411; 76 (1972), 407–424; 77 (1973), 391–403; *Journal of Field Archaeology*, 1 (1974), 117–148.

....
...../ΤΙΒΕΡΙΟΕΠΟΛΥ
ΧΑΡΜΟΕΟΚΑΙΑΧΥΡΙ
ΟΕΟΠΑΤΗΡΤΗΕΕΝ
ΕΤΟΒΟΙΕΕΥΝΑΓΩΓΗΕ
ΟΕΠΟΛΕΙΤΕΥΕΑΜΕ
ΝΟΕΠΑΕΑΝΠΟΛΕΙΤΕΙ
ΑΝΚΑΤΑΤΟΝΙΟΥΔΑΙ
ΕΜΟΝΕΥΧΗΕΕΝΕΚΕΝ
ΤΟΥΕΜΕΝ ΟΙΚΟΥΕΤΩ
ΑΓΙΩΤΟ ΠΩΚΑΙΤΟ
ΤΡΙΚΛΕΙΝΟΝΕΥΝΤΩ
ΤΕΤΡΑΕΤΟ Ω ΕΚΤΩΝ
ΟΙΚΕΙΩΝΧΡΗΜΑΤΩΝ
ΜΗΔΕΝΟΛΩΕΠΑΡΑΨΑ
ΜΕΝΟΕ ΤΩΝΑΓΙΩΤΗΝ
ΔΕΕΞΟΥΕΙΑΝΤΩΝΥΠΕ
ΡΩΩΝΠΑΝΤΩΝΠΑΕΑΝ
ΚΑΙΤΗΝΛΕΕΠΟΤΕΙΑΝ
ΕΧΕΙΝΕΜΕΤΟΝΚΛΤΙΒΕΡΙ
ΟΠΟΛΥΧΑΡΜΟΝΚΑΙΤΟΥΕ
ΚΑΙΤΟΥΕΚΛΗΡΟΝΟΜΟΥΕ
ΤΟΥΕΜΟΥΕΔΙΑΠΑΝΤΟΕ
ΒΙΟΥΟΕΑΝΔΕΒΟΥΛΗΘΗ
ΤΙΚΑΙΝΟΤΟΜΕΑΙΠΑΡΑΤΑΥ
ΓΕΜΟΥΔΟΧΘΕΝΤΑΔΩΕΕΙΤΩ
ΠΑΤΡΙΑΡΧΗΔΗΝΑΡΙΩΝΝΥΡΙΑ
ΔΑΕΕΙΚΟΕΙΓΕΝΕ ΟΥΤΩΓΑΡ
ΜΟΙΕΥΝΕΔΟΞΕΝΤΗΝΔΕΕΠΙ
ΕΚΕΥΗΝΤΗΕΚΕΡΑΜΟΥΤΩΝ
ΥΠΕΡΩΩΝΠΟΙΕΙΕΘΛΙΕΜΕ
ΚΑΙΚΛΗΡΟΝΟΜΟΥΕ
ΕΜΟΥΕ

Greek inscription on column from Stobi synagogue

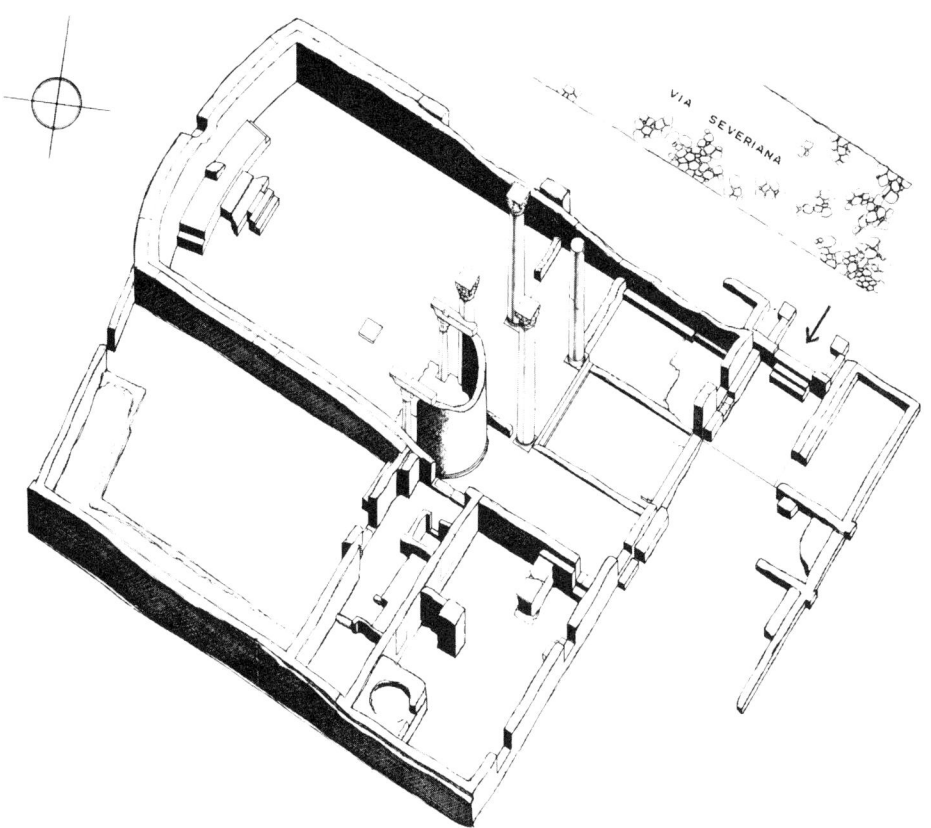

Isometric reconstruction of Ostia synagogue

View of *aedicula* and *propylaeum*, looking eastward — Ostia synagogue

Menorah, lulab, ethrog and *shofar* on *aedicula* at Ostia

Jerusalem, at the eastern end of the hall. As in many other synagogues, a bench runs along the southern wall. In a room adjacent to the synagogue on the south, a *menorah* was scratched on a plastered wall — an indication of the identification of this building.

Ostia.[6] Among the most important synagogue discoveries outside Roman Palestine is the synagogue brought to light at Ostia, the port of Rome; it was uncovered and restored in 1961–1962. This structure was revealed accidentally during preparations for a highway to the international airport on the coast, near the town. The synagogue was founded in the first century C.E., though the principal remains are of the fourth century C.E.

The fourth-century synagogue comprises a complex of rooms measuring 23.5×36.6 m. The main hall, measuring 12.5×24.9 m., is divided into three sections. It has three entrances, the middle one of which leads to the forepart, slightly lower than the rest of the hall, and paved in mosaics. From there, stairs lead to a *propylaeum* comprising four columns, forming the main entrance to the prayer hall, paved in *opus sectile*. This inner part is enclosed by walls which pass between the *propylaeum* and the walls of the hall. In the

[6] M.F. Squarciapino, "The Synagogue at Ostia," *Archeology*, 16 (1963), 194-203.

northeastern wall there is an opening, closed by metal bars. The southwestern wall was removed when a large *aedicula* was installed in the final phase of the building; in the initial phases there were two entrances beside the *propylaeum*. This *aedicula* entirely blocked the southern access to the interior of the hall. On the façade of the *aedicula*, which most probably served as the site of the Torah shrine, two columns bore architraves jutting out of the wall, ending in corbels and ornamented in relief with the *menorah* motif flanked by a *shofar*, *ethrog* and *lulab* — decidedly Jewish symbols. The location of this *aedicula* recalls that of the two *aediculae* flanking the entrances to the synagogue at Sardis (see pp. 177–183), which apparently held Torah shrines. There seem to have been *aediculae* on the front wall of the hall in the synagogues at Capernaum and Chorazin as well.

Adjacent to the curved back wall of the prayer hall was a raised *bema*. South of the prayer hall, abutting it, was a further space divided into two rooms — one apparently a kitchen with an oven and storage vessels *in situ*, and the other, larger, with benches along the southern and western walls. These rooms were undoubtedly related to the synagogue, for their northern doorways led toward the prayer hall, and it is assumed that they formed part of a hostel. On the east of the complex were remains of what can be regarded as a sort of narthex or vestibule.

In an inscription from the Ostia synagogue mention is made of a donor, one Mindis Faustus, who donated the Torah shrine (*kibotos*; see also pp. 185–189); this inscription is from the second–third centuries C.E. and, of course, cannot refer to the *aedicula*, which was built later. The inscription is contemporary with the Dura-Europos synagogue, in which a fixed place for the Torah shrine was found.

Beneath the fourth-century building are the remains of synagogue structures from the first century C.E. on; their plan is still unclear, though the excavators believe it somewhat resembles that of the fourth-century building.

Naro.[7] At Naro (Ḥammam Lif) in Tunisia, remains of a sixth-century C.E. structure were uncovered at the end of the nineteenth century, but the chance nature of the find, by a resident French army officer, precluded the preparation of a proper plan. The mosaics were removed and sold, part eventually reaching the Brooklyn Museum in New York. The fate of the other remains is unknown. The mosaic pavement depicted floral medallions containing animal and other motifs. One of the dedicatory inscriptions, in Latin, mentions the *sancta sinagoga*.

Above we have reviewed the remains of several ancient synagogues in the Diaspora, from the Hellenistic to the Byzantine periods. These structures represent only a small percentage of the synagogues which we can assume existed in the numerous Jewish communities of the Diaspora in antiquity. Epigraphic sources, for instance, reveal that there were about a dozen synagogues in ancient Rome. Various archeological remains containing Jewish symbols such as the

menorah, together with epigraphic and literary evidence, indicate the existence of some 140 synagogues in the Diaspora, and this figure probably represents only a fraction of the actual total.

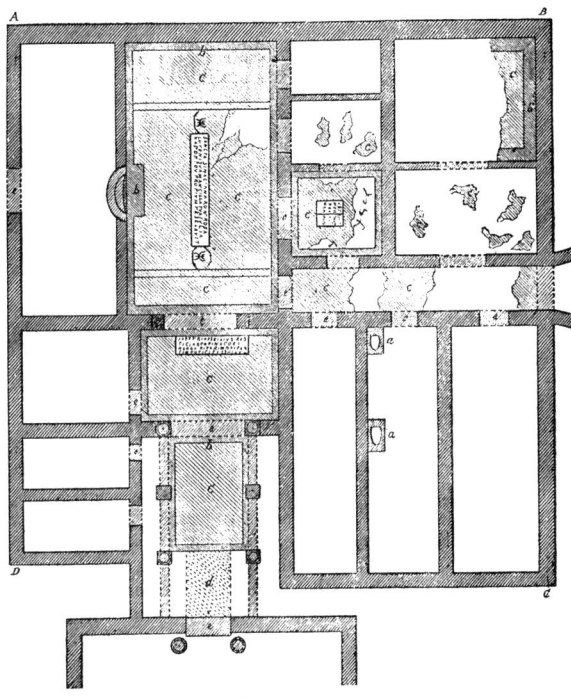

[7] Goodenough, *Jewish Symbols*, II, pp. 89–100.

Plan of Naro synagogue

Mosaic floor of Naro synagogue

The Synagogue of Dura-Europos

Lee I. Levine

Among ancient synagogues, the most sensational find, and the richest in its implications and ramifications, is that of Dura-Europos. Externally the Dura synagogue was modest in the extreme. It was located in a residential area and was originally a private house. In this regard there is no comparison with the architectural impressiveness of the Sardis structure (see pp. 177–183). The uniqueness of Dura, however, lay in its interior. The elaborateness of its wall decorations is otherwise unknown in ancient synagogue art.

Located on the Euphrates River in what is today Syria, Dura-Europos was founded by Seleucus I ca. 300 B.C.E. Built as a typical Greek town in a grid-pattern with walled defenses, a central agora, and temples dedicated to the traditional Greek deities, the city was one of the many foundations established by the Hellenistic monarch throughout his realm. Dura remained a Seleucid outpost until the mid–second century B.C.E., when it was captured by the Parthians; for the next three centuries the city flourished as a center for east–west trade. In the second century C.E., with tensions between Parthia and Rome at a peak, the city was captured by the Romans and remained under their control for almost a century. Dura was destroyed by the Persians in 256 or soon after, and was never resettled.

Nothing is known about the Jewish community of Dura from literary sources. The synagogue remains constitute our single source of information. The fact that the building was so well preserved is indeed fortuitous. It was located in the western extremity of the town on a street running parallel to the city wall. The Persian attack on Dura in 256 C.E. came from the west; from the other three directions the city was impregnable. In anticipation of this assault, the Romans reinforced the wall defenses with a ramp, which at its full extent encompassed a large part of the synagogue building. When the city eventually fell, those parts of the synagogue which had been covered over were relatively unaffected by the ravages of war.

Although it is unknown exactly when the synagogue was founded, it is clear that the building, in its communal phase (in contrast to

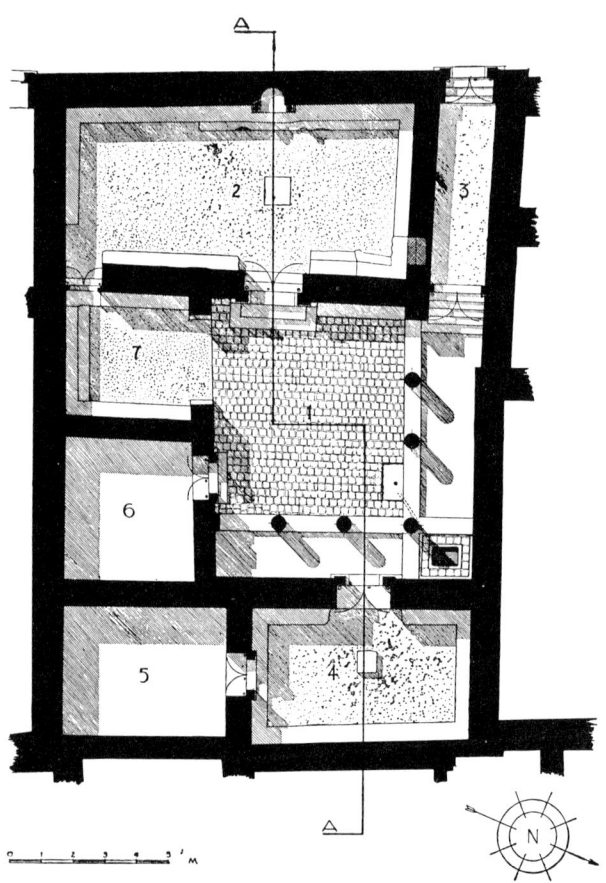

Plan of Dura synagogue: Phase I

its earlier usage as a private home), passed through two distinct stages. The later stage, to which practically all the extant remains belong, can be dated with precision. Several inscriptions tell of the dedication of the building in the year 556 of the Seleucid era and the second year of the emperor Philip (244/5 C.E.). The building thus existed for a decade before it was covered over in anticipation of the Persian assault. There are no indications, however, of the date of the earlier, more modest, synagogue building. If, indeed, the Jewish presence in the city was linked to the Roman garrison, with Jews serving as merchants and traders, it would date the community to the late second century C.E. The synagogue, in its first stage, was probably built about this time.

The earlier synagogue consisted of a series of rooms grouped around a central courtyard, 6.55 m. × 6.05 m. Entered from the northwest via a passageway (No. 3), the peristyle court (1) was paved with tiles. The rooms to the east and southeast (Nos. 4–6) apparently played no role in the synagogue ritual and were probably intended as a residence for the synagogue custodian, a hostel for wayfarers, or both. On the other hand, Room 2 to the west clearly served as the sanctuary proper. Although somewhat irregular, it was generally rectangular in shape, ranging in size from 10.65–10.85 m. to 4.60–5.30 m. There were two entrances, one near the center of the eastern wall, a second at the very southern extremity of that same wall. Benches were located on all four sides of the room, and in a few places there was an additional low pedestal, which might have served as a footrest, thereby compensating for the greater height of the benches in those places. In the middle of the room was a patch of white plaster probably concealing the foundation of some projecting object, subsequently removed. The focal point of the room was an *aedicula* used as a Torah shrine, located in the western wall opposite the main entrance. Between the courtyard and the side entrance of the sanctuary was Room 7, whose precise function remains elusive. It appears to have

served as more than a passageway to the main hall. Benches were built along three of its walls. If, indeed, there existed special quarters for women in ancient synagogues, an assumption which has recently been called into question, then this room would be a logical candidate. However, it may have been used for other purposes, religious, educational, or social.

The later synagogue building was larger and more ornate, indicating the increased prosperity of the Jewish community. In a number of features, this later building followed the pattern of the earlier structure: a "broadhouse" type building with worship oriented towards the long wall to the west, a courtyard adjacent and leading to the main sanctuary on an east–west axis, two entrances to the main hall from the east, an *aedicula* in the western wall of the sanctuary. At the same time, significant changes were also in evidence. The entrance to the entire complex was now re-located to the east, and the sanctuary proper and adjacent courtyard

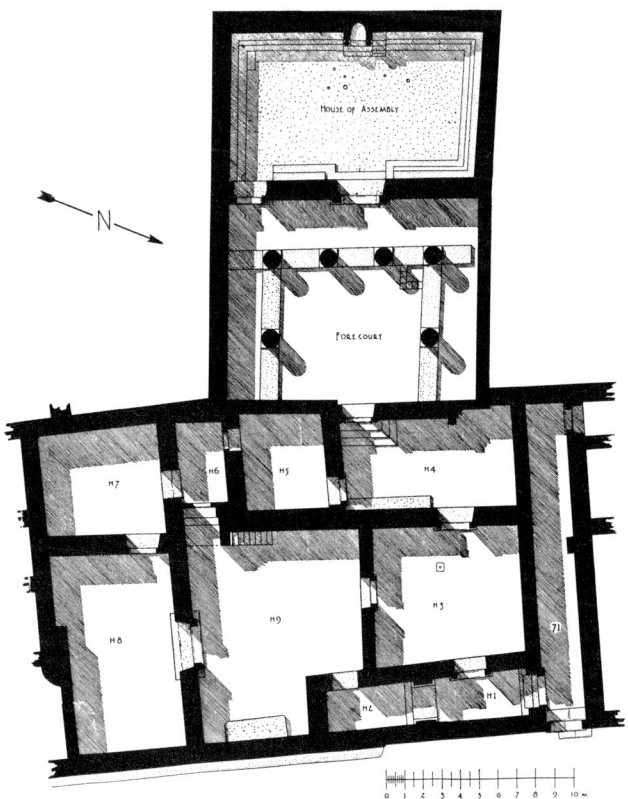

Plan of Dura synagogue: Phase II

173

were expanded to include the entire width of the former building. The assembly room was once again surrounded with benches; this time, however, seating capacity reached about 120 as against 40 of the earlier stage. Next to the *aedicula* was the elder's seat, clearly a place of honor and dignity within the room. Room 7 of the earlier phase was absorbed by the enlarged courtyard, and the problem of locating a women's section in this second stage becomes even greater. No special area seems to have been set aside for this purpose. If such an area existed at this time, it must have been as part of the main hall, which would have been partitioned off.

The major structural change of the synagogue complex involved an expansion to the east and inclusion of House H, 26 m. × 18 m., as part of the building. From an alleyway running down the street to the east, one entered a series of rooms which appear to have been divided into two separate suites. The first gave entry to the synagogue forecourt, through Rooms H 1, H 3 (a courtyard), and H 4. H 5 was a side room obviously associated with this suite. In addition, there was an inner suite to the south, consisting of five rooms with its own large courtyard, H 9. This area, more isolated from the regular flow of traffic to the courtyard and sanctuary, probably served as the residence for a synagogue official as well as a hostel for wayfarers.

The pièce de résistance of the Dura synagogue, however, is not the building itself, but its art. Literary sources as well as inscriptions mention the fact that synagogues were sometimes decorated with paintings; however, archeological excavations had previously uncovered only fragments. Now, suddenly, in this remote provincial town, a synagogue was discovered whose main hall was decorated on its ceiling and over all four of its walls. These walls were divided into five registers. The highest is missing; the lowest consisted of a continuous dado with panels depicting animal and human forms, masks, and imitation of marble incrustations. The three main registers in between contained a rich variety of scenes drawn from the biblical narrative (see below).

The only exception to the narrative character of the paintings was in the area above the Torah shrine, where representations were more symbolic in character. A façade stands in the middle of the face of the shrine's arch, probably intended to represent the Jerusalem Temple. To its right is a depiction of the sacrifice of Isaac; to the left, a large *menorah* with a *lulab* and *ethrog*. Above this area is a large section which is difficult to identify, simply because it had been so reworked in the short span of Phase II. At first, the decoration appears to have consisted of a large tree (the Tree of Life or a tree symbolic of the Torah), with two strange objects on either side: a table with a cushion (?) on top and a round object beneath, and some sort of stand featuring two lions standing on their hind legs. At a later point this area was divided in half. The lower portion bore a plethora of scenes: Jacob blessing the two sons of Joseph, Ephraim and Menasseh (lower right), Jacob blessing his twelve sons (lower left), and David depicted as Orpheus playing the harp to a spell-bound audience of animals with a lion in the center. The upper portion featured a seated monarch attended by his court. Various identifications have been suggested: Jacob and his brothers, the blessing of Moses, David, or the Messiah surrounded by the whole House of Israel. This central panel is flanked by four large figures:

Upper right:	Moses and the burning bush
Upper left:	Moses at Sinai or Joshua meeting an angel near Jericho
Lower right:	Moses or Ezra reading from the scroll
Lower left:	Joshua at Gibeon or Abraham receiving God's blessing

These scenes above the ark were clearly pregnant with meaning for the worshippers in the synagogue. The historical and symbolic associations were many. All persons and objects depicted are central to Jewish religious consciousness. The four wing panels serve to heighten the importance of this whole area, as does the fact that the scenes appearing on the

View of interior of synagogue, looking westward

Drawing of western wall above *aedicula*

various registers seem to lead into this central area.

Regarding these registers themselves, there is a general consensus regarding the identification of most panels. This is so despite the fact that some scenes were totally destroyed when the Roman ramp was made in 256 C.E. (particularly on the east side), while others are problematic owing to their poor state of preservation:

West wall:
  *Register A —
    North — Exodus
    South — Solomon and the Queen of Sheba
      Extreme left-hand panel is unidentifiable
    Register B —
    North — The return of the ark from the land of
      the Philistines
      Jerusalem and the Temple of Solomon
    South — Dedication of the Tabernacle with Aaron
      and his sons
      Israelite desert camp and the miracle of
      the well
    Register C —
    North — Pharoah and the infancy of Moses
      Samuel anointing David
    South — Mordecai and Esther
      Elijah resuscitates the widow's child
South wall:
  Register A — Obliterated
  Register B — Consecration of the Tabernacle
    Left-hand side obliterated
  Register C — The prophets of Baal on Mt.
    Carmel

* Moving from right to left.

Elijah and the widow of Sarepta
    Extreme left-hand panel unidentifiable
North wall:
  Register A — Right-hand side obliterated
    Jacob at Bethel
  Register B — Ḥannah and Samuel at Shiloh (par-
    tially destroyed)
    The battle at Evenezer
  Register C — Death of an important personnage
    at the altar (identification problematic)
    Ezekiel's vision of the dry bones
East wall:
  Registers A and B — Obliterated
  Register C —
    North — David and Saul in wilderness of Zin
    South — Belshazzar's feast (?)

Most of the copious scholarly literature on this synagogue has been devoted to the meaning of these scenes. All agree that they represent, in one form or another, high points in biblical history, when the hand of God was evident in guiding the destiny of the Jewish people. Nevertheless, the question arises as to the basis of the selection of these particular events, and the extent to which there is a central idea pervading all the scenes. Were these scenes selected at random, or is there a fundamental organizing principle underlying the choice?

Scholarly opinion is divided on this question. Rostovtzeff, Sukenik, and Kraeling assume that there was no overriding theme or comprehensive program dictating the selection other than a desire to memorialize important events, a kind of artistic *heilsgeschichte* paralleled in numerous literary passages, which likewise recounted these and other events.[1] Other scholars have suggested a variety of patterns. Several have seen each register as focusing on a different, though related, theme. Thus, du Mesnil de Buisson considers the subject-matter of one register to be historical, another liturgical, a third moralizing.[2] Sonne interprets the three regis-

[1] M. Rostovtzeff, *Dura Europos and its Art* (Oxford, 1938), pp. 100–134; E. Sukenik, *The Synagogue of Dura-Europos & its Frescoes* (Jerusalem, 1947), pp. 164–170 (Hebrew); C. Kraeling, *The Excavations at Dura Europos, Vol. VIII — The Synagogue* (New Haven, 1956), pp. 346 ff.

[2] Du Mesnil de Buisson, *Les peintures de la synagogue de Doura-Europas, 245–256 après J.-C.* (Paris, 1939), pp. 13–17.

ters as reflecting the rabbinic dictum regarding the three crowns: Torah, priesthood, and royalty.[3] Others suggest one particular theme which is reflected in all the panels, Wischnitzer — a messianic one,[4] Goodenough — a mystical one.[5]

Whatever the outcome of this debate, it is clear that the Dura synagogue has made a greater claim on scholarly attention than any other single Jewish archeological find. And rightly so. The Dura synagogue has opened up whole new vistas in our understanding of Jewish religious thought and artistic taste, and of the synagogue as a central communal institution. Scholars had speculated for decades about the existence of a developed Jewish artistic tradition in antiquity. Dura proved it. Much remains to be done in analyzing this art as regards its iconography, sources, and subsequent influence. Such research will undoubtedly enrich our understanding of this synagogue, Jewish art, and Roman provincial art generally. Finally, as the oldest datable synagogue of the post-70 C.E. period, Dura has provided much evidence regarding early synagogue architecture, and a clear picture of the evolution of an early synagogue building from domestic architecture.

C. Kraeling concluded his masterful and authoritative study of the Dura Synagogue with a summary worth our quoting here: "The Dura Synagogue is in a very real sense a chance discovery, an incident and an accident that could not be predicted and cannot be expected to occur soon again. But this by no means belittles its importance. The Synagogue brings to vivid expression the vigor and the piety, the high aspiration and the dignity of a relatively small and unimportant Jewish community of the eastern Dispersion in a frontier garrison city. At the same time, through this one structure we can look out into a vast panorama of historical development and relationships, finding new insights suggested everywhere. Here we find new suggestions for an understanding of the growth and development of synagogue architecture. Here the history of Jewish piety and of the development of its interpretative tradition is freshly illumined. Here the ancient Jewish use of art is restored to its rightful place in the total picture of ancient Judaism. Here we see in a new light the common front which Christianity and Judaism held against paganism, and the relationship between Jewish and Christian art. These are the things that give the Dura Synagogue its scientific importance."[6]

[3] I. Sonne, "The Paintings of the Dura Synagogue," *Hebrew Union College Annual*, 20 (1947), 255-362.

[4] R. Wischnitzer, *The Messianic Theme in the Paintings of the Dura Synagogue* (Chicago, 1948).

[5] E. Goodenough, *Jewish Symbols in the Greco–Roman Period* (13 vols; Princeton, 1952–68), Vols. 9–11, and especially Vol. 10, pp. 197-210.

[6] Kraeling, above, n. 1, pp. 401–402.

The Synagogue at Sardis

A. Seager

The city of Sardis, in western Turkey, 90 km. from the Aegean coast, was famed as the capital of ancient Lydia. It later became capital of an Achaemenid satrapy and remained an important center through the Hellenistic, Roman, and early Byzantine periods until its destruction in 616 C.E. by the Sassanid king Chosroes II. With a population estimated at 100,000 under Roman rule, it is perhaps the largest ancient city in which substantial synagogue remains are preserved.

The existence of a Jewish community at Sardis is recorded in ancient literature. If Sardis, called *Sfard* in Lydian and Persian, is indeed the *Sepharad* of Obadiah 1:20 as some scholars believe, then its Jewish community already existed during the Achaemenid empire. Josephus cites Roman decrees which safeguarded certain rights of the Sardis Jews. One decree notes that they had a place of assembly "from the beginning" and "in accordance with their ancestral laws."

View from the acropolis of the Roman bath-gymnasium complex, including the synagogue

Evidence of a later Jewish settlement at Sardis comes chiefly from the synagogue discovered in 1962 during excavations conducted by Harvard and Cornell Universities. It is the best preserved and by now the most thoroughly explored ancient synagogue of Asia Minor. It is the largest early synagogue extant and — important for the history of Diaspora Judaism — shows a Jewish community flourishing in a major Roman city during the talmudic period.

The synagogue has an unusual and unexpected setting. It is an integral and prominent part of a monumental public building complex, a Roman bath-gymnasium. The synagogue is flanked by the *palaestra* of the gymnasium and a row of shops lining a colonnaded, marble-paved avenue. This was a principal thoroughfare of the city, and perhaps the successor to the Persian Royal Road. The synagogue and other portions of the complex have been partly restored.

The entire complex was built on an artificial terrace as an urban renewal project following a devastating earthquake which struck Sardis in 17 C.E. It was much remodeled in its long history. Excavation below the floor of the synagogue showed several construction stages within the same building boundaries and with the floors at nearly the same level.[1] As originally planned, the synagogue site was to have been developed as a functional part of

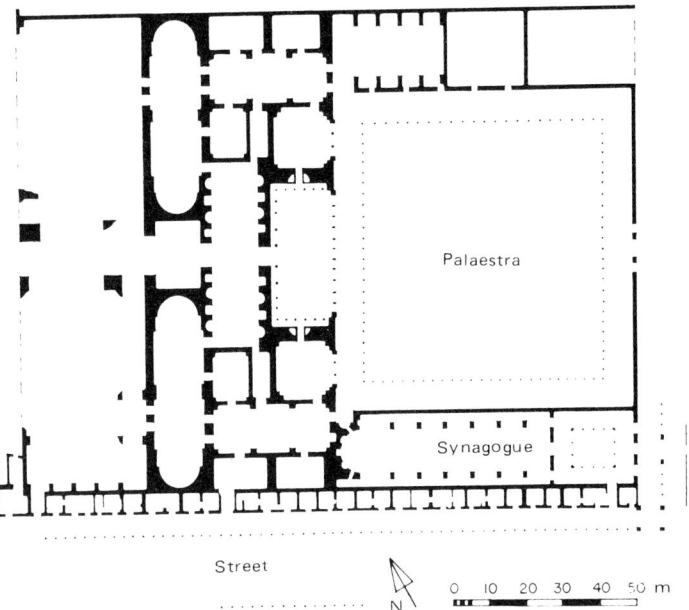

Plan of the Roman bath-gymnasium complex, including the synagogue

the pagan gymnasium. The plan of a later stage suggests that the building was used for a while as a civic basilica. Eventually, that part of the complex was turned over to the Jewish community for use as a synagogue. It was rebuilt and redecorated under Jewish auspices, accommodating the new use to a structure built originally for a different purpose, on a scale comparable to the original construction.

In its final form, ignoring for the moment some minor later partitioning, the synagogue consists of two principal rooms: a peristyle forecourt with a central fountain in the form

---

[1] See Andrew R. Seager, "The Building History of the Sardis Synagogue," *American Journal of Archeology*, 76 (1972), 425–435.

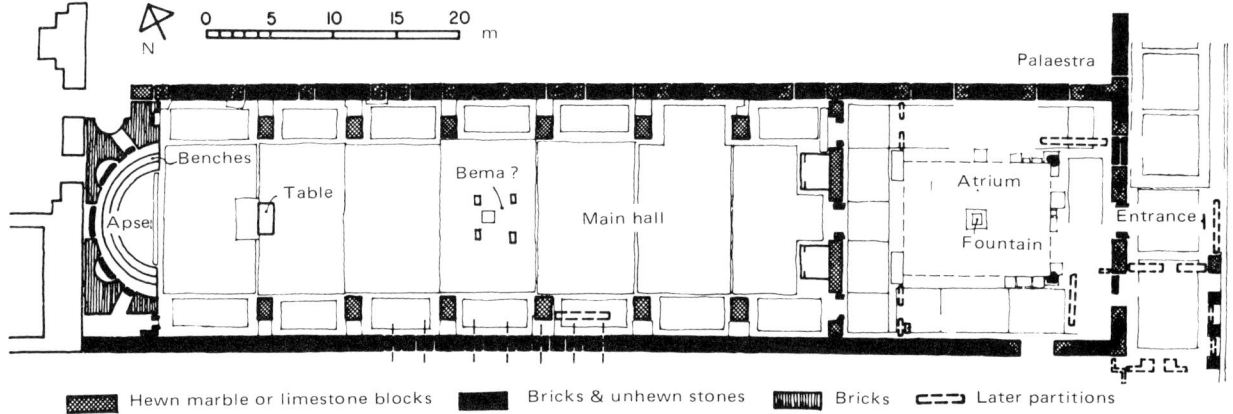

Plan of the synagogue

of a marble krater, and an assembly hall 54 m. long and 18 m. wide containing two rows of large piers and an apse at its western end. The axis of the rooms, emphasized by the symmetrical arrangement of furnishings, is roughly, but not exactly, east–west. The piers of the main hall originally rose to a considerable height. The roof probably was of wood trusses. Unlike many synagogues, there are no benches along the side walls of the hall nor in the court. The floors are paved with mosaics, except for the area around the forecourt fountain. Most of the mosaics are of elaborate geometric patterns. One panel, prominently placed in the hemicycle of the apse, is a finely-crafted figurative design showing twining vines growing from a golden urn filled with water, with a dedicatory inscription within a colorful wreath. Two peacocks flanking the urn were destroyed in antiquity. The lower portions of the walls were covered with marble decoration; small pieces of colored marble formed inlay panels of geo-metric, floral, and animal designs (including pomegranates, fish, and birds) which were set in an architectonic frame. According to an inscription found in the main hall, there were paintings higher up on the walls or on the ceiling, and fragments of brightly colored glass mosaic from the upper portions of the walls or piers were found among the collapsed masonry. As part of the restoration program, the floor mosaics were lifted from the disintegrating bedding and then relaid, and samples of the marble wall decoration were reconstructed.

We know from coins found beneath the floor that most of the mosaics were installed in the second half of the fourth century C.E., and so the building must have reached substantially its final form by that time. It was probably used as a synagogue even earlier, but most of our detailed knowledge concerns the building after the fourth century remodeling. Further modifications and alterations were made periodically, continuing until the build-

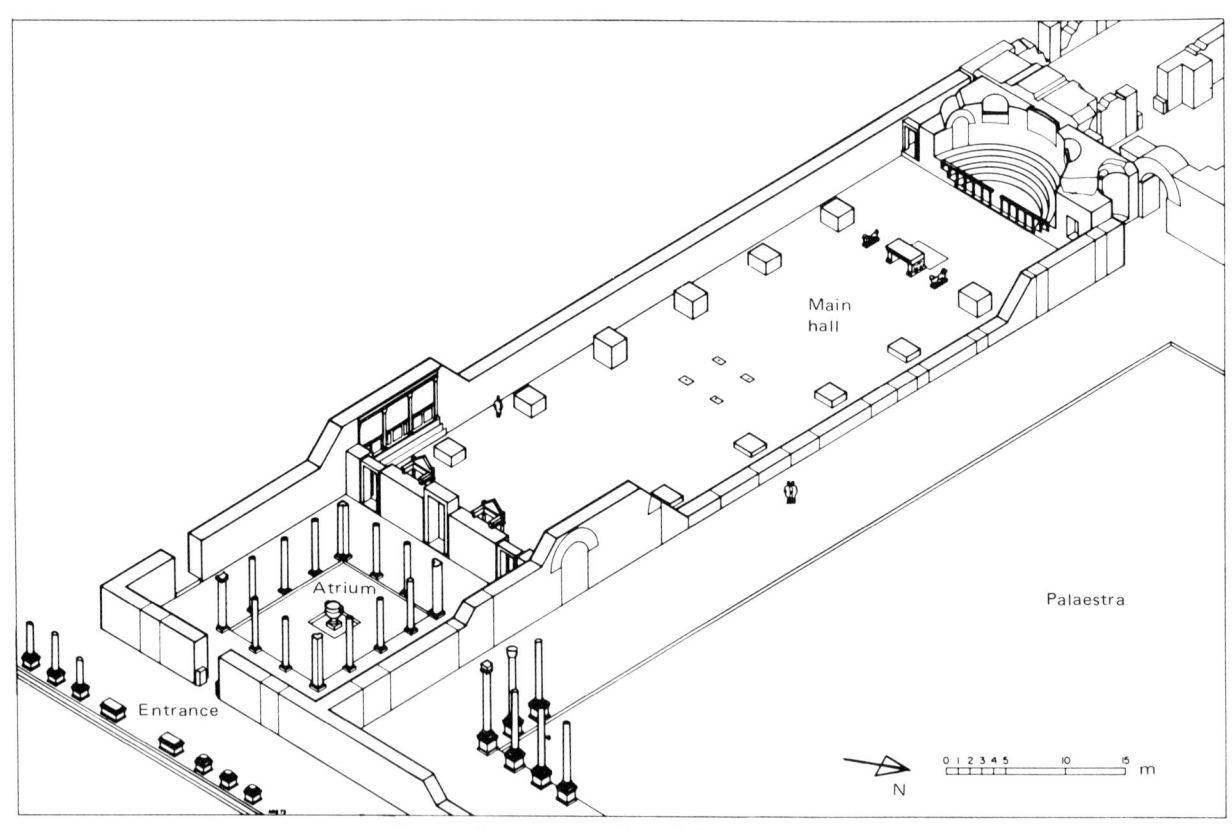

Isometric reconstruction of the synagogue

ing was abandoned when the city was attacked in the early seventh century C.E.

Among many objects of interest found within the building are a dozen representations of *menorot* and a spectacular *menorah* of marble, elaborately and finely carved, bearing the name Socrates. This *menorah* was more than 1 m. wide when intact. There are also more than 80 inscriptions (including fragments) in the floor mosaic and on plaques of marble wall revetment, giving information about the members of the synagogue and about some architectural features. Most of the inscriptions pertain to donations of interior decorations and furnishings made in fulfillment of vows. The great majority are in Greek. There are only a few fragments in Hebrew, one reading "Shalom." Of the inscriptions which do not pertain to donations, the most intriguing is a rectangular marble plaque found outside one of the doors to the synagogue (where it may have been moved by plunderers), enjoining in Greek: "Find, break open, read, observe."

A curious feature is the quantity of material

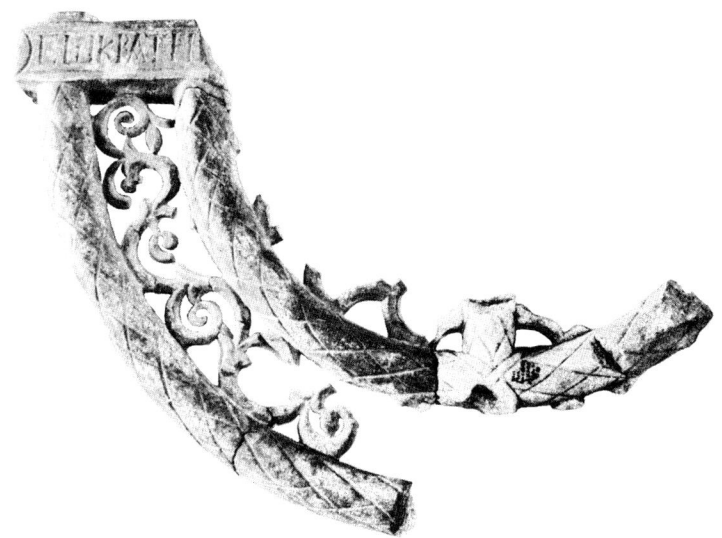

Fragmentary marble *menorah*, inscribed in Greek

reclaimed from other buildings and shrines and reused in construction of the synagogue. Parts of a Roman monument bearing eagles carved in relief were reused as supports for a great marble table set up in front of the apse. Two pairs of marble lions flanking the table are archaic or classical sculptures. Other spoils, including several Lydian and Hellenis-

Main sanctuary, looking east. Note the two *aediculae* flanking the main entrance

Main prayer hall, looking east from apse

tic monuments and inscriptions, were built within the piers and walls and are not associated with the use of the building as a synagogue.

There are two entrances to the synagogue, both leading to the forecourt. One is from the south, through a short passageway between two shops. The other entrance is from a colonnade with mosaic pavement on the east, through a door on the central axis. The colonnade area was severely burned during the raid of 616 C.E.

The forecourt also was found in a disrupted condition. Many pieces of the colonnade are missing, probably robbed for lime burning, but a few sections of columns, several bases, and three heart-shaped Ionic corner capitals remain. The columns are short compared with the columns of the *palaestra*; this suggests that the court was two stories high, but there is no concrete proof. A balustrade of openwork screens between the columns separated the fountain area and the surrounding mosaic pavement. One of the inscribed balustrade top-rails mentions a restoration or reconstruction (*ananeosis*).

The marble wall decoration of the forecourt was an addition, probably of the fifth century C.E., replacing an earlier wall-covering of plaster. The marble decoration included an arched frieze in shallow relief depicting urns and doves within bands of architectural ornament.

A subsequent modification in the forecourt was the insertion of thin partition walls aligned with the western colonnade, forming a narthex at the west end of the court (a similar change occurred in the synagogue at Beth-Alpha in Palestine). A marble basin on a tall pedestal, not connected to water pipes, was found against the east side of the southern partition wall.

Three doors (the northern one later blocked) led from the forecourt to the main hall of assembly. Upon entering, the grouping of apse, table, and lions provided an impressive focus at the end of the long architectural axis. Other furnishings were associated with that grouping; the marble *menorah* of Socrates, a small fragment of a bronze *menorah*, and an inscription recording the dedication of a *menorah* were all found nearby.

Despite the imposing setting, the apse at Sardis does not seem to have contained a Holy

Ark. There were three niches and two diagonal passages in the apse as originally built (probably when the building was used as a civic basilica), but these were later walled up and the curved wall of the apse was re-covered with marble. Having a patterned mosaic floor but no niches in its wall surface, the apse has no appropriate place for a Torah shrine. Around its curved wall, it does contain three tiers of benches which probably served as seats for the elders. Experiments have shown that approximately 70 persons could be seated here. A balustrade across the opening of the apse separated the area of the benches from the rest of the hall.

Neither is the huge marble table appropriate for a Torah shrine. The most likely use of the table was for readings or pronouncements. One of the Greek inscriptions found in the hall provides the relevant clue for this; it refers to the revetment of a *nomophylakion,* "the place that protects the Law." Thus we know that the Torah shrine was made in such a fashion that it could be decorated with marble. The table is ruled out as a Torah shrine because it had no revetments.

The Torah scroll was probably kept in one of two aedicular shrines built against the entrance wall, flanking the central door, on the Jerusalem end of the hall. Both shrines have been restored. All the Hebrew inscriptions found in the building lay next to the southern shrine, and it was here too that we found a neatly incised marble plaque showing a *menorah, lulab, shofar,* and two spirals interpreted as Torah scrolls.[2]

There was yet another fixed furnishing in the synagogue. Four stone slabs set into the mosaic in the very center of the hall, forming a square of about 2.8 m., supported a light-weight structure, probably a wood platform on marble colonettes. It may have served as a *bema.* A mosaic inscription set among the stone slabs mentions a "priest and teacher of wisdom."

[2] See Y. Shiloh, "Torah Scrolls and the Menorah Plaque from Sardis," *IEJ,* 18 (1968), 54–57.

Synagogue forecourt

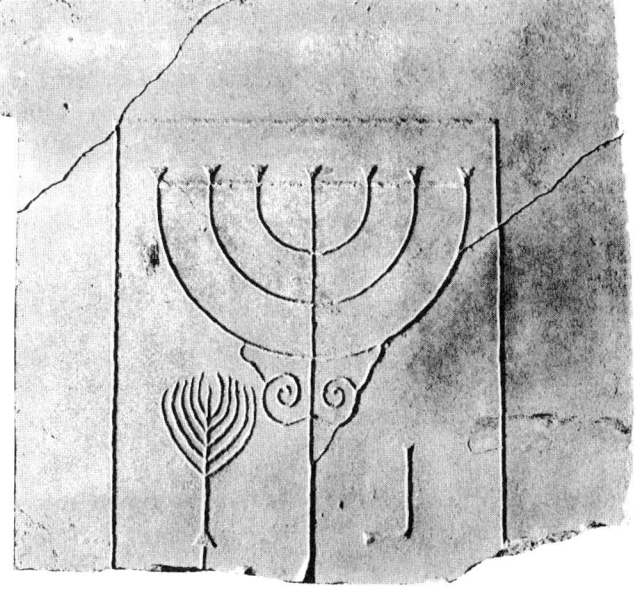
Marble *menorah* plaque

Not all of the furnishings were installed at the same time. The shrines were in place when the fourth century mosaics were installed, but the table and the *bema* stones intrude into the mosaic, as does the inscription of the "priest and teacher of wisdom." Nevertheless, these furnishings seem to have coexisted for a while. The hall probably had multiple uses, and the several focuses could have been associated with the different activities. Worshippers at prayer may have faced the shrines at the east end, while the Torah was read from the central *bema*. The west end with its benches conceivably functioned as a tribunal. The main hall or forecourt probably served some of the activities usually ascribed to annex rooms, including community gatherings and teaching. One or more of the three small rooms west of the main hall may have been occupied by Jews for part of the building's history, but the connection of these rooms to the synagogue proper is tenuous. It seems that no formal provision for annex rooms was made on the site.

Neither was there special provision for women at worship within the main hall. The piers could have supported a gallery or balcony which, according to traditional interpretation, would have been reserved for women. However, at Sardis there is no suitable staircase. Access to a second level would have had to be something like a ladder, which could hardly have been used regularly for public assembly. Apparently, women either worshiped together with the men or were excluded from the assembly hall entirely. (It is interesting in this connection to note that twelve of the dedicatory inscriptions mention wives as co-donors.)

The building shares many characteristics common to ancient synagogues. However, it lacks benches along the side walls and, as noted, a women's gallery, which are often thought typical of synagogues. Moreover the Sardis synagogue is unique in its site and in its program of wall decoration, inscriptions, and furnishings. Along with other synagogues recently discovered, it shows there was considerable diversity in ancient synagogue architecture. The building also changed through additions and modifications in the several centuries that it was used by Jews. It seems likely that underlying the architectural diversity is a variability of Jewish religious expression which has not yet been defined.

The prominent location, great size, and ambitious decoration of the synagogue attest a large, affluent, and influential Jewish population. The economic and social integration of Sardis Jews within the larger Roman community is shown also by the mix of owners of the shops along the colonnaded avenue; the contents of the shops indicate that some of the owners were Christians while others were Jews. A graffito on a clay jar found in one shop reads, in Greek: "Belonging to Jacob, Elder of the Synagogue." At least two synagogue members were goldsmiths, and Jacob seems to have been a jeweler. Inscriptions found in the assembly hall reveal the political position of the Jewish community. Often the names of donors are followed by the title "citizen of Sardis." Nine of the donors are identified as city councilors. Other titles include a record-office functionary in the Roman provincial administration, a former procurator, and a count.

The synagogue of Sardis provides much information about the later centuries of a Jewish community which may have existed there for nearly a millennium. Though the city was geographically remote from the centers of talmudic scholarship, the community was pious (indeed, piety is honored in the inscriptions). It also shared in the prosperity of the city under Roman rule and retained an important position in civic affairs through the first centuries of official Christianity. Though standards of craftsmanship and maintenance declined in later years, the synagogue fared no worse than other buildings in the city during the sixth and seventh centuries C.E.

Remains of a Synagogue at Corinth

G. Foerster

The Jewish community of Corinth was one of the most important in the Diaspora in the Hellenistic and early Roman periods. This commercial emporium in the northern Peloponessus was one of the focal points of the missionary activities of St. Paul, and it is recorded that he preached in the synagogue there. His *Letters to the Corinthians* are further evidence of the importance of the Jewish community of this city.

The history of the Jewish community there is obscure, and archeological discoveries provide little illumination. At the beginning of this century, a fragmentary inscription was found, reading [συν]αγωγὴ Ἑβρ[αίων — "Synagogue of the Hebrews." This is carved on what may have been the stone lintel of the synagogue.

In the excavation of the theatre at Corinth, conducted by the American School of Classical Studies in Athens, a unique architectural member[1] was discovered, measuring 39 × 69 cm. and 20 cm. thick. It had served as a capital for a half-column on one side and for an engaged pier on the other side. The former side bears an acanthus pattern in bas-relief, while the latter side shows three *menorot*, also in relief. Between the *menorot* are a bound *lulab* and an *ethrog*.

The branches of the *menorot* are comprised of round beads, possibly intended to conform with the biblical description of the *menorah* (Exod. 25 : 31 ff.). Above the branches is a bar, characteristic of late depictions. The two flanking *menorot* are without bases, as in certain reliefs from Naveh in the Golan and Chorazin in the Galilee (see pp. 98–115, 161–162). The central *menorah* has essentially no stem below the branches, but rests directly upon a two-footed base.

Such depictions of three *menorot* in a row are not common in Jewish iconography, and the central *menorah*, which differs here from the other two, replaces some other central motif, such as the Torah shrine.

This unique capital certainly comes from one of the synagogues at Corinth, the remains of which have yet to be located. There is no direct link between this capital and the above-noted synagogue inscription from the same site. In any event, the two finds apparently belong to the same period, the fourth–sixth centuries C.E.

Capital bearing triple *menorah* relief

---

[1] First published in R.L. Scranton, *Corinth* XVI (Princeton, 1957), p. 116, Pl. 130a–b, but largely overlooked by students of ancient Jewish art.

The Mosaics of Mopsuestia — Church or Synagogue?

M. Avi-Yonah

The ancient Cilician city of Mopsuestia, allegedly founded by the legendary hero Mopsus of Crete, lies north of the river Pyramos, on the road leading from Tarsus to Antioch. This is part of the Persian King's Highway from Susa to Sardis; today the site is occupied by the Turkish town of Misis. In 1955, a basilical building measuring 25 × 25 m. was excavated south of the river, beyond the walls of the old city. The extant remains included a narthex, the western part of the nave, and four aisles, two on each side.[1]

The entire building was apparently paved in polychrome mosaics. However, the shallow depth of the remains and the intensive cultivation of the orchard on the site — not to speak of inadequate archeological techniques — had resulted in the destruction of most of the pavement, and even the surviving parts have suffered severely. Of the three depictions in the nave, only one survives intact, apparently together with a fragment of a second depiction.

In the center of the complete scene, Noah's ark is surrounded by various animals. There can be no doubt as to the subject, for upon the cover of the object in the center is the Greek inscription ΚΙΒΩΤΟΣ ΝΩΕ Ρ, which may perhaps be translated as: "the ark of Noah the R[edeemer]," or "the r[edeeming] ark of Noah." The ark is depicted as a chest on four legs, a pictorial interpretation of the word κιβωτός, "box," "chest," applied in the Septuagint to both Noah's ark and the Ark of the Covenant.

Two rows of animals surround the ark. The outer row contains only mammals, except for a single crane. In the corners are fierce beasts — lion, panther, and rhinoceros (the fourth corner is damaged); between are less savage creatures: deer, camel, ox, buffalo, goat, and the like. No attempt has been made to show animals in pairs. The inner row, immediately around the ark, contains various species of birds, generally standing on a base-line. Noah and his family are not depicted.

Depiction of an ark as a chest is frequent in early Christian Bible portrayals, which are mostly based upon earlier Jewish art. In Asia Minor, local tradition connects the story of Noah's ark with various cities;[2] on the third-century C.E. coins of Apamea Kibotos in Phrygia, a large chest is portrayed, bearing representations of Noah and his wife; upon the ark is written ΝΩΕΙ, "Noah."[3] The procession of animals has only one parallel in a mosaic pavement, in the synagogue at Gerasa in Trans-Jordan, which was in use until its destruction in the fifth century C.E. (a church was constructed on its ruins in 531 C.E.).

The ark in the Mopsuestia mosaic is enclosed by a wide border containing rich floral ornamentation, mainly acanthus leaves, along with various geometric patterns. Amid the acanthus leaves, on a black background, are various animals. Many ritual objects are also depicted, such as chandeliers, candlestick lamps, and bowls with fruit.

In one of the mosaic fragments in the center

---

[1] The excavations were directed by L. Budde of the University of Münster. Results are published in L. Budde, *Pantheon*, 18 (1960), pp. 116–126; *idem, Antike Mosaiken in Kilikien*, I (Recklinghausen, 1969).

[2] Strabo 12, 8, 13; 576.

[3] A. Kindler, *Bulletin of the Ha'aretz Museum*, 13 (Tel Aviv, 1971), 24 (Hebrew).

The mosaic pavement in the western part of the nave, depicting Noah's ark

of the nave, part of a fish is depicted; the excavators believe this was part of a scene from the story of Jonah and the whale, though it may also be part of the zodiac sign of Pisces. The inner northern and southern aisles are paved with complex geometric patterns, devoid of images except for peacocks among vine tendrils.

In the outer northern aisle, where the floor is slightly raised, the story of Samson is depicted — the first such depiction known in a mosaic floor. This is a sequential depiction in nine scenes, in the order of events as described in the Bible. In most of the scenes, only a small fragment actually remains, but above each scene are biblical verses in Greek, closely

Two of Samson's foxes, tied tail-to-tail

corresponding to the Septuagint version (MS B of the Vatican). The scenes are arranged from right to left (east to west):

1) Samson rending the lion's whelp asunder (Judg. 14:6). All that remains of the scene is part of Samson's body.

2) The swarm of bees in the body of the lion (Judg. 14:8). Only the tree separating this scene from the previous one survives.

3) Samson's foxes (Judg. 15:4–5). Two foxes are bound tail-to-tail.

4) The story of Samson's wife and her father (Judg. 15:6). Only part of the scene is preserved, showing a woman in mourning seated beside a corpse.

5) Samson removing the gates of Gaza (Judg. 16:3). In the upper part of the scene, Gaza is depicted diagonally; below is Samson shown as a giant, with a woman striding before him (a detail with no biblical basis).

6) Samson sleeps while a Philistine shaves the seven locks of his head (Judg. 16:19). In the extant portion, at the bottom, Samson's hand is seen hanging over the edge of the bed. Two flower-pots stand beside the bed. The edge of Samson's head also remains, resting on an oval pillow, with the Philistine behind. A hand (Delilah's) holding a pair of scissors cuts off two locks; a third lock lies on the pillow.

7) The Philistines putting out Samson's eyes (Judg. 16:21). The scene is entirely lacking, and only part of the verse survives.

8) Samson and the "lad who held him by the hand" coming from the dungeon to the temple of Dagon (Judg. 16:27–30). Only a female head remains, with a Corinthian capital above. The woman's face is wracked by terror and suffering.

On the western side of the nave, near the door, there is a late repair in the pavement. Here, again, are Noah and his sons, the ark and the animals, depicted in a simple popular style.

Even in these meager, fragmentary depictions of the Samson cycle, two important details should be noted: Samson is always depicted as a giant, and the dress is clearly Byzantine rather than Hellenistic. These two factors distinguish the Mopsuestia mosaics from the depictions of the same story in the catacombs on the Via Latina in Rome.[4] Budde dated the Mopsuestia mosaics to the end of the fourth century or the early fifth century C.E., particularly on the grounds of stylistic parallels, and ascribed them to a church of St. Tarachus and other local martyrs. Mosaic floors depicting Old Testament themes are quite rare in Christian art, although a well-known exception is the floor in the church at Aquileia (313–319 C.E.) showing

[4] See A. Ferrua, *Le Pitture della nova catacomba di Via Latina* (Rome, 1960).

the story of Jonah and the whale. This tendency was given legal sanction in 427 C.E. when Theodosius II prohibited all use of the cross in floors (*Cod. Just.* 1, 8, 1); this restriction was subsequently extended to include biblical figures. A date later than the first quarter of the fifth century C.E. would, therefore, place the Christian attribution of the Mopsuestia mosaics, as well as the entire building, in great doubt. Several reservations can be raised concerning the early dating. The closest stylistic parallels may be found in mosaic floors of the *second* half of the fifth century C.E. on, as in the Church of the Nativity at Bethlehem.[5] The depictions are far removed from the Hellenistic tradition, which still survives in the biblical scenes in the Dura-Europos synagogue and in the early Christian catacombs. This process is well demonstrated by comparing the symbols of the zodiac in the synagogue of Ḥammath-Tiberias (first half of the fourth century C.E.) with those depicted in the Beth-Alpha synagogue (early sixth century C.E.).

We may therefore ask whether the building was, in fact, a Jewish synagogue rather than a Christian church. Old Testament depictions, which are lacking, as stated, in contemporary churches, commonly appear in synagogue floors (e.g., at Gerasa, Na'aran, and Beth-Alpha). Several further considerations support this conclusion.

In the entire area excavated, only one specifically Christian artifact was unearthed — a small bronze cross. Such an object may have been shifted and is not necessarily connected with the mosaic floors. Within the depictions themselves there is neither an inscription nor ornament indicating Christian symbolism. Budde's so-called "flowers of the cross" or "fields of crosses" are no more than ordinary floral patterns of this period, also found in synagogues. Moreover, all the motifs in the Mopsuestia floors (bowls, candelabra, lamps and fauna) have parallels in synagogues, especially at Japhia, Ḥusifa, Ma'on, and other sites in Israel.

Sleeping Samson being shorn of his locks by a Philistine

The easterly orientation, however, is not conclusive in identifying the nature of the structure, for all the known synagogues in Asia Minor (Sardis, Miletus, Priene and others) are oriented in the same manner as Christian churches everywhere.

In repaired parts of the floor — obviously following the original laying of the floor — there are also biblical scenes, the simple style of which reminded Budde of the depictions at Beth-Alpha. Since great care was taken in later periods to avoid depictions with biblical figures in church floors, as mentioned above, the supposition that at least in the period of the repairs the building was not in Christian hands gains further strength.[6]

[5] This is also the opinion of Professor Kitzinger of Harvard University.

[6] The fact that the Greek captions are derived from the Septuagint translation rather than from that of Aquila the

Whether these represent a church or a synagogue, they clearly witness the existence of a cycle of scenes illustrating the stories of the Bible — sequences with consistent depictions of the *dramatis personae.* This evidence antedates the Joshua Roll by several centuries, and is about a century older than the illuminated Vienna Genesis. In the catacomb frescoes in Rome and in wall mosaics in churches, these serialized illuminations were split up into individual scenes; in manuscripts, however, and surprisingly in the mosaics at Mopsuestia, the depiction is still in serialized sequence. Thus we have before us evidence of the origins of depictions in illuminated manuscripts treating Old Testament subjects. Such illustrations probably did not appear in manuscripts of the Bible itself, in either Hebrew or Septuagint Greek, but were intended merely to illustrate Bible stories. The Hellenistic character of the earliest illustrations of this sort is indicative of their origin — Alexandria, the greatest Jewish center outside Roman Palestine. The hellenized Jewish community there persistently sought to promulgate Judaism throughout the Hellenistic world, through both literature and complementary illuminations on Old Testament themes. Clearly, alongside translations into literary Greek — as, for example, the plays of

Ezekiel of Alexandria (second century C.E.) and the poems of Pseudo-Philo (also from Alexandria, after 70 C.E.), treating the Exodus from Egypt or the story of Shechem — graphic depictions were also devised for instruction of non-Jews, adapting figures known from Greek mythology. These basic depictions underwent metamorphosis in each new locale: in Mesopotamia they took on an oriental, Parthian character, and in Asia Minor, a Byzantine character. In this respect, the Samson mosaics at Mopsuestia represent a projection of ancient Jewish art and, as such, thus enrich Jewish history with a new and refreshing graphic dimension.

But why was the Samson cycle depicted at this site? The answer to this question lies in the remote past. Samson, the legendary hero of the Israelite tribe of Dan, is similar to other, non-Israelite legendary heroes — one of whom was Mopsus, the traditional founder of Mopsuestia in Asia Minor. The eighth century B.C.E. Phoenician inscriptions, discovered at Karatepe in Cilicia in 1946, mention a king from the dynasty of *MPŚ* (Mopsus). According to classical legend this Mopsus was noted for his riddles, as was Samson. Amongst his descendants was the king of the *DNNYM*, which name recalls that of Dan. The resemblance was apparently noted by the inhabitants of Mopsuestia, and when a fitting subject was sought for the floor of their house of worship, they naturally selected the Samson cycle from among the numerous biblical episodes before them.

Proselyte, which was of more widespread use among the Jews, is not in itself sufficient to refute our suggestion, for the statutes of the Emperor Justinian (*Novella* 146) make it evident that the Jews continued to use the Septuagint at least until the 6th century C.E.

ABBREVIATIONS

AASOR	Annual of the American Schools of Oriental Research
Ant.	Josephus, Antiquities
B	Babylonian Talmud
B.C.E.	Before the Common Era
b.	ben = son of
BASOR	Bulletin of the American Schools of Oriental Research
BIES	Bulletin of the Israel Exploration Society (Hebrew)
C.E.	Common Era
Cod. Just.	Codex Justinianus
IEJ	Israel Exploration Journal
J	Jerusalem (Palestinian) Talmud
JQR	Jewish Quarterly Review
LCL	Loeb Classical Library
M	Mishna
Nat. Hist.	Pliny the Elder, Natural History
PAAJR	Proceedings of the American Academy for Jewish Research
PBSR	Papers of the British School at Rome
PEFQST	Palestinian Exploration Fund Quarterly Statement
R.	Rabbi
T	Tosefta

GLOSSARY

ABBASID — An Islamic dynasty centered in Baghdad, 749–969 (in Palestine).

ACANTHUS — A plant whose leaves form the lower portion of the Corinthian column; used for other architectural decorations as well.

ACROPOLIS — A citadel or elevated part of a Greek city.

AEDICULA — A miniature shrine.

AMORAIM — Rabbinic sages in the talmudic period, 200–500 C.E.

ANTA(E) — Pilasters forming the ends of lateral walls of a temple cella.

APSE — A semi-circular or polygonal recess, arched or dome-roofed.

ARCHITRAVE — The horizontal beam of stone or timber spanning the interval between two columns or piers.

ASHLAR — Rectangular block of hewn stone.

ASTRAGAL — A rounded moulding often ornamented with a bead or reel.

ATRIUM — A central court, often before the entrance of a Byzantine basilica, as in synagogues and churches of the period.

BALLISTA — A military engine for hurling great stones.

BALUSTRADE — A series of pillars or columns supporting a handrail.

BARAITA — Early rabbinic tradition not included in the Mishna.

BASILICA — An oblong hall with a double colonnade and apse.

BEMA — An elevated platform in a synagogue.

BETH-MIDRASH — A rabbinic academy.

BOULETERION — A meeting place of a Greek council.

BROADHOUSE — A building whose focal point is situated on the long wall.

CAPITAL — The upper member of a classical pillar or column.

CATAPULT — An ancient engine for discharging darts and stones.

CENSER — A vessel in which incense is burned.

CHANCEL-SCREEN — A rail separating the clergy, choir or *bema* from the main part of a church or synagogue.

CODEX — A collection of Imperial decrees.

CONCH PEDIMENT — A domed roof of a semi-circular apse.

CORBEL — A stone bracket or timber jutting out from a wall to support a projecting feature.

CORINTHIAN CAPITAL — One of three Grecian orders; bell-shaped capital with rows of acanthus leaves.

CURIA — A name given to an assembly hall, particularly of the Roman senate house or those of ancient Italian towns.

DENARIUS — A Roman silver coin.

DIAPER — An ornamental design of diamond reticulation for panels or walls.

EGG AND DART (ovolo) — A quarter-round moulding whose typical ornament is the egg and dart.

ECCLESIASTERION — The meeting place of citizens of a Greek *polis*

ENTABLATURE — The horizontal superstructure carried by a colonnade (or by the equivalent superstructure over a wall) comprising an architrave, frieze, and cornice.

ETHROG — A citron used on the Sukkot holiday.

EX-VOTO — An offering made in pursuance of a vow.

EXEDRA — A recess or alcove with raised seats.

FAÇADE — The face of a building.

FLAGSTONE — Stones used for pavement.

FRESCO — A painting in water color on plaster before it is dry.

FRET — An ornament consisting of straight lines intersecting at right angles.

FRIEZE — The middle member of an entablature, often enriched with relief sculpture.

GENIZA — Depository for sacred books.

GEONIM — Heads of the Babylonian academy in post-talmudic period.

GRAFFITO — A drawing or writing scratched on a wall, or other surface.

GRAMMA — Unit of weight in the metric system.

GUILLOCHE — An architectural ornament imitating braided ribbons.

GYMNASIUM — A place for physical exercises and training.

HAGIOS TOPOS — Sacred place.

HALAKHA — An accepted decision in rabbinic law (pl. halakhot).

HAZZAN — Precentor who intones the liturgy and leads the prayers in synagogue; in earlier times, a synagogue official.

HEADER — A stone laid perpendicular to the face of the wall.

HELIOS — The sun god.

HEMICYCLE — Half a cycle.

HORROR VACUI — An artistic style avoiding the use of empty places.

IN ANTIS — Columns in between the two antae.

IN SITU — In the original place.

IONIC CAPITAL — A capital of the Ionic order, decorated with volutes.

KIBOTOS — The Greek word for chest, usually used for clothing and bedding, but used also for an ark.

LAVER — Basin or cistern for washing.

LINTEL — The horizontal timber or stone over a door or window.

LULAB — A palm branch, used on the Sukkot festival.

MEANDER — Ornamental pattern of lines winding in and out.

MEDALLION — A decorative panel or tablet.

MENORAH — A candelabrum.

METOPES — The square space between Doric triglyphs.

MIHRAB — The niche facing Mecca in the wall of an Islamic prayer house.

MIQVEH — A ritual bath.

MISHNA — Earliest codification of Jewish oral law, compiled by R. Judah the Prince ca. 200 C.E.

MONOLITH — A single block of stone shaped into a pillar or monument.

MYSTERIES OF ELEUSIS — A secret religious society in honor of Demeter and Persephone, located at Eleusis.

NARTHEX — The western portico in early Christian churches, for women, penitents, and catechumens.

NOMOPHYLAKION — "Protector of the Law," i.e., a Torah shrine.

NYMPHAEUM — A building in classic architecture for plants, flowers and running water, ornamented with statues.

ODEON — odeum — A building for musical performances and philosophic debates.

OPUS SECTILE — Paving or wall decoration made of shaped tiles of colored marble.

OVOLO — A convex moulding of quarter-circle or quarter-ellipse section, receding downwards.

PALAESTRA — A public building for the training of athletes.

PALUDAMENTUM — A military cloak worn by Roman generals and chief officers.

PAROCHET — A cloth covering for the Torah shrine.

PATRIARCHATE — The political and communal leader of the Jews in the Roman Empire in late antiquity.

PEDIMENT — The triangular gabled end of a ridged roof of classical Greek-style buildings.

PERISTYLE — A row of columns surrounding a court or temple.

PIER — A mass of masonry from which an arch springs.

PILASTERS — A rectangular column.

PIYYUTIM (pl.) — Hebrew liturgical poetry of the Byzantine period.

PLINTH — The lower square member of the base of a column.

PORTICO — A colonnade.

PRONAOS — The porch in front of the naos (cella) in a Greek temple.

PROPYLAEUM — An entrance before a building or group of buildings.

QUADRIGA — An ancient chariot drawn by four horses harnessed abreast.

ROSETTE — A carved or moulded conventional rose on a wall.

SAMARIA OSTRACA — Sherds containing records of oil and wine shipments found at Samaria.

SAMARITANS — Inhabitants of Samaria.

SANHEDRIN — Highest court of justice and supreme council in ancient Jerusalem.

SARCOPHAGUS — A stone coffin.

SATRAPY — An administrative division of the Persian empire.

SEAT OF MOSES — (Cathedra of Moses) — A special chair where the head of the Jewish community sat.

SEPHARAD — Name found in Ovadiah 1:20, interpreted as a reference to Sardis.

SEVENTH YEAR — The sabbatical year when Jewish agricultural activity in Israel is to cease.

SHEPHELAH — Low lying plain located between the coast and Judaean hills.

SHEMITAH — See "Seventh Year."

SHOFAR — A ram's horn.

SIFRE — A midrash to *Numbers* and *Deuteronomy*.

SOCLE — The lower part of a wall, as well as a low plain block or plinth, serving as a pedestal to a statue, column, or vase.

STELE — An upright slab forming a Greek tombstone or carrying an inscription or design.

STOA — A portico or detached colonnade.

STRETCHER — A stone laid with its side parallel to the face of the wall (header and stretcher).

STUCCO — Plaster or cement used for coating wall surfaces or moulding into architectural decorations.

STYLOBATE — A continuous base supporting a row of columns.

SYRIAN GABLE — A triangular pediment with its base cut into by an arch.

TABULA ANSATA — The frame of a Roman inscription which has a triangular ear on the right and left side.

TALMUD — A large corpus of Jewish civil and ceremonial law. Two compilations exist, one from Palestine, ca. 400 C.E., the other from Babylonia, ca. 650 C.E.

TANNAIM — Rabbinic sages of the mishnaic period — pre-200 C.E.

TANNAITIC — Rabbinic traditions of the mishnaic period — pre-200 C.E.

TELESTERION — Square hall with rock-cut seats like a theater, found in Eleusis where the mysteries were practiced.

TERMINUS ANTE QUEM — The date before which.

TERMINUS POST QUEM — The date after which.

TERRA SIGILLATA — Pottery made in moulds. In modern archeology the term is restricted to fine red-glazed tableware in use throughout the Roman Empire.

TESSERA — A small cube of stone, glass or marble used in making mosaics.

TETRASTOON — A building composed of four stoas.

TITHE — The tenth part of the annual produce of agriculture.

TOPONYM — The place name of a country or district.

TORUS — A rounded convex moulding used principally in the bases of columns.

TOSEFTA — A collection of teachings and traditions closely related to the Mishna.

TREFOIL — Three-lobed ornamentation.

TRICLINIUM — A Roman dining room, originally with couches on three sides.

TRIGLYPH — Grooved tablets alternating with metopes in the Doric frieze.

TRUSS — A projection from the face of a wall, often serving to support a cornice.

UMAYYAD — An Islamic dynasty centered in Damascus, 635–749 C.E.

ZEALOTS — A Jewish sect in Jerusalem, active during the revolt against Rome, 66–70 C.E. The term is often used with reference to all Jewish revolutionaries.

ZODIAC — A belt of the celestial sphere divided into twelve equal parts called signs.

BIBLIOGRAPHY

I. GENERAL

Avi-Yonah, M., "Places of Worship in the Roman and Byzantine Period," *Antiquity and Survival* 2:2–3. (*The Holy Land. New Light on the Prehistory and Early History of Israel.* The Hague and Jerusalem, 1957.)

—— and Stern, E. eds. *Encyclopedia of Archaeological Excavations in the Holy Land.* 4 vols. Jerusalem, 1975–78.

Baron, S., *The Jewish Community.* 3 vols. Philadelphia, 1942–48.

Finkelstein, L., "The Origin of the Synagogue," *Proceedings of the American Academy of Jewish Research,* I (1930).

Goodenough, E., *Jewish Symbols in the Greco-Roman Period.* 13 vols. Princeton, 1953–68.

Hengel, M., "Proseuche und Synagogue," *Tradition und Glaube. Fest. für K.G. Kuhn.* Göttingen, 1971.

Huttenmeister, F., *Die Antiken Synagogen in Israel,* 1. Wiesbaden, 1977.

Kohl, H. and Watzinger, C., *Antike Synagogen in Galilaea.* Leipzig, 1916.

Levy, I., *The Synagogue: Its History and Function.* London, 1963.

May, H.G., "Synagogues in Palestine," *Biblical Archaeologist,* 7/1 (Feb. 1944). (Reprinted in the *Biblical Archaeologist Reader,* ed. by N. Freedman and G. Wright. Garden City, N.Y., 1961.)

Rabinowitz, *Bulletin for the Exploration of Ancient Synagogues. Vols. 1–3.* Jerusalem, 1949–1960.

Rivkin, E., "Ben Sira and the Non-existence of the Synagogue," In: *The Time of Harvest: Essays in the Honor of Abba Hillel Silver,* ed. D.J. Silver. New York, 1963.

Saller, S.J., *The Second Revised Catalogue of the Ancient Synagogues of the Holy Land.* Jerusalem, 1972.

Shanks, H., *Judaism in Stone; the Archaeology of Ancient Synagogues.* New York, 1979.

Sukenik, E.L., *Ancient Synagogues in Palestine and Greece.* London, 1934.

II. SECOND TEMPLE PERIOD SYNAGOGUES

Corbo, V.C., "L'Herodion di Giabal Fureidis," *Jerusalem Through the Ages.* Jerusalem, 1968.

Foerster, G., "The Synagogues at Masada and Herodium" (Hebrew), *Eretz-Israel* 11 (1973).

Guttman, S., *Gamla* (Hebrew). Tel-Aviv, 1977.

Ma'oz, Z., "A Synagogue from the Time of the Second Temple" (Hebrew), *Israel Land and Nature,* 3 (1978).

Yadin, Y., *Masada: Herod's Fortress and the Zealots' Last Stand.* New York, 1966.

——, *The Excavation of Masada 1963/64, Preliminary Report.* Jerusalem, 1965.

III. SYNAGOGUES OF THE GALILEE

Avigad, N., "On the Form of Ancient Synagogues" (Hebrew), *All the Land of Naphtali.* Jerusalem, 1967.

Corbo, V.C., and Spijkerman, A., *Cafarnao I–III.* Jerusalem, 1972–75.

Dothan, M., "The Aramaic Inscription from the Synagogue of Severus at Hammath-Tiberias" (Hebrew), *Eretz-Israel,* 8 (1967).

——, "The Representation of Helios in the Mosaic of Hammath-Tiberias," *Academia Nazionale dei Lincei,* 365 (1968).

Foerster, G., *Galilean Synagogues and Their Relation to Hellenistic and Roman Art and Architecture* (Hebrew). Diss. — Jerusalem, 1972.

——, "Notes on Recent Excavations at Capernaum," *Israel Exploration Journal,* 21 (1971).

Loffreda, S., "The Late Chronology of the Synagogue of Capernaum," *Israel Exploration Journal,* 23 (1973).

——, "The Synagogue of Capharnaum — Archaeological Evidence for its Late Chronology," *Liber Annuus,* 22 (1972).

Meyers, E.M., Kraabel, A.T., Strange, J.F., "Ancient Synagogue Excavations at Khirbet Shema', Upper Galilee, Israel, 1970–1972," *AASOR,* 42 (1976).

——, Kraabel, A.T., Strange, J.F., "Archaeology and

Rabbinic Tradition at Khirbet Shema'," *Biblical Archaeologist*, 35/1 (1972).

Sapir, B., Neeman, D., *Capernaum; History and Legacy, Art and Architecture*, The Historical Sites Library N1/9. Tel Aviv, 1967.

IV. SYNAGOGUES IN THE BETH SHEAN AREA

Bahat, D., "A Synagogue Chancel-Screen from Tel Reḥob," *Israel Exploration Journal*, 23 (1973).

——, Druks, A., "Beth Shean — Ancient Synagogue," *Revue Biblique*, 78 (1971).

Ben-Dov, M., "Remains of a Synagogue at Kokhav Hayarden" (Hebrew), *Eretz Shomron*, Jerusalem, 1973.

Demsky, A., "The Permitted Towns in the Boundaries of Sebaste According to the Reḥob Inscription" (Hebrew), *Qadmoniot*, 11 (1978).

Zori, N., "The Ancient Synagogue at Beth Shean" (Hebrew), *Eretz-Israel*, 8 (1967).

——, "The House of Kyrios Leontis at Beth Shean," *Israel Exploration Journal*, 16 (1966).

V. SYNAGOGUES OF THE GOLAN

Kochavi, M., (ed.), *Judea, Samaria and the Golan. Archaeological Survey 1967–68*. Jerusalem, 1970.

Oliphant, L., "Exploration North East of Lake Tiberias and in Jaulan," *Palestine Exploration Fund Quarterly Statement*, 18 (1885).

Schumacher, G., *Across the Jordan*. London, 1886.

——, *The Jaulan*. London, 1888.

VI. SYNAGOGUES OF JUDAEA AND THE SOUTH

Mayer, L A., Reifenberg, A., "The Synagogue of Eshtemo'a — A Preliminary Report," *Journal of Palestine Oriental Society*, 19 (1939–40).

Ovadiah, A., "Excavations in the Area of the Ancient Synagogue at Gaza," *Israel Exploration Journal*, 19 (1969).

Safrai, S., "The Synagogues in the Southern Judean Hills" (Hebrew), *Immanuel*, 3 (1973–74).

Yeivin, Z., "Inscribed Marble Reliefs from Khirbet Susiya Synagogue," *Israel Exploration Journal*, 24 (1974).

VII. INSCRIPTIONS AND SMALL FINDS

Lieberman, S., "A Preliminary Remark to the Inscription of 'En Gedi" (Hebrew), *Tarbiz*, 40 (1971).

——, "The Halakhic Inscription from the Beth Shean Valley" (Hebrew, English summary), *Tarbiz*, 45 (1975/76).

Mazar, B., "The Inscription on the Floor of the Synagogue in 'En Gedi — A Preliminary Survey" (Hebrew), *Tarbiz*, 40 (1970).

Mirsky, A., "Aquarius and Capricornus in the 'En Gedi Inscription" (Hebrew), *Tarbiz*, 40 (1971).

Naveh, J., *On Stone and Mosaic, The Aramaic and Hebrew Inscriptions from Ancient Synagogues* (Hebrew). Jerusalem, 1978.

Sussman, Y., "A Halakhic Inscription from the Beth Shean Valley" (Hebrew), *Tarbiz*, 43 (1973/74).

Urbach, E., "The Secret of the 'En Gedi Inscription and its Formula" (Hebrew), *Tarbiz*, 40 (1970).

Urman, D., "Jewish Inscriptions from Dabbura in the Golan," *Israel Exploration Journal*, 22 (1972).

Yeivin, Z., "Chorazin," *Israel Exploration Journal*, 12 (1962).

VIII. SYNAGOGUES OF THE DIASPORA

Budde, L., *Antike Mosaiken in Kilikien. 1. Recklinghausen*, 1969.

Du Mesnil de Buisson, *Les Peintures de la synagogue de Doura Europos, 245–256 après J-C*. Paris, 1934.

Gutmann, J., *The Dura Europos Synagogue — A Reevaluation 1932–72*. Missoula, 1973.

Hanfman, G.M.A., "The Ancient Synagogue of Sardis," *The World Congress of Jewish Studies*, 4, 1 (1967).

Kitzinger, E., "Observations of the Samson Floor at Mopsuestia," *Dumbarton Oaks Papers*, 27 (1973).

Kraeling, C., *The Excavations at Dura Europas. Vol. 8 — The Synagogue*. New Haven, 1956.

Mitten, D.G., *The Ancient Synagogue of Sardis*. New York, 1965.

Seager, A., "The Architecture of the Dura and Sardis Synagogues," *The Dura Europas Synagogue, a Re-evaluation (1932–1972)*, J. Gutmann ed., Missoula, 1973.

——, "The Building History of the Sardis Synagogue," *American Journal of Archaeology*, 76 (1972).

Sonne, I., "The Paintings of the Dura Synagogue," *Hebrew Union College Annual*, 20 (1947).

Squarciapino, M.F., "The Synagogue at Ostia," *Archaeology*, 16 (1963).

Sukenik, E.L., "The Mosaic Inscriptions in the Synagogue at Apamea on the Orontes," *Hebrew Union College Annual*, 23 (1950/51).

——, *The Synagogue of Dura Europos and its Frescoes* (Hebrew). Jerusalem, 1947.

Wiseman, J., & Mano-Zissi, D., "Excavations at Stobi, 1970–72," *American Journal of Archaeology*, 75–77 (1971–1973).

——, & Mano-Zissi, D., "Excavations at Stobi, 1973–74," *Journal of Field Archaeology*, 1 (1974).

——, & Mano-Zissi, D., "Stobi: A City of Ancient Macedonia," *Journal of Field Archaeology*, 3 (1976).

Wischnitzer, R., *The Messianic Theme in the Paintings of the Dura Synagogue*. Chicago, 1948.

INDEX